SEDUCTION BY THE STARS

SEDUCTION
BY THE
STARS

An Astrological Guide
to Love, Lust, and
Intimate Relationships

Ren Lexander and Geraldine Rose

BANTAM BOOKS
New York • Toronto • London • Sydney • Auckland

SEDUCTION BY THE STARS

A Bantam Book / February 1995

All rights reserved.

Copyright © 1995 by Ren Lexander and Geraldine Rose

Book design by Richard Oriolo

Library of Congress Cataloging-in-Publication Data

Geraldine Rose.
    Seduction by the stars : an astrological guide to love, lust, and intimate relationships / by Geraldine Rose & Ren Lexander.
        p.   cm.
    ISBN 0-553-37451-6
    1. Astrology.   2. Interpersonal relations—Miscellanea.   3. Dating   (Social   customs)—Miscellanea.   4.   Love—Miscellanea.
5. Astrology and sex.   I. Lexander, Ren.   II. Title.
BF1729.P8G47   1994
133.5—dc20   94-17150
                                                                CIP

Published simultaneously in the United States and Canada

Bantam Books are published by Bantam Books, a division of Bantam Doubleday Dell Publishing Group, Inc. Its trademark, consisting of the words "Bantam Books" and the portrayal of a rooster, is Registered in U.S. Patent and Trademark Office and in other countries. Marca Registrada. Bantam Books, 1540 Broadway, New York, New York 10036.

PRINTED IN THE UNITED STATES OF AMERICA

BVG   20   19   18   17   16

TABLE OF
SEDUCTIONS

INTRODUCTION

ARIES
March 21st to April 20th

CANCER
June 22nd to July 23rd

LEO
July 24th to August 23rd

VIRGO
August 24th to September 23rd

LIBRA

September 24th to October 23rd

SCORPIO

October 24th to November 22nd

SAGITTARIUS
November 23rd to December 21st

CAPRICORN
December 22nd to January 20th

AQUARIUS
January 21st to February 19th

PISCES
February 20th to March 20th

FURTHER READING

SEDUCTION BY THE STARS

INTRODUCTION

■ ■ ■

Most astrology books are primarily geared toward self-knowledge: toward increasing your awareness of what makes you tick.

This one isn't.

Seduction by the Stars is geared toward teaching you how to handle *other* people and *their* astrological peculiarities.

This book is an invaluable collection of tips and tactics on how to get the person you're after or deal with the one you've got. It covers all phases of the relationship: from the first magical meeting of eyes across a crowded room to the final poignant "get lost."

Within the covers of this book, you will discover:

What attracts you to Libras (they're so well groomed and decorous, aren't they?)

How to get a Leo interested in you (and destroy your credit rating in the process)

How to get an Aries into bed (run away until you catch them)

What a sexual relationship with a Sagittarius is like (pack your vitamin pills)

How to handle a relationship with a Cancer (keep the Kleenex and homemade soup on hand)

How to end a relationship with a Scorpio (and live to tell the tale)

Quite frankly, this book could be a dangerous weapon if it fell into the wrong hands. The wrong person could use it to cut a ruthless swath through the ranks of the opposite sex.

Of course, we would never condone lies or deception designed to get someone into bed. That could never lead to anything truly worthwhile.

Nevertheless, there is such a thing as putting your best face to the world and so maximizing your chances of success. We all have a solid, reliable side to our nature—which is what a Taurus needs to be reassured by. We all have a fun, spontaneous side—which is what the Gemini needs to kindle the spark. We all have a part of ourselves that likes to be mothered—so why not let a Cancer do it? It's a simple question of how best to present yourself to initiate interest.

Once interest is provoked, you face the often delicate question of how to move this abstract mental and emotional connection toward physical moaning and groaning. It's here that this book becomes your best friend. Where else could you learn how and why to Vamp a Scorpio, how and why to Dare an Aries, how to execute the Public Provocation Proposition on a Gemini, how to commit *Cogito Ergo Fornicatio* with an Aquarius, how and why to Pig Out in the Park with a Taurus?

You will find outlines for more than a hundred seductions in *Seduction by the Stars*—ranging from the traditional Sickeningly Sincere Candlelit Dinner to such outrageous scenarios as the Gothic Thriller and the Twilight Zone Naughty.

Not only can these be used to move your relationship over the hump of the first sexual encounter, they are also invaluable aids for restimulating a relationship that's sagging sexually.

Beyond the issue of getting a prospective partner into the sack and keeping them coming back for more, there is the very tricky question whether the two of you are sufficiently compatible to turn randiness into relationship: whether that bed prospect who initially had you melting at the knees will turn out two weeks later to be an inconsiderate slob who bores you silly. *Seduction by the Stars* will help you enter into such *liaisons dangereuses* with your eyes wide open—or at least as wide as lust-narrowed eyes can be pried.

Astrology in general—and this book in particular—can also help you to acknowledge the foibles of your lover and take the bad with the good. With understanding come acceptance and tolerance.

Finally, there is the vexed and thorny question of how to bail out of the decaying hulk of the relationship with as few scars as possible should tolerance sag or passion wilt.

To all such questions and more, you will find invaluable answers in *Seduction by the Stars*.

First, however, a brief astrology lesson will help you get the most out of this book.

Mini Astrology Lesson

■ ■ ■

Some people will read this book and think "Hold your horses, I know a stay-at-home Sagittarius. Wait a minute, I know a sex-mad, messy Virgo. Hang on, I know a submissive Leo, a quiet shy Gemini, an unreliable Capricorn, an organized Pisces, an independent-minded Libra, a Cancer who's a lousy cook."

Don't bother writing to us. We know, we know, we know already. Maybe you even know an anorexic Taurus (hard to believe but anything's possible).

Please remember that of necessity, this book investigates the archetypes of the Sun signs. The Sun sign is the one part of their horoscope that everyone knows. It is based on the Sun's annual passage through the twelve signs of the Zodiac, during which the Sun spends about thirty days in each sign.

The truth of the matter is that each of us is a lot more than just our Sun sign. Each of us is a unique combination of influences from the Sun, the Moon and all the planets of the Solar System at the time of our birth. If you want to investigate to that depth, only a visit to a professional astrologer can help you. Nevertheless, your Sun sign remains the fundamental core of your character.

After your Sun sign, the next two most influential factors in your horoscope are the sign rising at the time of your birth (the Ascendant) and the sign occupied by your Moon.

The Ascendant

The Ascendant or Rising Sign is the sign of the Zodiac that was crossing the eastern horizon at the time of your birth.

This changes approximately every two hours. Accordingly, even twins born as little as five minutes apart could have different Ascendants, which would make for a critical difference in their horoscopes and therefore their personalities.

Your Ascendant determines many of the tactics you use in your interactions with other people; it affects the way you present yourself; it shapes the persona you build in interacting with other people and the external world. It's your modus operandi.

If you find, for instance, that the gentle, caring man you've met doesn't seem to fit the personality profile of the typical Aries—well, perhaps it's because he has a Pisces Ascendant. Or, if you find that only about half of what you read in this book applies to your submissive Leo lady, perhaps accommodating Libra crossed the horizon at the time of her birth.

The Moon Sign

Your Moon sign is the sign of the Zodiac occupied by the Moon when you were born.

The Moon sign indicates the emotional conditioning you underwent in your formative years. It can be thought of as an imprint or legacy from your early home environment and especially from the way your mother related to you when you were a child.

As an adult, you experience the Moon sign as a bundle of deep-seated emotional needs that must be fulfilled. In times of stress and pressure, people tend to retreat into their Moon sign. They then exhibit the emotional needs and characteristics of that sign—often more than the characteristics of their Sun sign.

So if you are puzzled as to why that otherwise self-effacing Virgo you're dating sometimes lashes you with a stinging tongue, it could be because she has Moon in Scorpio. Or if you can't understand why your otherwise homebody Cancerian man is always planning a jaunt overseas, perhaps his Moon is in Sagittarius.

Finding out your would-be lover's Ascendant and Moon sign will give you much greater understanding of how to handle them than you could obtain by researching their Sun sign alone.

To find out your lover's Ascendant and Moon sign, you need to know the time of day and place of their birth. Then consult an astrologer or, more economically, have these details calculated by one of the many astro-computing services (check your phone book or local New Age magazine).

Then, armed with not one but three key pieces of information, you will have a significantly better astrological profile of the object of your desire. Having found out, for example, that your Libra has a Scorpio Ascendant and Moon in Aquarius, you will read not only the Libra section but the Scorpio and Aquarius sections as well, and the three together should give you a very useful handle on how to enter into and carry on a relationship with your intended.

Ultimately, there is no substitute for having a complete horoscope cast by a professional astrologer. If you are contemplating a serious continuing relationship with someone, spare no effort to find out the exact location, date and time of their birth and rush to the nearest astrologer to have them vetted—even if you have to wine, dine and charm their mother to extract the data. It could save you months of fruitless pursuit and years of frustration—not to mention helping you avoid the agony of a broken heart, countless hours of psychotherapy and the decimation of your bank account.

On the Cusp of a Dilemma: Which Sign Do I Read?

Should the object of your desires happen to have been born on a day when the Sun changes signs, it's possible they were not born under the sign they have been mistakenly reading for years in the magazines.

On March 20, for example, the Sun generally moves out of Pisces and into Aries. If they were born on this day you need to give their time of birth to an astrologer, who can make a calculation and tell you definitively into which sign their Sun falls.

Very, very few people are actually born at the precise moment when the Sun moves from one sign to the next. Unless they are one of these rare people born right "on the cusp," they will be one sign or the other. Remember that the Sun sign reveals the true nature of a person, the essence of his or her character. Getting it right once and for all could turn out to be a major factor in the progress of your love life.

ARIES

March 21st to April 20th

...

Methinks yon Aries has a

lean and hungry look

The Lure of an Aries

■ ■ ■

What charm.

That smile, that confidence, that presence, that aura of energy.

Surely this person could take hold of life and swallow it whole.

How could anybody come across so well, so quickly?

Hold on to your horses (or, rather, your rams), you've just met an Aries.

What is likely to draw you to an Aries is their initial impact: their raw energy, their outgoing nature, their air of self-assurance, their chutzpah.

Aries have an all-out approach to life and sex. They are achievement-oriented dynamos who love nothing better than a challenge. (Of course, not all Aries are in charge of their lives and earmarked by fate for automatic success—but don't tell them that; they all like to think they are.)

If you haven't had sex for a while and you're desperate and dateless, this is the Sun sign least likely to shilly-shally around. Aries are not noted for their patience. Once genuinely interested in anyone or anything, they look for quick returns and immediate results—especially in sexual matters, which hold a particular fascination for them. Their sexual drive is raw and primeval.

Aries men secretly identify with Tarzan—and so do Aries women!

If you have recently come across a book on obscure sexual positions, Aries, being natural athletes, are the sign most likely to want to try them all. What's more, they find it very hard to ignore a dare.

If you want the other person to take the initiative, Aries is also for you. Perhaps you are exhausted from the hunt and you want to be chased for a change. Consider, then, a person born under the sign of the Ram. Male or female, they prefer to chase rather than be chased.

If you hanker after an incandescent, *brief* affair that creates so many sparks it lights up the night sky, Aries is the sign for you.

Now take a deep breath, pause a moment, and be warned. Aries are natural initiators. This is the sign most likely to impress at the first meeting or the first frenzied session of passion. However, the long-term prospects may not be all that the short-term excitement leads you to expect.

How to Interest an Aries

■ ■ ■

To interest an Aries, you must appear *interesting* rather than *interested*. There are two fundamental points to remember:

1. Aries are suckers for image and are always concerned about the impression they make.

2. They love a challenge.

You must skillfully cater to both these foibles. You must let them know that you find them interesting but you must *not* let them think you are a sexual pushover. *Never* tell them they fascinate you—especially if they do.

Perhaps the best technique is to make it obvious that you find Aries an interesting conversationalist but don't let them think you are sexually enamored. Try to convey interest in *them* but, if anything, appear rather uninterested in getting them into bed; Aries want to think they got *you* into bed—that way they feel they had their way and got what they wanted. They love to win and to feel they came out on top.

Key tactic: Charm and withdraw.

An integral part of the charming phase will be the way you present yourself physically. Aries must be convinced they look good standing next to you. You must be an asset to their ego.

So do not wear your old favorite sloppy clothes. Above all, never appear at any function inappropriately dressed. Aries' favorite color is red. A red dress, a red necktie, a red scarf, even red socks will be appealing.

For a big date, dress to kill. If you're short on chic, rent, borrow or buy. The same applies to your house or apartment if you intend the seduction to take place there. They need to see that you have possessions that reek of success. Display your status symbols shamelessly. Direct them to your leather sofa. Conspicuously switch on your Bang & Olufsen. Aries are not impressed by modesty. An ideal status symbol is a sports car—especially a red one. If you don't own a red sports car *yet*, mention that you are checking some out. Tell them that just the thought of driving your own sports car gets your motor running. Many Aries (especially the men) spend decades of their lives planning how they can acquire one. If you want to get an Aries' serious attention, cater to this fantasy and hire a sports car for a week—or for a weekend.

Impress dynamic Aries as being ever ready for action. Never appear tired. Never yawn.

It's always a good idea to slip in a remark or two about your well-known acquaintances. Aries are impressed by name-dropping. They love the big time—which is where they feel they deserve to be.

Talk about your job if it is impressive enough, university degrees, sports triumphs, business coups, film scripts you are about to have produced— anything that can increase your status in their eyes. Better still: get someone else to tell Aries about you on your behalf. Ask a friend to list all the amazing achievements you are just too cool to mention yourself. (It's not that Aries is swayed by humility, but they want someone whose self-confidence is so high that they wouldn't waste going on about their triumphs.)

Above all, the thing to convey to Aries is a sense of destiny about you and your career. Fate has singled you out for something truly momentous in the near future. You're on the way to the top; the big time is just around the corner.

Suggested opening line: "I'm going skiing next weekend. Someone's dropped out. Are you free?"

What to talk about: Success, status, winning, who you know, what you know about who you know, how you are destined for fame and fortune, their brilliant career, your brilliant career, red sports cars.

Where to take them: A good curry restaurant or other spot where the rich and successful congregate and where Aries can dress to be noticed, skiing weekends, down the coast in your red sports car, Club Med holidays, martial arts classes. If you are required to join them in their favorite sport, make sure you cut an attractive figure—but it may be a mistake to win by too much.

What to give them: Red things—red T-shirts, red hats, red lace underwear, a red sports car! Buy them something associated with their favorite sport.

Consider books on making money and life at the top. Remember that they like to make a great impression wherever they go—perhaps you can think of something that will help them do so.

How to Seduce an Aries

■ ■ ■

Key tactic: Run away until you catch them.

Never chase an Aries if you want to get one into bed. Aries like conquests and challenges. Aries respond to playing hard to get more than any other sign. Fawn over them, lavish praise on them, give them single-minded devoted attention and they will lap it up. They will. But they won't be sexually interested in you. Feign mild indifference and they will pull out all the stops to win you over. You must keep them intrigued and uncertain.

To seduce an Aries, present yourself as a challenge. Never forget that Aries is ruled by Mars, the God of War. It must have been an Aries who coined the expression "All's fair in love and war." To Aries, love is warfare. They want the challenge, the battle and the conquest. Once they feel they have conquered you, you're history.

Above all else: never let them feel they have conquered you *before* you've had sex together. If you do, you may never get that roll in the hay.

The art of seducing an Aries is in the timing. While the Ram is chasing you, they'll feel very horny—very horny indeed. But once you have confessed you desperately want them, you're no longer a challenge. You've surrendered, so you've automatically become much less desirable. They may not even want to go through with the act—though the male Aries is unlikely to forgo at least one perfunctory boink if only to add another notch to his belt.

Accordingly, you must keep to an absolute minimum the time lapse between indicating you want to do it and doing it. Which leads us to . . .

Seduction 1: The Pounce

The directest of direct methods: pounce.

Aries understand sudden and dramatic beginnings.

The minute the door to the apartment closes behind them, take them in your arms and give them a kiss that goes on for as long as it takes you to rip their clothes off.

Perhaps you don't need to wait until you reach their apartment. You could pull the car over somewhere secluded and go for it. Or find a more creative use for the broom closet at work. Let your imagination go. Remember—Aries is a natural athlete.

If you are *sure* that the vibes are right and that your target is in pure Aries mode, you could dispense with preliminaries and go straight for the direct grope. This gives Aries a wicked thrill. It's crude, rude and raw. They'll be impressed: here is someone who doesn't mess around. (See Sagittarius, the Grab.)

Seduction 2: The Challenge

Key tactic: Keep presenting yourself as a challenge.

At this point, you've presumably got Aries on the boil with your about-to-hit-the-big-time image. You need also to have subtly conveyed that, while you are Mr. or Ms. Supercool on the surface, there is a latent Mt. Vesuvius underneath ready to burst forth when the right Pompeii comes along.

By this stage, Mr. or Ms. Aries won't be able to figure out why you haven't leapt on them already. (Aries seldom have a low opinion of their sexual magnetism.) Now is the time for tactic 2(b): you reveal why you have held yourself back from jumping all over them. You hint that you are probably too much for them to handle. You're a heartbreaker. You feel guilty about all the emotional carnage you've wrought. You're basically a good person but . . . well . . . it's not your fault other people fall in love with you . . . you don't ask them to and, well, frankly, some people just can't keep up with your level of passion.

Some Sun signs would run a mile from such egomaniacal revelations, but

Aries like directness and relate to inflated egos. If this tactic works, they will regard you as even more of a challenge.

Mr. or Ms. Aries will now reply with something like, "You don't have to worry about me. I can take care of myself. I can handle it."

Look them in the eye and . . .

Seize the moment.

If you are in a restaurant, feel them up under the table. Ask the waiter for the bill, reach for your wallet or purse with one hand and use your other hand to make your way up their thigh. Maintain a nonchalant expression.

Aries go for an illicit thrill. You don't have to worry about making it to your place for your first passionate encounter. Improvise.

You must impress them with the overpowering nature of your raw lust. You want them *now*.

If you are in the living room, don't wait to get them into the bedroom. Immediacy is everything. If you don't jump at this point, the moment may be lost forever.

Don't hit them at 2 p.m. with the revelation that you are dying to get into their pants if you really do have to go back to work. Aries is likely to go away and think about it. This is dangerous. "Huh, well, they're really infatuated with me. Well, of course they are," they'll think.

You are now an ex-challenge. Other people who are more of a challenge will start to pass through Aries' mind.

You've blown it.

No, you must be ready to rush them to the nearest motel or parked car within minutes of confessing your desire. Be prepared. If you leave an Aries to go in search of condoms, they may not be there when you get back.

You must be reaching for the brastrap or jockstrap within five minutes (maximum) of any admission of lust.

Seduction 3: The Outrageous Move

If progress in passion is stalled, try the Outrageous Move. (This seduction is a close relative of the Pounce.)

Say you find yourself in a long conversation with an Aries at your place and are wondering how to make the quantum leap from endless chitchat to kissing, groping and the full fireworks. The solution is to short-circuit this procedure with the Outrageous Move.

Without a hint of warning, make your move—even in midsentence. ". . . and so I really think (*zip!*) . . . that unilateral (*tug!*) . . . negotiations (*rip!*) . . . should not prejudice . . . (*ahh!*)"

Be bold and brazen. Select one or more items from Column A to be suddenly connected to one of their items in Column B.

Column A	Column B
tongue	buttons
fingers	zippers
teeth	bra
toes	neck
lips	ear
	big toe
	thighs

The response you are looking for is shocked pleasure. The response you are *not* looking for is shocked horror. But if that's what comes, consider switching quickly into Seduction on the Battlefield and getting your timing right at the second foray.

Seduction 4: Seduction on the Battlefield

Aries love the smell of battle, the adrenaline of confrontation, the excitement of a clash of wills. In the Aries psyche, it is a very short step from conflict to sexual arousal. They can find a heated argument a major form of foreplay.

Your goal is physical, but you can enter this seduction from either the physical or the mental arena. Consider these battlegrounds:

Chess

Card games

Tennis (squash, racquetball, etc.)

Water sports (fighting for possession of a ball in a swimming pool, perhaps?)

Intellectual debate

The intellectual debate could be your best bet because it can be prolonged or suddenly interrupted. Engage them in a vigorous debate on . . . whatever. Get them really steamed up. Obviously you are going to subscribe to the opposite position to the one you know they hold. If they are rabidly right-wing, become a born-again socialist. At the point where you see their martial momentum reaching take-off point, *you* take off. Grab them. Kiss them with vicious intent; rip their clothes off. In military terms, this would be a full frontal assault. (See Seduction 1: The Pounce.)

Seduction 5: The Initiation

It's part of the challenge psychology of Aries that they like to boldly go where no one has gone before.

This is one sign to whom you can confess a secret sexual longing that's never been fulfilled . . . yet. This alone might tempt them to participate. Confess you're a virgin. They will want to deflower you. Confess your ignorance of oral sex, confess your lifelong desire to be tied up with black stockings. Aries will be tempted.

Seduction 6: The Pretend Virgin

While either sex could try this with an Aries, a woman will probably be best able to carry off the Pretend Virgin seduction.

The aim here is not to lie, but to indulge this Aries fantasy of deflowering maidens and by pretending you are one. You may even like to assume a role: the chaste Southern belle, the convent-trained innocent, the sixteenth-century village maid.

Or you may just act as if you were a sixteen-year-old would-be sexpot still in possession of her virginity, eager to dispose of it but a bit frightened too. Pout. Look innocent. Gasp. "You *will* be gentle with me, won't you, since it's my first time and all?"

Aries will know you're playacting but should be unable to resist playing along with you and will be straining to unleash himself upon you and relieve you of your pretend virginity.

Seduction 7: New Mounts to Conquer

Aries love new thrills—even if they are only variations on the theme of an old thrill. The trick is to present the Aries with the opportunity to make a new entry into the erotic database.

Think: "What new possibilities do I have to offer that they may not have tried before?"

Perhaps you could be their first redhead, their first priest, their first nun, their first schoolteacher, their first ex-hooker, their first rock star, their first film director, their first ballerina, their first politician, their first member of the Secret Service.

Can you offer some status that will allow them to glow in having "conquered" you? Are you related to royalty, to Madonna, to Michael Jackson, to Rasputin, to Casanova? Are you about to have your first role on the screen, about to have your first best-selling book published?

Can you offer some new, unusual venue they haven't tried before: yacht, plane, train compartment, treehouse, rowboat, tent, hot-air balloon, billiard table, swing, ambassadorial suite at the Hilton?

Seduction 8: Unexpected Bedfellows

Aries have a reputation for being easily sexually aroused first thing in the morning. If you know there is a sexual charge between you and an Aries, why don't you try rising at the crack of dawn and contriving to crawl into bed with your Aries to see what happens?

Perhaps you could scheme to stay overnight at their place after ensuring that your car won't start. Or maybe you've made sure your Aries is in the adjoining motel room. Knock on their door at 6 a.m.; move straight toward the prewarmed bed. They'll get the idea.

WARNING: Some of these Aries seductions are rather . . . er, sudden. You need cast-iron self-esteem to engage in any of the "shock tactic" seductions for Aries (or the other Fire signs, Sagittarius and Leo). If you don't have it, forget it. If you fall flat on your face, Aries will not hesitate to spread a wildfire version of what didn't happen in which you star as an Oscar-winning nerd. You must have a prepared selection of drop-dead comeback lines such as:

"Nobody told me they were in therapy for sexual dysfunction."

"Obviously I'm too much for them to handle."

"Hey, I thought they were hot stuff. I didn't know they were a wimp."

Seduction 9: The Dare

Aries find it very hard to resist a dare. Suggest something outrageous. Get them to one of the following locales:

Between floors in their office building. Press the stop button.

The stairwell at work.

The boss's desk after hours.

The front row at a movie theater.

Make a move. Say something provocative. "I'm game. Are you?"

Even if this seduction doesn't come off, they'll be impressed by your sheer audacity. It should be good groundwork for Seduction 1, 3, 4 or 7.

Other good Aries seductions:

The Instant Seduction (see Gemini)

Seduction by Curiosity (Gemini)

The Five-Star Seduction (Leo)

A Streetcar Named Desire (Leo)

The Reverse Grab (Scorpio)

The Vamp (Scorpio)

Jungle Drums (Sagittarius)

The Grab (Sagittarius)

The Egomaniacal Sales Pitch (Sagittarius)

The Tarzan-and-Jane (Sagittarius)

Sex with an Aries

■ ■ ■

Now that you've got your Aries into the bed, it's time to lather up their ego. Tell them every honest (or even halfway honest) positive thing you can think of. Her breasts drive you crazy. His biceps are amazing. Her butt drives you wild. His equipment is monumental.

Remember: Aries are ego-obsessed. But all egos are built on the fragile inner child. Many Aries are so convinced of their own wonderfulness that they themselves never understand just how fragile their ego is.

(Of course, you will meet Aries with fragile egos working hard to maintain a convincing front. If you do, you'll soon realize that their primary obsession is to build up their confidence and self-esteem. In which case, your appreciation of their sexual delights could be worth far more than a whole year with an expensive therapist.)

Postcoital praise will go a long, long way with an Aries.

Aries women (as well as the other Fire signs, Leo and Sagittarius) are very impressed in the bedroom by the me-Tarzan-you-Jane approach. They like sex a bit on the wild side. Mars, the ruling planet of Aries, is the planet of *male* sexuality. Remember that the symbol of Aries is the Ram—not the sheep. Aries women can have a very male-like sexual appetite—including the desire for conquest. Ms. Aries usually doesn't mind calling a fuck a fuck and probably prefers that you do too. If you want to do something a bit out of the ordinary, suggest it in plain language and she'll be tempted.

Remember: they love a challenge. If it's a first for them, they are likely to give it a go on those grounds alone. Moreover, if it's a first for you, they are likely to want to get in on the act. If you are aiming to dispose of your virginity, Aries would just love to initiate you. (Though, frankly, you'd probably be better off going for a more patient, caring sign—consider a Capricorn or a Pisces.)

On the other hand, if you're one of those guys who has a secret worry that your equipment is smaller than the national average, the Aries woman is not for you. Aries women are most likely to be impressed by *big things* and have never believed those magazine articles that say size doesn't matter.

If you are bedding an Aries man, he needs to be reassured that he is hung like the Empire State Building—or at least up to the national average—especially if he isn't.

Aries love to be told that any aspect of their sexual performance is the best you've ever had. You probably won't need to exaggerate their manual skills—Aries are infamously handy.

THE BIG WARNING: Aries are notorious for being typhoons of passion at the beginning of relationships but fading into sporadic zephyrs the longer the relationship goes on.

Maybe this is because they are already seducing the new boy or girl on the block—mentally, anyway.

They must be certain you are ready for lust at the squeak of a zipper; and yet, at the same time, they must perceive you as nonchalant and a little uninterested—so that they can feel they sexually conquer you each time. This is where sexual relationships with Aries can get quite tricky. They want attention but will shun you if they perceive you as a subservient lapdog. Aries often create their own Catch-22: they want you to be besotted by them but despise you if you are.

If you sense that your Aries lover is just beginning to lose interest in you, the best way to respark them is with something different, something they haven't tried before. Aries loves to perform and be admired, so try staging your own fantasy role-play: master-slave, schoolgirl-teacher, chaste virgin and crusading knight, pillaging Hun and village maiden, bored housewife and traveling salesman. Emphasize the "initiation" element.

Never forget that Aries like to be dared by something they haven't tried yet. They especially like to be challenged by public sex. Invite them to go down on you in the second row of the movies. Try sexual congress, fully clothed, standing underneath a bridge. Suggest that the two of you try to work your way through the Kama Sutra. Try working your way through every seduction scenario in this book!

Remember that they are easily aroused in the morning. Try mounting your Aries partner before they have fully woken up. Some Aries really go for this.

If the flame of Aries passion is starting to sputter, one way to reignite it is to start talking about breaking up—or actually to break up. Kiss them goodbye. Once you are heading into the sunset, you are again a challenge and your desirability rating automatically soars.

A less dramatic version of this is simply not to phone them for a few days so that they begin to worry and suspect you are losing interest. They are sure to suspect that you are in pursuit of someone else. If you can get them battering at your door and then give them the sexual night of their life, you've got it made—for a few more weeks anyway.

How to Handle a Relationship with an Aries

■ ■ ■

Having commenced a sexual liaison with an Aries, your best bet is to explain that you are only interested in a two-month relationship—maximum. Hint that most people become sexual bores in a matter of weeks. Say it's a sad fact of life that most people can't cut the mustard in the cot for any longer than a couple of months—at least the spicy mustard you must have.

Here is a challenge to gladden the heart of any Aries. They now must perform truly splendid sexual stunts—so splendid that they will convince you how extraordinary they are and defy your theory of the two-month burnout.

What to do after two months?

This may indeed be the time to end it, you know. Think about it seriously.

If not, let it drift on past the two-month deadline for a while. They will certainly point out to you that you have been together for more than two months. "Really? Jeez. Well, things are going pretty well. But I don't want a long-term commitment." You might hint that you've never had a relationship with anyone for longer than four months because *nobody* has ever maintained your sexual interest or kept up with you sexually for that long. Hint that they would have to be the most interesting person and best boink in the country. Another challenge to bring joy to an Aries heart.

And, after that, what about long-term commitment?

Well, yes, long-term commitment . . . er . . . hmmm . . . maybe . . . but keep in mind that you must always present a challenge to an Aries. They must always see it as a challenge to win your affection or sexual interest. Once they think they've got you totally hooked, you're history.

"And Alexander wept, for there were no worlds left to conquer."

Alexander the Great, an Aries, having conquered the entire world by the age of twenty-one, was grief-stricken because there was nothing left to conquer. Remember this, and keep something in reserve that the Aries must strive to conquer.

With many Aries, it can be a serious mistake to admit you're in love with them.

The first time—or even the first few times—they hear you say "I love you," they will be most gratified. "This person is mine. They have been overwhelmed by my good looks, talent and sexual magnetism." Soon after this, however, they will get bored and start to take you for granted. They've vanquished you—not only your body but your mind, your heart and your soul—and now they want someone else to overpower. They're bored with you. They will project this feeling onto you: *you're* the one who's boring.

So be circumspect about any confessions of undying love.

To keep an Aries interested in you, keep them off balance. Two excellent ways to do this are:

1. hint that they are boring;

2. tell them they are boring.

Deep down, many Aries are convinced that they are the most interesting person in the room/the suburb/the country/the galaxy. If you hint that they are worn out, boring or passé, a proton bomb will be unleashed inside their egos, and a previously tired or dispirited Aries will become energized before your very eyes. They will start being sexy, seductive, scintillating, as they set out to reconvince you that they are the most interesting, most sexual person in the known universe.

To get the most out of your relationship with an Aries, keep them tantalized, tempted and on their toes. As long as you can do that, you will retain their interest. If you fail in this task, well . . . there are eleven other Sun signs.

Your first challenge, then, is to keep them on their toes—but the second challenge is to stay on your toes too. Love can be a battleground with an

Aries. Ever-competitive Aries aims to be the dominant force in any relationship and can be quite ruthless in achieving this.

Aries would rather display anger than vulnerability. They often resist self-
exploration and self-knowledge, as they fear this would expose inner frail-
ties that they simply do not want to know about. They resist admitting
vulnerabilities for fear that this would make them appear weak and place
their partner in the dominant position. On the other hand, if you display
your vulnerability, they could go for your emotional jugular, or simply
discard you as a wimp. If you are the sentimental type (for example, a
Cancer or a Pisces), you may be well advised to focus your groin on another
sign of the Zodiac.

If you enter a relationship with an Aries, you have to be prepared for
stand-up, toe-to-toe psychic slugfests. Indeed, with some Aries, a sure sign
that they have lost affection for you is when they stop arguing with you.

Aries are incredibly competitive—even with the ones they love. This puts
an Aries-lover in a no-win situation. If you lose the battle, you'll lose their
respect. Aries disdain losers. However, if you win the battle, they may flee
this frightening prospect of equality in a relationship.

If their partner exceeds them in appeal, luck or success, it can plunge
them into a vortex of envy and jealousy. Frustrations in any aspect of their
lives—career, financial, social—will also fill them with anger, which they
will want to take out on someone.

Be mentally, physically and spiritually ready for the fray or you may be
sliced to ribbons in the knife-spoked wheels of the Aries fighting chariot.

Aries are at their best at the beginning of a relationship. They are sexual
dynamos: excited and exciting. It is this initial impact that draws people into
long-term commitments with Aries; unfortunately Aries are often not suited
to the long haul. The agony for the partner is thinking that they can relight
the Ram's fuse and respark that initial incandescent energy and connection.
All too often, it simply can't be done. You must either accept the reduced
level of passion or move on.

A final warning: sexual exclusivity is difficult for Aries, but they will
expect you to be their exclusive sexual property.

Must-Do's

Reassure the Aries male that he is abundantly equipped or at least equal to the national average.

Reassure Aries of both sexes that their technique is outstanding.

Dress well.

Keep them convinced that there is a potential sexual adventure just around the corner.

No-No's

Don't appear too interested, but don't appear uninterested.

Never let sex fall into a pattern.

Never tell an Aries you are in love with them.

How to End a Relationship with an Aries

■ ■ ■

Aries cannot comprehend why anyone would want to end a relationship with them. They can quite understand why they would jettison some boring been-around-too-long for a new target, but why would anyone discard someone as sexy and dynamic as they are?

If they drop you, your feelings won't be taken into account. If you drop them, you have committed the unforgivable and the inconceivable.

There are some signs with whom you can remain friends, but Aries is not usually one of them. If they broke up with you, it is because you are "boring"—so why would they want to know you any longer? If you broke up with them, you have cast a slur on their wonderfulness. The only way they can rationalize this is to change their opinion of you: obviously you are emotionally inadequate, if not mentally imbalanced.

Your best bet may be to apply cooling balm to their singed ego as you push them out the door. "You're too exciting for me . . . I need more peace and quiet . . . I can't handle your huge energy . . . You deserve someone much better than me." That sort of rubbish.

Breaking up with an Aries is dangerous. They will not be overcome by paroxysms of jealousy (as a Scorpio would be), but they may be driven into an absolute fury caused by dislocated ego.

All thwarted Fire sign types are capable of letting the air out of the tires on your car, and possibly scratching nice little goodbye notes such as I HATE YOU, DROP DEAD, YOU ASSHOLE in the paint.

If at all possible, engineer the situation so that the termination of the relationship appears to have been orchestrated by them. This protects their ego. One good way of getting Aries disenchanted with you is to become a fawning sycophant, hanging on their every word and giving in to their every whim.

Above all, the thing to avoid is this: the Aries suggests that you break up and you just say, "Yes, okay, I think that's a good idea." This will intrigue them—"How could they give *me* up so easily; they should be devastated by the loss of *me*; they should be weeping or having a spontaneous nervous breakdown—they must be stronger than I thought."

Before you know it, they will want you back. Aries like dramatic starts and restarts—and they love the chase. As you are walking away from them, you again become a quarry to be pursued.

If you really do want it to be over—definitively over—then, as soon as they suggest you break up, bury your face in a pillow and sob convincingly. Leaving in tears will convince them that you were actually too weak to be of interest. Clearly you are a wimp and of no further use.

Once the relationship is over, Aries generally haven't got the slightest interest in their ex-partner's feelings.

Arians at Their Best

■ ■ ■

Arians are a Molotov cocktail of raw sexual energy and personal magnetism. They are active, dynamic, outgoing, passionate, courageous, frank, inquisitive and wild. They are great self-starters and initiators. They can help you rediscover your joie de vivre, your sense of humor and the meaning of lust and life.

Arians at Their Worst

■ ■ ■

Arians have an overpowering desire to dominate. They are unashamedly prepared to use sarcasm, bullying, belittling, haranguing, door-slamming and verbal cruelty to maintain the dominant position in a relationship.

They can be overly competitive, vain, self-righteous, pushy, confrontational and reckless.

While Aries can be a volcano of passion at the start of a relationship, their passion can fade in the long haul.

They can be so obsessed with their own ego, status and future or past successes that they completely lack concern for the feelings of others. In consequence, partners can come to feel that Aries has merely used them to satisfy their own ego-centered ends and transitory carnal urges.

Sexy Arians

■ ■ ■

Diana Ross, Warren Beatty, Casanova, Marlon Brando, Elle Macpherson, Billie Holiday, Omar Sharif, Julie Christie, Dudley Moore, Charlie Chaplin, Wilhelm Reich, Alec Baldwin, Shannen Doherty, Steve McQueen, Gabriela Sabatini.

Unsexy Arians

■ ■ ■

Doris Day, Wayne Newton, Anthony Perkins, David Frost, Rod Steiger, Nikita Khrushchev, Fatty Arbuckle, Debbie Reynolds, Hayley Mills, Francis Ford Coppola, Elton John, Tiny Tim.

TAURUS

♉

April 21st to May 21st

...

Newton's First Law of Taurodynamics:

Objects maintain a state of rest unless acted

upon by a nuclear bomb.

Newton's Second Law of Taurodynamics:

Force $=$ mass $\times$ anger

Newton's Third Law of Taurodynamics:

For every action there is an equal and

opposite nonreaction.

The Lure of a Taurus

■ ■ ■

If you are looking for a relationship that is safe, with no nasty surprises, if you are looking for someone reliable and predictable, someone who will not lightly cast you aside for another, someone who will be loyal and will not hear of others criticizing you (though that someone may periodically put the boot into you themselves), Mr. or Ms. Taurus could be your ideal companion.

If you're in a state of chronic unease as part of the psychological after-shock of an on-again, off-again relationship or one where you didn't know whether you actually were in a relationship, consider the steadfast Bull.

Taureans are great homebodies, so if you are looking for a lover who is not going to bleed your bank account and will be perfectly happy with evenings in and home-cooked meals, this could be the Sun sign for you.

While every astrologer knows about the small percentage of lean Tau-reans, ninety percent tend toward the short and chunky—indeed, even the ones who aren't short can look that way because they are so thickset. Taurean men can have great solidity and strength, and could be irresistible if you're into barrel chests, biceps and pecs and the great outdoors.

Taurean women can have a lovely "earth mother" quality about them, but if anorexic models are your ideal of feminine pulchritude, most Taureans won't fit the bill. They are inclined to put on weight if they look sideways at a lettuce leaf—and they aren't likely to be looking sideways at it, they are more likely to have already devoured it, along with more fattening fare. By contrast, if you like love handles to hold on to, and especially if you're a breast man, consider Ms. Taurus. What's more, their legs aren't bad and they often have absolutely beautiful skin.

Indeed, some Taureans can be just plain beautiful all around. Taurus is ruled by Venus—the planet of love, sensuousness and beauty. The more Venusian Taurean can have the looks of a professional model and a refined taste for the elegant, the erotic and all pleasures of the senses.

Taurus is the first Earth sign of the Zodiac, and we do mean Earth. They are often great nature lovers and gardeners. This is one of the few signs that will accept a cheap camping trip as a romantic event. They are practical, down-to-earth, no-nonsense.

Constancy, consistency, devotion, reliability: if these are the qualities you desire, look no further than for someone born under the sign of the Bull and Venus, the planet of love.

How to Interest a Taurus

■ ■ ■

Key tactic: Find out what their values are and mirror them.

Taureans don't believe opposites attract. They expect their partner to share their values, their tastes, their opinions, their hobbies. Find out what they believe in and, as much as is honestly possible, agree with them. They want you to like the same books, the same movies, the same music, the same banks, the same cough medicine, the same toothpaste, the same mayonnaise.

Taureans are conservative and not at all intrigued by the eccentric, different or bizarre. In fact, they are downright suspicious of nonconformity. They will be comforted to learn that your tastes and values are the same as theirs.

Earthy, practical Taurus is most unlikely to be impressed by the sort of short-term superficial success that could fascinate an Aries. Flashy clothes and name-dropping are of no interest to them. They want to hear that you have a steady job and money in the bank.

If you want to impress a Taurean, emphasize your establishment qualities. Steady, secure, sensible is the way to come across if you want them to do likewise.

Taureans are very interested in family lineage and tribal life. Don't say anything negative about your parents; Taureans are great believers in genetics. They want to inspect your pedigree. They want to know that your family is respectable and sane. Tell them your clan has been living in the same house for three generations. Very solid, very reassuring.

Taureans will take note of your love of nature. They will be pleased to hear that you like to go hiking in the woods and highly impressed if you know the botanical names of plants.

The proverb "A bird in the hand is worth two in the bush" was coined by a

Taurean. Indeed, the original Taurean version is "Half a bird is worth three in the bush."

Talk about safe money—conservative investments, property, having it in the bank. Stay well away from any chat about gambling—which for a true Taurean would include the stock market. In fact, anything that isn't blue-chip or government-backed may well be labeled gambling.

Do everything you can to impress them with your solid, dependable, commonsense, down-to-earth nature.

Don't get involved with a Taurean unless you have a full frontal approach to food. They don't want to hear that you are picky, fussy or allergic. They want a hearty eater who can dig in with them. (Warning! Do not share a communal plate with them because you may come away hungry—divide it in half. Throw out your chopsticks if the Taurean is using a spoon—unless you are on a starvation diet. Taureans are notoriously fast eaters. But don't ever complain that they eat too quickly. They will get terribly offended. To them, wolfing is natural.) If a Taurean cooks for you, bring your appetite. Your desirability may drop if you decline a second or third helping. Skip lunch if necessary.

And then there is the legendary Taurean sweet tooth. Come bearing gifts of chocolates and sweets. How could they resist the would-be lover who arrives armed with chocolate hazelnut cake and a bottle of good port for a cozy evening noshing in front of the fire?

Suggested opening line: "You must try this cake. Can I get you some?"

What to talk about: Food, nature, your houseplants, gardening, family history, paintings, music, pottery, property, your belief in traditional values, the need to get the country (society, education, etc.) back on track, anything that supports reestablishing the establishment.

Where to take them: All dates must involve eating; go for nice spots, but nothing too flashy or trendy—trips to art galleries, pottery and craft shops, the opera, concerts, museums; camping trips, picnics, walks in parks; day trips to historical gardens and houses, nurseries, garden centers, farms.

What to give them: If possible, find out about some favorite thing of theirs that has finally worn out after decades of use and buy them one *exactly the same* (or as near as possible). They will compliment you on your taste. Other good presents are old books with leather bindings, prints and pictures, houseplants, historical novels and videos, antique kitchenware and traditional food. Try Scottish shortbread, old-fashioned chocolates and other sweets, whatever they had when they were young; not new, not different, what they are used to—with the possible exception of a microwave oven, for home cooking quickly!

How to Seduce a Taurus

■ ■ ■

Key tactic: The way to a Taurean's sexual organs is through the stomach.

Taureans love food. The only happy Taurean is one with a full stomach.

Watching a lowly grub transform into a beauteous butterfly is nothing compared with observing the metamorphosis undergone by a hungry Taurean becoming a full, calm and happy one. To watch a hungry Taurean stuff his or her face is to watch an angry bull become a placid cow, a snarling Mr. Hyde become a beneficent Dr. Jekyll.

Never try to hold a conversation with a hungry Taurean. Never come between them and a meal—never even suggest waiting ten minutes. If you want to get into a Taurean's good graces and stay there, feed them. If you're a good cook, they will be putty in your hands.

Never commit the sin of inviting your Taurean for a meal that takes two hours to reach the table. This is a primary Taurean turn-off and will be taken as evidence of lack of consideration. A microwave could be considered a legitimate Taurean marital aid.

Keep the fridge well stocked with tidbits and gourmet treats ready to offer them the instant they walk in the door. This will ensure that they visit you frequently.

By now, you should have grasped the fundamental principle: you lure a Taurean to bed with a trail of food. Appetizer in the dining room, informal main course in the living room, dessert in the bedroom.

You could never seduce a hungry Taurean. It would be rape. Taurean logic: stomach first; sex second.

There is bound to be some particular sweet your Taurus cannot resist. Find out what it is. Never invite them back to your place for coffee.

You must say, "Would you like to come back to my place for coffee and cake?"

If the scene of the seduction is to be your place, Taurus is probably the only Sun sign likely to be interested in the framed photograph of your grandfather. Reminisce about Gramps. You were so fond of the old boy that you've kept his spectacles.

At this stage, you shouldn't be aiming to overexcite your Taurean. Rather, your aim has to be to make them feel *safe*. You need to get them mellow, make them confident that you are not going to do anything at all unorthodox or wild.

And since Taureans feel safest in familiar surroundings, their own bed is probably a better couch of seduction than yours.

Seduction 1: The Nudist

Nudity is a big turn-on for Taureans. They like *flesh*.

And they like to know what they are getting into! They don't like surprise packages. They like to check you over before it's too late.

Don't worry if you don't have the greatest body in the civilized world. They just like bodies. They are not usually into erotic underwear or striptease or slowly undressing you—they are into flesh, nudity and getting it off. Being confronted with naked flesh is a major form of Taurean foreplay.

The challenge, then, is to find a legitimate, wholesome way to get your gear off—and, even better, to get both of you naked simultaneously.

Here are some tried-and-true scenarios for offering your Taurean a sneak preview of delights to come.

Seduction 1(a): Venus or Adonis Rising from the Waves. Arrive at their place hot and sweaty after physical work or exercise.

Apologize and request the use of the bath. Forget to lock the door. Treat them to your repertoire of Bizet, Puccini and Andrew Lloyd Webber. (Singing in the bath is a common Taurean hobby—remember, they like you to share their values!) Make sure your towel falls in the water and call out for them to bring you a dry one. Or ask for a drink.

If they deliver the goods, ask them to join you in singing the chorus. If the vibes are right, make a grab.

Après bath, smother yourself in talcum powder and saunter out draped only in a towel that threatens to fall off at any moment.

Sit discomfitingly close to them. Watch them sweat.

Ask them to apply talc or moisturizer to your back. The towel may slip a bit. This is a good time to ask for a neck rub, a back rub . . . "Ouch, it's my tennis muscle . . . lower back . . . down there . . . farther down . . . farther . . ."

We leave the rest up to you.

Seduction 1(b): The Dorothy Lamour. A good scenario for getting both of you nude simultaneously—and apparently unpremeditatedly—is skinny-dipping.

This is a very, very good suggestion if you have the use of a friend's private pool or have one of your own.

Perhaps you can find a way to combine skinny-dipping with the Taurean love of nature.

Imagine this: It's a warm day. You and your Taurean date are driving in the country and you just happen to take an interesting little side road and just happen to stop by a pond or stream and it is so hot but neither of you brought a swimsuit. Oh well, why not just strip and jump in? It's more natural, after all. If swimming in the nude surrounded by nature doesn't get your Taurean aroused, you may have to start wondering about their hormone levels.

Other possibilities for mutual wet nudity include a private sauna or hot tub.

Seduction 1(c): The Rubenesque Seduction. You may also try the subtler technique of perusing a book of artistic nudes with them. Or take them to an art gallery and wax romantic about the Arcadian nudes. If they are particularly taken with one, buy the print, have it framed and present it to them. You could be rewarded. A sort of seduction by art gallery.

Seduction 2: Necking

The sign of Taurus rules the neck. For Taureans, the neck is a major erogenous zone. They can be quite turned on if you kiss and nibble their neck. A hot tip is to target the back of the neck, a neglected erogenous zone in the West but very popular in the East.

You might start out by offering to give them a neck and shoulder massage, then venture a peck or two, a nibble, a kiss. If you are favored with responsive squeaks or groans, keep focusing on the neck while you explore other zones with your hands.

Seduction 3: *Déjeuner sur l'Herbe* or Pig-Out in the Park

To make it very difficult for a Taurean to say no, combine nature and food.

(If your particular Taurean isn't crazy about nature and the great outdoors, move the following scene to your backyard or dining room.)

Organize a picnic in a secluded dell. Pack the blankets, pack the pâté, the cold chicken, the desserts, the condoms placed delicately under the cheesecake in the picnic basket.

As you are laying out the first course, talk of nature. You feel one with Mother Earth. Aren't animals inspiring? So natural and uninhibited. Here in the greenery, you experience your body as part of nature. You feel natural. You feel physical. Modern urban life is all in the head, isn't it? We need to get back to the earth, etc.

This should all be smoothed over with a very fine bottle of wine.

The first course has been devoured by your Taurean target; only now may you venture a kiss or two. But don't stand between them and dessert.

Make your move the instant dessert disappears. Mr. or Ms. Taurus is likely to be so caught up in the combination of earth, nature, food and animal passion that it will be difficult to say no.

Be aware that Taureans are legendary postlunch nappers. You must jump in through the window of opportunity while they are sensuously mellow but before their eyelids (and other things) begin to droop.

Having landed your Taurean, you too may now nap. As Taureans themselves so much enjoy the postprandial forty winks, they are unlikely to complain about your rolling over and going to sleep.

Seduction 4: The Tom Jones

Move the pig-out from the park indoors, and you have the basis of the Tom Jones Seduction. If you've never seen that unforgettable scene from the movie *Tom Jones*, rent the video.

The way you devour chicken should leave your Taurean in no doubt that this is what you want to do to them. Consider what is possible with a drumstick. Consider the tearing of flesh off the thigh; consider nibbling your way up the leg, pausing to lock your dining companion's gaze before proceeding to suck meaningfully on the end.

Consider the uses of a stalk of asparagus, traditionally eaten with the fingers, dripping with butter. Reach for the tip with your tongue.

Consider what is possible with fruit. Consider the potential of a half-peeled banana and moistened lips. Consider what can be done with a bunch of grapes—or perhaps just two grapes placed slowly in the mouth and rolled around languidly before the final biting and swallowing.

Men should rehearse what they can do with the plump end of a fig.

Hopefully the Taurean will join in the spirit of things and start devouring food in like manner. See if you can turn it into a salacious competition. After which, there is only one truly suitable dessert . . . them.

The Tom Jones is an earthy, primordial seduction to be used on Taureans who have a sense of fun. It's to be avoided with Librans and Virgos. This seduction is perfect whenever language is a problem. The way you approach a spoonful of ice cream may be all the sexual Esperanto you ever need.

Seduction 5: The Finger-Licking-Good

The more recent version of the Tom Jones seduction is the famous fridge scene from 9½ Weeks. (Again, rent the video if you need some tips.)

Instead of feeding yourself à la Kama, you feed your Taurean à la Sutra.

Pop strawberries and cream in their mouth. Lick any spillage from their face. Hold a large strawberry in your mouth and get them to take it from you. Simultaneously tear flesh from a drumstick. Tease them with food you almost put in their mouth but not quite. Move them smoothly from eating out of your hand to eating you.

This seduction scenario may be intertwined with Pig-Out in the Park or the Tom Jones seduction.

Other good Taurean seductions:

The Instant Breakfast (see Gemini)

The Declaration of Love (Cancer)

The Intimate Evening for Two (Cancer)

Sex with a Taurus

■ ■ ■

A classic Taurean progression is: love, sex, then passion.

They often want to love someone before they have sex with them; then have sex without displaying real physical passion. It may be only at a more advanced stage of the relationship, after they start to feel really safe, that they let their considerable passion and sensual potential loose on you.

They are more likely to discover passion after a bit of practice. But there is a lot of earthy lust in there and, once a Taurean is sexually engaged, their passion can last a lifetime. Indeed, once their libidos are let loose, Taureans can be veritable gluttons for sex. Quantity, quality and yet more quantity.

Patience with your Taurean in the early stages could be a good investment. You have to help habit-dominated Taurus establish good sexual patterns with you. You may have to gently break them in like a car or a new pair of shoes.

Taureans don't equate regularity with boredom. They can handle the idea of a regular 3 p.m. session every Sunday with no problem at all. To them, this means you are dependable, whereas other Sun signs will think you are taking them for granted or that you are just plain boring.

Taureans are tough, so they can take sex at times of the day or night that would ruin the passion and performance of others.

Your earthier Taurean is not usually interested in exploring your entire repertoire of coital positions. They admire staying power and reliability. So long as you can keep working away for half an hour in the one position, that's just fine. If you can't, try a Gemini. Once a Taurean discovers a sexual position that really works for them, they are not generally interested in researching the rest of the Kama Sutra. If you try to maneuver them into a nouvelle position, they may worry that you are secretly intending to inflict something kinky on them.

Any novelty at all in sexual position or technique needs to be approached in such a way as to make it appear safe, acceptable, normal. Taureans are generally not into the wild side of sex. For them, sensual pleasure is more important than excitement. They are sense- and body-oriented. Aim to cater to and participate in their love of touch, sight, sound and taste.

To really spice up your sex life, think oral (they do). Whipped cream and fruit judiciously applied could result in ecstasy. You may have large laundry bills, but it will be worth it. Invest in aerosol bottles of whipped cream or, even better, jars of chocolate sauce.

When it comes to oral sex, don't be shy about raising your hand and saying, "Yes, please." Ms. or Mr. Taurus might surprise you.

The secluded outdoors will usually have a continuing appeal to this earthy sign. Picnics, moonlit strolls on the beach, camping trips and vacations in the country will definitely present opportunities for clothesless encounters of the physical kind.

How to Handle a Relationship with a Taurus

■ ■ ■

Memorize this irregular verb: *I am strong-willed, you are stubborn, he is pig-headed.* All three of these people are Taureans.

Taureans are *stubborn*—or, in their terminology, determined.

We all know that if two people are to create a mutually satisfying relationship, compromises and adjustments must be made. That is, all of us know this except Taureans. Getting a Taurean to change is about as much fun as having a circumcision reversed.

Taurus is the sign of the Bull. Picture yourself trying to budge a placid but huge bull by pushing against him; now you have some idea what you are up against when trying to get a Taurus to change.

Always remember: *Taureans love the rut they are in.*

Be prepared to listen to all their moans about their job, their boss, their family and their life, but don't, for heaven's sake, suggest they should actually do anything about it.

These phrases were invented by Taureans:

"People just have to take me as I am."

"People just have to love me as I am."

"Why should I change for anyone?"

Many women are attracted to men on the basis of wanting to reconstruct their personality. "I can get him to open up, I can get him to communicate, I can make him more loving, I can change him." If this is your inclination, *do not become involved with a Taurean.*

Let's say you've got a Taurean with an irritating habit you want to eradicate—you want them to give up smoking or junk food, pick up after themselves, put down the toilet seat. You can nag them until you are blue in the face. Pointless. You can scream at them. Waste of energy. You can threaten to leave them. Did they hear you?

The only way to get them to change is to *have a stranger say it to them.*

There you are. This is the previously unrevealed secret key to effecting change in Taureans—if you must try to change them at all. Don't ask us why it works. You could nag them for years about their weight problem. Futile. The worst Taureans are virtuoso naggers themselves but have the responsiveness to nagging of a cement block.

What you need to do is organize some stranger to make a casual comment—about their weight, for example. Whammo, they'll come back home absolutely determined to reform their eating habits.

Why is it so? All we can do is make this suggestion. Taureans believe everybody should love them just as they are. If they toss their underwear on the floor all the time or go to sleep in front of the TV while still refusing to let you change the channel, that's just how they are—people should simply accept it. After all, it's their TV, it's their clothes, it's their floor. (Possession is ten-tenths of Taurean law.) Anybody who wants them to change in any way obviously does not love them. If you are upset by tripping over their underwear or having to watch what they want to watch even when they're not watching it, it just shows that you don't really love them.

However, a passing stranger doesn't have any vested interest in changing them. So if the stranger gently suggests that they are filthy pigs, maybe they'll realize that they are a bit porcine after all, and perhaps they'd better do something about it.

Try paying a succession of (brave) strangers to hint at areas that need improvement. We say *brave* strangers because Taureans do have a temper. Did we say temper? We left out nouns like fury, rage, holocaust, volcanic eruptions, and adjectives like homicidal, maniacal, overwhelming, catastrophic.

Taureans may be slow to anger, but if you do anger one—*watch out!* Every object and person in the vicinity will be endangered.

Remember that big, slow, gentle bull you were pushing against? Consider what happens when that bull becomes angry; consider that huge bulk galvanized into total fury; consider all this charging at you at 30 mph with sharpened horns. This is the angry Taurean in action.

Key tip: Find out what makes them angry and avoid doing it.

Words, objects and people tend to go flying in all directions when a Taurean gets mad. Make sure you are not the one who gets them angry, but if you are stupid enough to do so, *immediately* absent yourself for at least two hours, preferably two days. Never try to talk to or reason with an angry Taurean. (Would you try to talk to an angry bull?) Before returning to the scene, phone to make sure it's over and it's safe to return.

Make no mistake, no matter how placid or slow to anger your Taurean partner might be, they have the capacity to become a human tornado. They seem to have only two states: placidity and volcanic rage, with no real in-between. They do not get "a little angry."

They can bottle up annoyances for many years, and then they all come out as if a dam has burst. Taurus will then rake up all the muck on you for the last twenty years and catalog all your flaws, faults and mistakes.

At such times, they will come across as insufferably holier-than-thou—as if they had all the answers to life, which they worked out when they were sixteen. (Indeed, Taurus is perhaps the sign most likely to have easy worldly success at an early age.)

The worst of Taureans have no concept that other people have different needs, different callings, different destinies.

At their worst, Taureans can use their temper to cow their partner into submission. Beware the Titanic Taurean Temper Tantrum and their attempts to dominate using that and jealousy.

And always remember: they are not after a partner who wants to "do their own thing." They believe in the attraction of identicals.

Must-Do's

Feed them.

Keep in mind: They love the rut they are in.

Present your most conservative, respectable front.

Agree with all their values and tastes as much as possible.

Never help yourself to their possessions without permission, and maybe not even then.

If they get mad, run away.

No-No's

Never ever come between a Taurean and food.

Never try to hold a conversation with a hungry Taurean.

Never try to change them, even in small ways.

Never criticize members of their family or their relationship with their family. Listen to all their complaints about their family but never ever say anything against them yourself.

Never get them angry.

How to End a Relationship with a Taurus

■ ■ ■

If your relationship is rocky, you'll never get a Taurean to go to counseling or read self-help books. If the ongoingness of the relationship relies on their changing, the relationship is doomed. It's time to abandon ship.

But remember and be warned: Taureans are obsessed with security and continuity. They are allergic to change. More than any other sign, they will attempt to protract an unsatisfactory relationship.

Taureans need to be weaned from a relationship. Sudden change can cause shock and even nervous breakdowns. It might be best to slowly keep changing the nature of the relationship a bit at a time. Start to see them just a little less, then keep seeing them but stop bonking them, then see them less still. Slowly, slowly, slowly. When it comes to a head and they ask you what's wrong, try to emphasize how much you like them and want to be their friend, but say you're afraid you're just not the right person for them. They need someone more solid and dependable. Hint that you are heading for financial ruin caused by wild, speculative investments. Set out to convince them that their life would be more stable, more secure and even financially safer without you in it.

Above all, do not get them mad. It might be best not to tell them you want to break up within smashing distance of your best dinner service. Otherwise the breakup might be more widespread than you originally imagined.

Taureans are very possessive. At the end of a relationship they can get very territorial. "I want my iron back. You used my electricity, you owe me fifty percent of the bill. You burned my teakettle. I want it replaced. You left a mark on my coffee table. You owe me three-quarters of a jar of coffee." If you've lent them something, you may not get it back, but they will want back their toothbrush as well as their one-quarter-remaining tube of toothpaste.

Taureans are hard to shift. Ending a relationship is much more difficult if it involves their moving out of your place.

Taureans at Their Best

■ ■ ■

You can look forward to fidelity, regular sex, regular meals and a regular, stable, home-based life. You will share bounteously in their love of the sensual pleasures: art, music, food, sex. You will bask in a feeling of security—knowing that you can trust the devotion, loyalty and steadfastness of your mate, not to mention their good sense with money and their practical approach to life.

Taureans at Their Worst

■ ■ ■

You'll find yourself in the clutches of an unrefined, gross materialist who will treat you as a possession and try to enforce this ownership through the threat of Titanic Taurean Temper Tantrums. You will find yourself apoplectic with frustration in trying to motivate or change this intractable, ultraconservative, sluggish slob. You will be heartily sickened by the way they stay under the family thumb while simultaneously milking their parents for money. You will long for someone more spiritual, lively and independent.

Sexy Taureans

■ ■ ■

Rudolph Valentino, Gary Cooper, Fred Astaire, Tchaikovsky, Shakespeare, Cher, Audrey Hepburn, Stevie Wonder, Shirley MacLaine, Al Pacino, Ann-Margret, Margot Fonteyn, David Byrne, Candice Bergen, Janet Jackson, Jack Nicholson, Michelle Pfeiffer, Al Pacino, Grace Jones.

Unsexy Taureans

■ ■ ■

Adolf Hitler, Queen Elizabeth II, Immanuel Kant, Glen Campbell, Bing Crosby, Shirley Temple, Karl Marx, Ho Chi Minh, Orson Welles, Salvador Dalí, Liberace, Fats Waller, Raymond Burr, Dennis Hopper, Rupert Murdoch, Socrates, Willie Nelson, Perry Como, Jack Klugman, Sigmund Freud.

GEMINI

♊

May 22nd to June 21st

■■■

I'm not schizophrenic—

we're a Gemini.

The Lure of a Gemini

■ ■ ■

They bounce into the room already talking before the door opens. Their eyes sparkle as they tell you about their day, the class they just started and oh, how are you and where did you get that great shirt and how much did it cost and have you seen that new movie yet why don't we catch it later no I think I'd rather—that book looks interesting, can I borrow—oh, can I use your phone, I just need to make a quick—

You've just been hooked by the sparkle, vivacity and energy of a Gemini.

If you're a refugee from a predictable, humdrum existence, Gemini is for you.

If you like sex to be bookended by lively conversation, Gemini is for you.

If you want someone who looks and thinks young for their age, Gemini is for you.

If you want to have a fling with someone who hasn't got the time to feel guilty about it, Gemini could be the Sun sign for that too. They can be quite amoral (note: not *immoral*). They also need and like lots of experiential titillation (which you will be required to provide lest you be disposed of overnight, so watch out).

If you want someone who can reach full sexual arousal in a breath and peak almost as quickly, consider the electric, spontaneous, vivacious Gemini. The quickie is a favorite course on their sexual menu.

Gemini women—and, to a lesser extent, the men—often have a delightful elfin or pixieish quality. Gemini women tend to be on the short side and rarely get fat. They often have a tomboyish (though not unfeminine) side.

If you are looking for an older, more experienced person, next to Capricorn, youthful and enthusiastic Gemini is your best bet. Whatever their age, if interested in you, they will approach sex and seduction with youthful vigor and enthusiasm. Moreover, they usually look five to ten years younger than their chronological age.

(In fact, many Geminis are a better value in their thirties and forties when they are more grounded, less ratty and less likely to be involved with shallow, unreliable people. In their youth, they can't discriminate between hyperstimulation and quality—in people or in anything else. In consequence, they mismatch themselves simply because they are hooked on short-term trendiness, excitement and glamour.)

The symbol of the Gemini is the Twins. With Gemini you could be getting two—or three—partners for the price of one, all in one trim, youthful package. What more could you want?

How to Interest a Gemini

■ ■ ■

Key tactic: You must quickly—indeed, immediately—establish yourself as one of the most mentally stimulating people they've ever met.

Geminis love ideas. They are information freaks. You need to be brimming with stimulating ideas and *au courant*. Sprinkle your intelligent remarks and observations with the latest buzzwords.

Talk about whatever new thing you're studying. They're very impressed by anyone who is learning anything. They will be interested in *whatever* it is you're a student of—Egyptian hieroglyphics, French, German, conversational Swahili, herbalism, yoga, Indian cooking.

Above all, don't present yourself as a dodo. Never talk about football to a Gemini unless they confess to an interest in it first. They may take such a reference as a signal that you are not intellectually up to scratch. Talk instead about the book you are writing. If you're not writing one, talk about the one you would write if only you had the right, stimulating lover to give you the inspiration.

It is very important that you don't interrupt them while they are talking—even though they will cut you off in midsentence constantly. They know they do it—they just can't help themselves. When they realize what they have done, they will say, "I'm sorry—what were you saying?" (And then probably break in again as you try to finish what you'd started to say.)

But . . . *you must listen.* Don't interrupt. Make the occasional incisive, stimulating remark. Keep them talking. It shouldn't be hard.

If you don't know much about one of their pet topics, feign deep interest and keep them raving on.

Be prepared to be intellectually tested. Their biggest insult is to accuse someone of having a mediocre mind. They equate this with being sexually mediocre. If they suspect that you are even a little bit of a dullard, you're not going to make it to first base.

Geminis can actually get quite turned on if you can beat them in an intellectual argument. They find it very exciting to be bested in logical argument by a member of the opposite sex. The women in particular are very turned on by discovering that a man is their intellectual equal—or superior.

Geminis love words and plays on words. If you can drop some clever sexual pun, it will grab their interest. They love word games like Scrabble. You might interest them by seeking their help with a cryptic crossword.

Geminis love flirting and making subtle sexual innuendos and cleverly wicked allusions. They will be very impressed by your daring if you can match them in this game.

Above all, never appear old and stodgy.

After the initial contact, phone them or drop over as soon as possible. They get bored quickly, so don't delay a week until the first date. You must aim to see them within twenty-four hours.

Geminis are suckers for trends and fads. They're hooked on novelty, and they like to be up-to-date and informed. So when planning a date, think Californian. Geminis want to explore the latest food in the latest "in" places to be seen, followed by a trip to the latest movie.

They like their food well presented but are not generally big eaters. Some are downright picky. Japanese restaurants are a good bet. So is food that is served communally, so that they can help themselves to the bits they like— perhaps Middle Eastern or Chinese. Fastidious table manners are a must. Some Geminis can be revolted by the sight of people pigging out. For a Gemini, the company and the conversation are likely to be just as important as the food. Take them to some outlandish restaurant serving some previously unheard-of food that has suddenly become the new-wave cuisine— Mongolian buckwheat cakes, Nigerian yam patties, that sort of thing.

Variety, variety, variety, spontaneity, stimulation and more variety. For Gemini, variety is the spice of life.

Never be late for a date with a Gemini, but never complain if they are— which is not unlikely. Don't be too shocked if they are an hour late. No need to take this as a sign that their affection for you has diminished. They were probably doing their best to be on time—it's just that they had a few dozen important things to do—oh, and, of course, they just couldn't get off the phone.

You need to like their friends. Ms. Gemini is quite likely to say, "Oh, you must meet Michael, you'd really like him. And Warrick, he's fun. And drop in and meet Will next Saturday—he's into everything you're into." Before you know it, she has organized a meeting with you and Michael and Warrick and Will—and you discover that one of the things that Will used to be into was her. In fact, they are all ex-lovers of hers.

Smile and try to get along with them all—they're probably interesting.

Suggested opening line: "Do you go to the movies much? I've just started work on a screenplay about a teacher who salvages these hopeless kids by helping them start up a part-time business recycling . . . but I'm not sure what they could be recycling. Golf balls? Skateboards? Then again, an underground magazine could have more opportunities . . . more opportunity to explore new concepts for disadvantaged teenagers. Then again, I thought, why not an FM radio station—maybe a pirate radio station? What do you think?"

What to talk about: Anything and everything; change topics all the time, preferably in midsentence.

Where to take them: The newest, most-talked-about place in town—even somewhere outrageous, the latest movie, the latest exhibition, the latest musical, somewhere serving the new fad food. No need to tell them where you are taking them beforehand; just turn up, grab them and go. Take them on a touring vacation with lots of action and exploration. Generally Geminis are urban people, so don't overdose them on country rambles—they generally prefer the bright lights and energy of the city.

What to give them: Books are always a safe bet: new releases, the latest exposé on the lives of the rich, royal or randy. Also T-shirts with witty captions or cartoons, tickets to the hottest show in town and anything to do with communication—stationery, handmade paper, an answering machine, fax machine, portable telephone. They love knickknacks. They get a genuine buzz from clever curios.

How to Seduce a Gemini

■ ■ ■

"If it were done when 'tis done, then 'twere well it were done quickly."

Carpe diem. Seize the day. Not just the day—the hour, the minute, the second. If you don't, in a heartbeat it can be gone forever. If a Gemini wants you, grab them *now.*

If you are out with a Gemini on the first date, throw away the book of dating rules. Forget rules like: *I don't go to bed on the first date, it has to happen in private, it has to be in bed, there has to be plenty of time for before and afterward.* Mentally expunge them and go with the moment. If you don't, you could miss out on having a relationship with that Gemini altogether.

It could have been wonderful; it could have been one of the great relationships of your life. Very true. But you'll never convince them of that . . . *après le moment.* You've missed the moment so you've missed out. Forever.

Imagine this scenario. It is the first date. You are back at your Gemini's place and incandescent passion is virtually setting fire to the black leather sofa.

But you pull back from proceeding to the actual deed. You've got big things on at work tomorrow. You have to get up at 5 a.m. You feel serious about this person, there's real chemistry here, you want time to savor the event, to give a good account of yourself. It's late. So you postpone the big moment . . . to the second date, when there will be more time.

The next day you call up your Gemini. Is this the same person? They've lost interest in you. They seem to have forgotten that the hot scene on the sofa ever took place. Do they have short-term memory loss? They say there's really no electricity between you. In fact, they're not interested in even seeing you again.

What? What's happened here?

What's happened is that you've missed that critical moment with the Gemini. And it will never come back. You've blown it—forever.

Don't think it couldn't happen to you because this exact scenario is a true story from the life of one of the authors of this book—in their astrologically ignorant days.

That's just Geminis for you.

Geminis are notorious for mentally auditioning would-be sexual play-mates. If you haven't gotten a Gemini into bed within six days, they may have already mentally undressed you, had you and decided you weren't worth the trouble. Been there, done that.

If things heat up, never ever postpone your first physical encounter with a Gemini for any reason whatsoever. They are noted for superquick passionate responses. If they are turned on in the living room, don't move to the bedroom. If they want you in the car, do it there and then. Five minutes from now they may have lost interest in you forever. Five minutes? It may only be thirty seconds.

And don't drag the foreplay out too long either. All those feminist tracts telling you that women need long, slow foreplay don't mean much to your average Gemini. Forget foreplay, even twoplay might take too long. If they want it, they want it *now*.

And don't drag the sex out too long either. Geminis like long foreplay and long sex *sometimes*. But their quicksilver minds get bored very easily. They could be clawing your back with passion, then, two minutes later, staring at the ceiling wondering when in the hell you're going to get it over and done with.

That's a Gemini for you.

Mind you, they also have the reputation of being masters of foreplay. They are often superb manual craftsmen. Not only are they quickly aroused—they are quick at arousing their partner as well.

By definition Geminis are changeable, spontaneous, flexible. There is no best place or time or situation. The important thing is to act while the moment is *hot* and the juices are flowing. Never forget that they can dry up faster than a faucet in the desert. They turn off as fast as they turn on. Their response to everything in life including sex and lust is quick, short, sharp and terrific.

There can be a cockteasing element in the more negative Gemini female (and, indeed, the equivalent in some of the Gemini men). Watch out for this. They know they have the capacity for being vivacious and titillating. A Gemini might drop quite a few hints and suggestive remarks, but this may not mean they actually intend to do the deed—at least with you. They like to test out their titillation rating. You can get more mixed signals from a Gemini than any other Sun sign.

So be careful. "No" always means *"No!"* even from a Gemini flirt.

Seduction 1: The Instant Seduction

"Strike while the iron is hot" has to be the watchword when seducing Geminis. Accordingly, if you meet a Gemini and sense that the attraction is mutual, you must be scheming how to get them into bed—or against a wall—as soon as possible after hearing those magical words, "I'm a Gemini."

Aim to bed them within forty-eight hours. The longer the period of seduction, the higher the risk of failure. You must take advantage of any spare time they have—even if it's only half an hour. You must be prepared to put your own life on hold until you've got them over the first hump.

Here, in order of alacrity, are some suggestions:

Seduction 1(a): The Absolutely Instant Seduction. This unpremeditated seduction is only for those who are ever ready with portable contraception—and lucky.

The idea of this seduction is to sweep your Gemini off their feet at the very first meeting—and at the place of meeting.

How you accomplish this will depend on your particular Gemini and where you meet. If, for example, you meet at a party, suggest a stroll in the garden. See what you can do around the back of a large elm tree. Or perhaps there is a garden shed handy. Or tell them that the host has this great etching in his bedroom you must show them. If there is no etching when you get there say, "I lied because I just had to get you alone." Make a move and see what happens.

Seduction 1(b): The Instant Coffee. Perhaps the most traditional of all modern, fast-track seductions. This seduction is often a prelude to the one-night stand—though repeat performances may be an option.

You meet, you talk until you can't wait any longer and then invite them back to your place for kissing, groping and bodily intertwining. (Translation: "Would you like to come back to my place for a cup of coffee?")

Seduction 1(c): The Instant Lift. A close second for popularity in modern fast-track seductions is the Instant Lift. Here you ask the person if they would like an opportunity to invite you in for a cup of coffee, i.e., for a session of kissing, groping, etc. (Translation: "Can I give you a lift home?")

This is sometimes also a prelude to straining car-seat springs.

If you get them home and they miss their cue and don't invite you in for coffee, ask if they could lend you a book on that subject you were talking about. Or insist on walking them to the door.

Seduction 1(d): The Reverse Instant Lift. A bit subtler than the Instant Lift is the Reverse Instant Lift. Here you ask, "Could you give me a lift home?"

If they don't have a car, suggest sharing a taxi.

The Reverse Instant Lift can sometimes be an amusing follow-up to the Instant Lift. "Can I give you a lift home?" "Actually, I have my car with me." "Oh good, then could you give me a lift home?"

If necessary, make some excuse about having had one too many drinks to be truly safe driving. Or tell them you forgot that you actually didn't bring your car, but came with a friend. Or say nothing. The amusement value alone could be the driving force in getting you to first base.

Seduction 1(e): The Instant Phone Call. Having met a Gemini earlier in the evening and said goodnight, calculate how long it will take them to get home, and phone them about five minutes later. Tell them you just had to share some thoughts you had after that great conversation. Geminis are phone-aholics, so this talk could go on for a while. If the Gemini sounds wide awake (which is likely), say you're finding talking to them such a buzz that you know you won't sleep for hours. "I know, why don't I come over with a bottle of wine so we can talk some more? I've got this great book I must lend you too. Would you like me to pick up some pizza/cake/whatever on the way?" As soon as you get in the door, get them talking again—make your move.

Seduction 1(f): The Instant Breakfast. The morning after meeting them, first thing, call them up and say you're coming over with breakfast. Say you know this place that makes the most amazing croissants (or bagels or whatever's trendy).

Tell them to go back to bed—this is room service.

Seduction 2: The For-a-Good-Time-Call Seduction

Geminis are in love with their telephones. The long telephone chat is a major part of their social life.

Combine this insight with the Gemini susceptibility to surprise tactics and you have the For-a-Good-Time-Call Seduction. Anything that comes out of the blue they find highly stimulating.

Call them in the evening from your car phone or the pay phone around the corner. Your aim is to get them interested over the phone. Ideally, you want them to utter those romantic Gemini words: "How soon can you be here?" If you succeed, you must materialize promptly. Be on their doorstep within minutes of hanging up.

Good approaches are:

"I found our talk earlier tonight so stimulating, I just had to share these other ideas with you . . . are you busy? Can I come over and talk some more?"

"I had to phone you. I wanted to get an early night but I just couldn't sleep. I couldn't get you out of my mind. You looked so fabulous yesterday. Are you free? Would you like me to come over?"

"I've been thinking about you all day. I had the most amazing dream last night. You were in it. Couldn't tell you about it over the phone. Are you busy? Can I come over?"

Seduction 3: The Fax of Love

A more techno-hip version of the For-a-Good-Time-Call Seduction is the Fax of Love. It's the cyber-yuppie version of Grandma's love letters.

The idea is to carpet-bomb your Gemini with a B-52 run of faxed messages—messages that start off with innocent invitations, progress to flirting and climax in the downright suggestive.

Turn it into a competition to see who can come up with the wittiest innuendo.

You may be able to use this technique to seduce someone you haven't even spoken to yet. You can also use it to protect your ego from a full frontal turndown. It's quick, it's economical and it's pre-trendy.

Aim for your final fax to read, "I'll meet you downstairs at 5:30 p.m." and their final fax to read, "Okay."

You must present a facsimile of eagerness and persistence.

Here are some messages to consider:

"I saw you at the party. Are you free tonight?" (If the reply comes back "No," reply, "Suggest you cancel. Forget the rest. I'm better.")

"You made a big impression on me. I'd like to have a chance to make a big impression on you."

"Correction to last fax: I'd like a chance to make a big impression into you."

"Do you like your eggs boiled, fried or scrambled?"

"Would you like to try out my electric toothbrush?"

"Are you a clock-watcher? I like to watch."

"If music be the food of love, faxes must be the score."

"Is the plural of fax fux?"

This seduction may be combined with other Gemini seductions such as Seduction by Curiosity and . . .

Seduction 4: The Wild Escapade

One excellent tactic for getting inside the electric Gemini skin is to suddenly propose a totally over-the-top, outlandish escapade. Geminis are very spur-of-the-moment. Out of the blue, announce that you are going to another city to see a controversial show or exhibition and have a spare ticket—would they like to come? They'll be impressed by your daring and spontaneity; they will find it very hard to say no to someone who obviously understands the thrill of the ad hoc adventure.

Seduction 5: The Public Provocation Proposition

The most outrageous of all Gemini seduction scenarios is the Public Provocation Proposition. This technique is only for the brave or the psychic. The PPP has only two possible outcomes: electrifying success and mortifying failure. It is based on the Geminian biological equation: mental stimulation = instant lubrication. The basic "Three Ps" Technique is to drop *in public* a brazen, non-sequitur declaration of sexual intent while staying totally cool. You must be deliciously provocative without being vulgar.

An example. You are dining with a small group that includes Mr. or Ms. Gemini. You've got the Gemini's brain at the boiling point with brilliant repartee on, say, the changing roles of men and women in society. Hook your Gemini into direct eye contact and say smoothly—so that others can hear—anything from the following list:

"Personally I don't mind women [or men] on top. I think that's where I'd like to see you. Care to workshop the idea back at my place?"

"You realize it's not your brain but your body that's driving me wild. But I'd be willing to wait until you've finished your dessert."

"Could you wait twenty minutes for coffee? That's how long it takes to drive back to my place."

"Is it true what they say about Geminis being sexual virtuosos?"

"Freud could have been right after all—everything may be connected with sex. I don't know about you, but this conversation is getting me really turned on. Could I drive you home?"

"Would you like to come back to my place and feel my etchings?"

"It was a great meal. What would you like for breakfast?"

Anything else you think you can get away with.

What you are looking for is an immediate twinkle in the eye of the Gemini and the attempt to suppress a smile. This is your sign of success. Failure will be clearly indicated by a glass of wine over your head.

The PPP is to be handled suavely—in a cool, understated way. It is not for the uncouth, the inarticulate or those who blush easily. Good luck.

Seduction 6: Seduction by Curiosity

Many possible seductions are included in this category. But they all involve tapping into the huge Gemini propensity for curiosity. Straight to the gonads via the frontal lobe.

Most Geminis will admit that they had sex with at least one person just out of curiosity.

How you pull off Seduction by Curiosity will depend on what physical and technical delights you use to intrigue them.

Remember, you can be daring and brash—they like that sort of thing. You could try one of the following:

"Wouldn't you like to stop fantasizing about me and get down to the real thing?"

"I read somewhere [i.e., this book] that Geminis mentally undress people they are attracted to and sexually test-drive them in their mind. Have you run me through yet? How did I rate? Wouldn't you like to find out for real?"

"I dreamt about you last night." It is 100 percent certain the Gemini will be desperate to know about the dream. Be reluctant to reveal all. Be coy. Confess that you feel a bit embarrassed about uncovering such a Rabelaisian blockbuster in your own subconscious. Clearly they have had an amazing effect on you. They've released all sorts of latent primal urges. Any red-blooded Gemini will now be absolutely determined to wrench this juicy story out of you. See whether they will let you act out the bawdy tale.

Other good Gemini seductions:

The Outrageous Move (see Aries)

Unexpected Bedfellows (Aries)

The Dare (Aries)

The Passport to Unscheduled Delights (Sagittarius)

The I'm-Available (Sagittarius)

The Stop-I-Can't-Wait (Sagittarius)

The Loose End (Sagittarius)

The Marcel Marceau (Capricorn)

Seduction by Humor (Aquarius)

The We-Shouldn't-Do-This-So-Let's (Aquarius)

Sex with a Gemini

■ ■ ■

A fling with a Gemini could be a veritable laboratory of sexual experiments.

Geminis have probably already thought of everything you've ever thought of. Quite likely they have tried a few more things than you'd suspect. Perhaps they may even teach you a thing or two. They have a reputation for trying anything at least once. Let your imagination go and you might find that your Gemini got there first.

Geminis have a legendary ability to do two or more things at once—they are quite likely to want three or four parts of their anatomy stimulated simultaneously even though you've only got two hands. Flexibility and dexterity are required. And they are quite capable of calling out instructions. Don't worry about not knowing what to do next. They'll probably tell you. Indeed, you may have to endure running commentaries during sex.

Sex in pitch darkness is out, but subdued lighting—candles and dim lamps—is a good idea. Geminis like to be visually stimulated and hate the idea that they might have missed out on something. Mirrors could be a plus.

Gemini rules the hands. Your biggest delight with a Gemini lover is likely to be the delightful things they can do with their digits. They are the original "octopus" of teenage sexual legend. They pride themselves both on their manual dexterity and their ability to bring partners to fever pitch. This has led to their well-deserved reputation for being masters of foreplay.

Remember that sex can actually go on too long for a Gemini. Give up all notions of impressing the Gemini with the one-hour bonk. They'll just get bored. They'd prefer a superintense ten-minute-or-less first-rate fuck. Quality and intensity—not quantity and endurance.

This may also be a problem if you enjoy receiving oral sex but it takes you more than two minutes to achieve climax. They can get bored giving oral sex. Challenge ambidextrous Gemini to do something with their hands, their feet and their mouth—simultaneously!

Geminis *love* variety. To keep a Gemini interested in sex, offer them lots of variety.

The simplest way to offer variety is in changes of venue: gardens, garden sheds, parks, boats, different rooms in the house, behind the stacks in the university library, backseats of cars. Let your imagination go.

Be ever ready for the ad hoc foc.

They need a rapid turnover of stimulation. You have to arrange this for them.

Key tip: Organize spontaneous sexual adventures.

"Pack your bags, we're off to Bali for two weeks. You have to be ready in two hours." They'll be ready.

Geminis tend to live off nervous energy rather than physical energy. They need a lot of sleep but are often erratic sleepers; quite a few are insomniacs. Late-night sex is not recommended, as it cuts into their beauty sleep. Geminis are more likely to appreciate daytime sex. They are high-voltage individuals and sex is likely to wake them up rather than put them to sleep.

So they won't appreciate having you roll over and go to sleep afterward—they've been sparked up and want to talk . . . or they want to do it all over again. That way nobody gets any sleep.

Geminis must be sure that there is a brain attached to the gonads. The minute they suspect that you are not intellectually up to scratch, you've had it.

To reheat a Gemini whose passion may be fading, you must reconvince them that you are indeed the most interesting person they've ever met and not the boor they've started to suspect you are.

They are also very put off by physical ineptitude. Only those with good motor skills need apply.

And they don't like blubber much either, so watch your weight.

How to Handle a Relationship with a Gemini

■ ■ ■

They have a saying in Melbourne, Australia: "If you don't like the weather, wait five minutes." This saying applies *par excellence* to Geminis. If you don't like a Gemini's mood, wait five minutes.

Unfortunately, the corollary of this is: If you do like a Gemini's mood, wait five minutes.

The plus side of this Gemini changeability is that they don't harbor resentments or jealousies. They may be furious with you one minute but it can blow over the next and be forgotten. If they are angry with you, screaming at you, take a deep breath and silently remind yourself: "In ten minutes, this will pass and they'll like me again."

Another plus is that they rise to the occasion in all sorts of unexpected emergencies. They adapt and improvise. You need someone to accompany you to an important business dinner and they have to be ready in fifteen minutes—ring your Gemini. You've been kicked out of your dwelling. Ring your Gemini. You need a report for work, your housework is spilling over the window ledges, the flu is coming on. Ring your Gemini. They'll probably write your report, do your laundry and make you a hot toddy—all at the same time.

A downside of this changeability is that it can be difficult to organize things in advance. As they can't predict what they will want to do in two minutes, how can you predict what they will want in two weeks?

One solution is to provide them with the spontaneity they need. Tell them to leave a night free but don't tell them where you are taking them—or, indeed, whether you are taking them anywhere. Turn up with some wild proposal.

When they experience the variability of a Gemini, many people form the opinion: "They can't make up their minds." This is a mistake. They do make up their minds most definitely—and very quickly. It's just that ten minutes later they may change it entirely. In fact, they may change it in midsentence. "I think I'll go to a movie and no I'll stay home and catch up on chores."

This is not indecisiveness. To a Gemini, it is only common sense. They have changed their mind in accordance with the changing stimulus from the outside and their own ever-shifting inclinations. It would be downright illogical not to change their mind when everything else has changed, wouldn't it?

You may find that your Gemini lover waltzes in for a two-hour stay, spends half the time on your phone, puts the receiver down and says, "Must go now. Give you a call," then dances out the door and leaves you wondering, *What about my quickie?*

Their need for immediacy can make them very impatient. You have to be the patient one; you can't expect it from them.

When a Gemini's up, everyone's up. They can't understand why others would be sleeping when they are awake. They need to wake you up so they have someone to talk to—but don't make the mistake of waking them up. If you are someone who gets going slowly and whose idea of prebreakfast communication is a series of grunts, be prepared for a few morning run-ins with a Gemini.

Geminis are not noted for being great savers. They seem to have a knack for frittering money away—they're unable to resist the latest fad or film. So your finances may need watching if you are in a relationship with one.

They also chafe under normal working hours. It is not atypical to find a Gemini working an erratic schedule in two or three part-time jobs rather than suffering the bondage they perceive in nine-to-fivedom.

Perhaps you can help them get their business together. They make the world's best salespeople and have great ideas—perhaps you could lend a steadying hand to help them get their working and financial life in order.

If your expectations are to settle in domestically and be looked after by a parent substitute, don't go for a Gemini. They are not noted for establishing calm domestic castles. They whizz in and whizz out, creating a home that is more of a calling port in between sorties.

You may well share a wonderful home-cooked meal—sometimes, perhaps even frequently, but not regularly or at any fixed hour. A quick snack or the bistro down the street is often their mealtime solution to their overpacked schedule.

To get the most out of a Gemini you need to develop an inner calm as they whirl around you, dashing from one activity to the other. They need a grounded person to provide a center point for their spinning orbit. However, the danger in being this quiet calm center is that they will find you boring. You need to tread the fine line between stability and predictability.

Key tip: Keep learning something new all the time.

This will keep them convinced that you are interesting. It will also give the two of you something new to discuss, dissect and debate.

You will probably have to develop great tolerance for the legendary Gemini flirtatiousness, and be willing to look on as they flirt with friends and strangers. That's just the way they are. Getting jealous about it won't do you or the relationship any good.

Think young, be open to new ideas all the time, be patient and tolerant, keep the spare tire at bay and you are likely to hold on to the wild, wonderful, wacky Gemini—and so get two or three lovers for the price of one.

Must-Do's

Be mentally alert and have a razor-sharp wit.
Be able to make on-the-spot decisions.
Have quick physical responses.
Organize the occasional wild, spontaneous trip.
Surprise them with genuine surprises. No hints.
Give them bizarre knickknacks. Replace roses with sunflowers, a potted cactus or a hard-to-find book.

No-No's

Grossness.
Boorishness.
Being bored.
Being boring.
Being overweight.
Being lethargic.
Asking them to shut up.
Interrupting them.
Fumbling.

How to End a Relationship with a Gemini

■ ■ ■

Geminis frequently end up friends with their ex-lovers. You might just be honest with them. Say that you are burned out, that you need to be alone for a while. Tell them they've worn you out. You need a quieter life.

Above all, for a smooth exit, never suggest that you're bored with them as a person or as a sexual partner. This is a very big no-no indeed. Say instead that they are sexy, good-looking and fascinating but that it's just not working out for you.

They could be the ideal fireside companion for future discussions of dilemmas in your love life. They can be the ideal confidant and advisor. They may even set you up with future dates.

If you want them to get over you, act boring and stodgy. Suddenly lose all interest in going out anywhere. Sit around looking tired, scruffy and unkempt. Refuse to talk to them. Refuse to listen to them. Acquire flab. Lose interest in sex. That should have you out the door in about an hour.

Geminis at Their Best

■ ■ ■

You'll never have a dull moment. They're always turning up with a new idea, a new place to go and a new book to read. They're energetic, versatile, sociable, curious, articulate, witty, vivacious, entertaining.

Geminis at Their Worst

■ ■ ■

Gemini will napalm your peace of mind and shatter your tranquillity with their high-strung disposition. They don't know when to shut up and their conversation can be a verbal junkyard of gossip, half truths, white lies and unfinished sentences. They can be superficial, capricious, short on concentration, amoral, emotionally fickle, unreliable, unpunctual and lacking in long-term perspective. At their very worst, they'll drive you bananas.

Sexy Geminis

∎ ∎ ∎

Isadora Duncan, John F. Kennedy, Marilyn Monroe, Judy Garland, Johnny Weismuller, Tony Curtis, Tom Jones, Paul McCartney, Errol Flynn, Joan Collins, Suzi Quatro, John Wayne, Clint Eastwood, Prince, Michael J. Fox, Johnny Depp, Stevie Nicks, Isabella Rossellini, Kathleen Turner.

Unsexy Geminis

∎ ∎ ∎

Queen Victoria, Henry Kissinger, Pat Boone, Jim Nabors, Bobby Darin, Stan Laurel, Boy George, Marquis de Sade, Barry Manilow, Bruce Dern, Gene Wilder, James Belushi.

CANCER

June 22nd to July 23rd

■■■

"I took my boy to a psychiatrist.

Dr. Freudenheimer said Sheldon had

an Oedipus complex."

"Oedipus shmedipus.

What does it matter, so long as

he loves his mother?"

The Lure of a Cancer

■ ■ ■

If you are suffering from a deficiency of mothering—perhaps your sexual self-esteem (if not your actual gonads) has been pulverized by a Scorpio, perhaps your bank account has been shredded by a Leo, perhaps you have been run ragged by a Gemini—then comforting, domestic Mr. or Ms. Cancer may be the soothing balm you need.

Affectionate, nurturing, softhearted, sympathetic, responsive: if these are the qualities you are looking for in a lover, Cancer is definitely one to consider.

If nesting in a cozy house or apartment with homemade soups and lots of hugs and togetherness sounds good to you, well, it generally sounds good to Mr. or Ms. Cancer too. They are the homebodies of the Zodiac and are sold on the concept that happiness = domestic bliss.

Because of this, Cancerians are generally a bad choice for a quick fling.

They are a very good choice if you want either to mother your partner or be mothered—or both.

They can often be shy and sensual—a very appealing combination. They almost beckon to be seduced.

And if you're ready for children in your life, chances are Cancer is too.

How to Interest a Cancer

■ ■ ■

Key tactics:

1. get them to mother you; and/or

2. you mother them.

Cancerians love to be fussed over and spoiled—and they like to do the same for others.

One ploy for gaining Cancerian interest is to expose your wounded, tragic soul. Reveal how your past partners have cruelly broken your tender, vulnerable heart. Bare your soul and show them your emotional bruises.

If they see that you have been hurt in some way by life—particularly by a heartless former lover who didn't appreciate your sensitive nature—it will bring out the mother in Cancer. Hopefully, they will want to take you under their wing and coddle you.

They, in turn, tend to be very sentimental, emotional—even mushy. Cancer is the Sun sign that wears their heart on both sleeves.

If they return your confidences by telling you how their heart was broken, give them *total* sympathy. Never suggest that it may in part have been their responsibility. Instead, tell them that obviously this person did not appreciate their sensitive, warmhearted qualities. Obviously the former lover was cold, uncaring and cruel. Unlike you. You can be trusted. You're all heart.

Tell them that you have this wonderful recipe you would like to cook for them. Invite yourself over to prepare it. Don't suggest they come to your place—go to their home, which is where they most like to be.

They are megaromantics. Let them know that you are too. Talk about the 1930s movies you love. Invite them over to watch a great sentimental classic on video. Tell them you'll cook your special soup and watch the movie with them—plus you'll make homemade bread. (Frozen, ready-to-bake dough may come in handy here!)

If you do take them to your place, make sure your kitchen is well stocked. It should look as if you could survive a two-month siege. Arrange fruits and vegetables creatively in bowls. Do ikebana with bunches of parsley and dill.

Always arrive at their place bearing comestibles—especially "comfort" food like soup, fresh bread, scones, preserves.

You must be seen as a safe homebody. Drop by with new recipes and invite your Cancerian to cook them with you. Putter with them in the garden—raking up the leaves or painting the fence.

Key tip: Above all else, convey that you understand that happiness lies in domestic bliss.

Let it be known early on that you worship your mother. The only excuse you ever need offer for not being able to keep a date is that you have to see your mom.

Ask after their mother frequently. If she is no longer alive, ask what she was like. Encourage them to reminisce at length. As much as possible, emphasize the qualities you have in common with their mother. She baked great pies. You *love* pie and you've got a great recipe for rhubarb pie. Their mother liked to garden. You *love* gardening and can't wait to get a patch of your own.

Occasionally you will find a Cancerian who had a very bad time with their mother. In this case, the idea is to sympathize *totally* and mother them as much as possible.

The subconscious of the Cancerian male has a motto: "I want a girl just like the girl who married dear old Dad."

One difficulty you're bound to encounter is that Cancerians tend to be moody and easily hurt. A common Cancerian tactic for protecting against future hurts is to pick holes in potential love partners and look for reasons why they are totally unsuitable. In this way they fend off any emotional pain—and a lot of pleasure as well.

Hide your flaws as much as possible. If you get wind that they dislike some aspect of your character or manners, say, "Oh yes, I'm working on it. It's just the way my mother taught me to behave—conditioning, you know. Goes back to childhood. But I'm working on it."

A BIG WARNING: Cancerians believe in love at first sight. Or, rather, love at first bite—if they taste your cooking and it's just like Mom used to make, they're in love.

They are quite capable of discussing how many children you would like to have as early as the first date—or after the first sexual encounter anyway.

The danger signal is when they suggest you meet their mother. Once you have met their mother, it will be assumed that you are unofficially engaged.

Suggested opening line: "My mother used to make a sauce similar to this. Do you think there's tarragon in it? I'm going to have a bit more. Can I get you some?"

What to talk about: All elements of domestic bliss—recipes, cooking, decorating, children, building a spare room, clever tips you've acquired on how to lower your electricity bills, where the best fruit market is, your mother, their mother, your cats, their cats, your dogs, their dogs, soap operas, the good old days, the British royal family and its marital problems. Gossip about friends and acquaintances. (Be warned, though, that Cancerians generally gossip in order to find fault with people and pass judgment on them—you could be included.)

Where to take them: Remember that they are stay-at-homes—even when they go out they still like to feel at home—so consider restaurants with names like Martha's Kitchen, Grandma's Eatery. Also consider kitchenware stores, haberdasheries, museums, antique shops, flea markets and visiting your mother. Consider too all the things you can do at their place: entertaining friends, cooking big old-fashioned dinners, watching videos, gardening, furniture restoration, neighborhood walks.

What to give them: Teddy bears, recipe books, romantic novels, biographies of old movie stars, videos like *Gone With the Wind*, *It's a Wonderful Life*, Fred Astaire and Ginger Rogers movies, something for the kitchen (especially if it is "old-world") and, as the relationship develops, Victorian lace nighties and cozy pajamas. If appropriate, give a kitten or puppy. If they already have pets, they'll be impressed if you bring presents for the pets— chicken livers for the cat, a bone for the dog.

How to Seduce a Cancer

■ ■ ■

The seduction must be based on 1930s movies: Clark Gable and Carole Lombard, Nelson Eddy and Jeanette MacDonald, that sort of thing.

Dinners, dancing, arm around the waist, flowers, chocolates, candles on the table, a meal preferably cooked by you, holding hands while you pop exquisite chocolates in their mouth. Music should be unashamedly romantic—Chopin, collections of great love songs, etc.

Cancerians are great cuddlers. So it's lots of cuddling at the early stages— but no sexual maurauding. This isn't an Aries you're dealing with. Cancerians need to feel safe and secure. They need to be gently guided into sexual union.

The key indicator to watch for is a "starry-eyed" look on their part. From then on, you should be just fine.

Cancerian women like their breasts tended to. You could try the hand on the shoulder sensitively dropped to the breast when the time is ripe. Pay her compliments about her bosom.

If you are sending out signals to a Cancerian male, display your cleavage to advantage. Titillation—to a Cancerian—can be just that.

Seduction 1: The Intimate Evening for Two

Plan an archetypal romantic dinner at home.

Make your first move during the coffee on the sofa—preferably in front of a fire warm enough to encourage the discarding of jackets, sweaters, etc.

Cancerians are touchy-feely, so the idea is to move them toward a situation where this is easy. Consider slow dancing cheek to cheek: set the CD player going, reach for their hand, pull them close. If they mold against your body nicely, your chances are good. (For other tips, see the Cuddle Litmus Test, Pisces.)

Key phrases that Cancerians love to hear are: "We were meant to meet." "We were meant to be together." "I think fate brought us together." "We were destined to meet." "It's fate." That sort of deterministic, anti-free-will stuff.

As you continue to move slowly, begin kissing them gently. All in time with the music. Listen for the first distinctive Cancerian squeaks, grunts or groans of pleasure. If you hear this, you are well and truly on the way to third base.

Seduction 2: The Reverse Seduction

Cancerians have a great fear of being used. One way to get them past this is for you to express your fear of being used.

Make them feel that they are the ones who have taken the initiative and pushed you beyond your doubts. "I feel strongly toward you. I really do. You're obviously a genuine caring person. But I've just been hurt so many times in the past that I don't know if I can trust again. I just don't want to be used."

What you are looking for is for them to say, "I know what you mean . . . I don't want to be hurt either . . . I'd never hurt you."

If you can get them to say, "I'd never hurt you," you should move into trembling kisses, then slowly undressing yourself and them and . . . the rest.

Seduction 3: The Polite Withdrawal

Like the Reverse Seduction, the Polite Withdrawal is a way to get your Cancerian past the fear of being used.

After much kissing, cuddling, nibbling and romantic canoodling, reluctantly but politely pull yourself away. Say how wonderful and special the evening has been, but that it's perhaps too early in the relationship for anything too heavy. You're serious about them and don't want to lose their respect. You're really worried that it might be too early in the relationship— for them. You don't want to risk ruining things because this may be the most important relationship of your life. You don't want to rush *them*. You think this may be the real thing, and want them to be as sure as you are.

Now be irresistibly drawn back to kissing them. With monumental difficulty tear your lips away . . . again. "No, I want to wait. I don't want to rush you. I want you to know you're safe with me. I don't want to spoil it. I want you to know that I have—" Lose track of your speech because you are gazing into their eyes so deeply.

"I . . . I . . . I . . ." Give up trying to find words and kiss them again.

What you are working toward is for them to interrupt all this procrastination, take the initiative and cut off your ramblings by kissing you or reassuring you: "No, I want you to stay," or "Will you just shut up and get on with it."

If this doesn't happen and you don't see that starry-eyed look, you may be with a very insecure Cancer indeed. You may have to wait until another night—until they make it plain that they definitely wouldn't feel you were using them if you stayed the night.

Seduction 4: The Declaration of Love

Cancerians fall in love very easily and look for long-term emotional commitment. This is definitely a Sun sign to whom you can make a declaration of love before sexual consummation. "I love you. I'll never hurt you. I just want to express my love for you. I hope you feel for me half of what I feel for you. I really do love you."

Obviously it's not advisable to say these things unless they're true. What you are looking for is an admission that they love you or are starting to fall in love with you. Then you move to Seduction by Assumption (see Libra). If they seem a bit coy about plunging into coital bliss, say, "But we love each other. This is the most romantic night of my life. I want to make it the best night of both our lives in every possible way. It will be beautiful."

If you can say this without developing instant dental cavities, you should be okay.

Seduction 5: The Romantic Movie Move

If you can't quite play the whole megaromance bit yourself, maybe you could get a movie to do it for you. Get some incredibly romantic video to watch with them. Consider films such as *Love Story*, *Dr. Zhivago* or *The Private Lives of Elizabeth and Essex*.

Start crying openly. Hold their hand. Start kissing them as soon as the end credits start rolling. Move on.

Seduction 6: The Stray Dog Seduction

Cancerians have a fetish for taking in stray dogs and cats. The idea of this seduction is to aim to have yourself added to the list of strays that have already moved into their home.

Having been forced to flee your home to escape emotional carnage, arrive on the doorstep just before dinner with a backpack containing the Cancerian basics: a well-thumbed copy of Keats, your CD of Beethoven sonatas, a video of *Gone With the Wind* and a photo of your mother. Do this preferably on a cold and rainy evening. Knock tentatively on the door, your hair dripping with water, asking if you could possibly be put up for the night.

If you play it right—making every effort to observe and imitate their domestic rites and rituals (stacking the dishes their way, fluffing the cushions, wiping down the kitchen table *spotlessly*, gaining the acceptance of their cats), it may take you only a short time to become part of their household unit.

It is then a short step from the narrow cot in the spare room to the palatial couch of Venus and Adonis in their bedroom.

As to how you actually play Venus to their Adonis or Adonis to their Venus, well . . . it depends. You could try stealing into their bedroom in desperate need of "just a cuddle," or you could try Seduction 2, 3 or 4.

Seduction 7: The Romeo and Juliet Balcony Scene

This is a shortcut—either into the Cancerian's boudoir or to wearing a bucket of water.

This is to be attempted only if you are (a) athletic, (b) capable of reading poetry without smirking, (c) a ham, (d) a Monty Python fan.

Let's face it, you'd have to win the Cancer's amusement and romantic Brownie points for even trying this one.

On a moonlit, balmy summer evening, position yourself under the Cancer's bedroom window. Come equipped with roses and chocolates. Throw small pebbles at the window to attract attention. The instant the Cancer leans over the balcony or windowsill, sing or recite something suitably romantic. Recommended readings: Byron, Shelley, excerpts from the balcony scene in *Romeo and Juliet*, Robbie Burns, Keats.

If you can't quite handle all this retro-Cancerian nostalgia, bring the scenario into the nineties and hire a karaoke system to serenade them. Become a modern troubadour. Plug in your system and mime or sing some suitably romantic number. What this is will depend on the taste of your Cancerian. Consider: Harry Connick, Jr., Pavarotti, Julio Iglesias, Madonna, Barbra Streisand.

Your Cancerian may well rush you inside simply to stop the neighbors from coming out to stare.

(P.S. If they do pour water over you, beg to come in to dry off and avoid pneumonia. Appeal to guilt and the Cancerian's caring nature.)

Other good Cancerian seductions:

The Tom Jones (see Taurus)

The Flower Shop (Leo)

The True Confession (Virgo)

The Slap-and-Tickle (Virgo)

The I-Need-You (Virgo)

The Cuddle Litmus Test (Pisces)

Portents of Passion (Pisces)

The Bath (Pisces)

Seduction by Lethargy (Pisces)

Whispers in the Dark (Pisces)

Sex with a Cancer

■ ■ ■

Shy yet sexual, Cancerians—the women in particular—need to be gently guided toward lust. Initially they are looking mainly for romance. Use this as a key to unlock the voluptuous sexuality inside every Cancerian.

They conceal their physical desires, even from themselves, because they so fear rejection. They need a romantic merging with their partner to feel that lust is safe and justified.

Key tip: Maintain the romance.

Make it clear that you've been sent to help them realize their most romantic fantasies. Find out what these are and go to great lengths to make them come true. Try role-playing on the theme of the great lovers of history. Cleopatra and Marc Antony. Romeo and Juliet. Tristan and Isolde.

Continually think of romantic scenes and scenarios. Candlelit baths can go over very well with your Cancerian. Consider moonlit strolls along the beach, regular gifts of flowers, romantic keepsakes (even a locket with your photo inside).

Think tactile. Cancerians love the soft touch. Give them massages ranging from the therapeutic to the erotic.

The Cancerian is not naturally a sexual adventurer or an experimenter. However, they are easily influenced.

They are famous groaners and squealers—as anyone who has heard them eating will testify. This tendency toward vocalization during sex should be encouraged, as it helps to bring the animal out of its shell.

Cancerians have a secret desire to dominate. See how far you can encourage this in the sexual arena. Encourage the Cancerian woman to assume the dominant position. Perhaps you could offer to be her sexual slave.

Cancerian sexuality can have an infantile quality. They may act very goo-goo girlish (even the men). Perhaps you could play along with this and encourage it as a form of sexual play. Consider role-plays based on fairy stories: Sleeping Beauty, Cinderella, Beauty and the Beast. The adult versions may end with more than a kiss. Try fantasies based on historical scenes of forbidden love and desire: Guinevere and Lancelot, the lady and the young priest, the pharaoh and the high priestess.

With Cancerian women, the biggest sexual danger looms when they become mothers. There can be a total transfer of affection to the child, leaving the man very much out in the cold. As mothers, Cancerians have a tendency to become born-again virgins, as if motherhood is so sacred that it must not be sullied by sexual contact. After motherhood, emotional warmth and closeness are often all the Cancerian woman wants.

Cancer rules the uterus. Female Cancerians can be more than a bit obsessive about their periods and be perpetually premenstrual, post-menstrual or transmenstrual. You have to be prepared to listen to the ins and outs of her cycle. You may need to keep track of it in your diary.

Good grief. Even Cancer men can seem to suffer from PMS.

How to Handle a Relationship with a Cancer

■ ■ ■

The hardest thing to cope with in a relationship with a Cancerian is moodiness. Traditionally Cancer is the moodiest of all signs. Observe the Moon, see how it waxes and wanes. Cancerians are ruled by the Moon and their moods wax and wane accordingly.

Always keep your antennae up. Learn the signs that reveal when their mood is about to change. If they are in a mood, tread carefully and wait.

And if you're involved with the sort of Cancerian female whose life revolves around her periods, *don't* make the mistake of asking, "Do you have PMS?" If you do, she is likely to fly off the handle. "Men! Every time they do some unbelievably stupid thing that irritates the shit out of you, they blame it on your PMS." The fact that she actually does have PMS will only worsen this tirade against you.

The symbol of Cancer is the Crab—and this is exactly what they can be: crabby.

They can be terribly upset by the merest trifle. You'll need to become a good apologizer.

They can go from a fairly even emotional state to tears welling up or uncontrollable anger and a fit of pique in a matter of seconds. Always have tissues on hand. Be prepared to see them blubber in public.

Cancerians can suffer from bad cases of what psychoastrologer Judith Bennet called the Glass Head Syndrome—i.e., expecting that loved ones should just *know* what they want or why they are upset (when often Cancerians don't know themselves). If you can't automatically tell, it's because you don't *really* love them.

Cancerians seem to find it impossible to keep their moods and feelings to themselves. They don't realize how tiring they can be when they let their emotions hang out all over the place all the time. They tend to blame other people for their moods: it's your fault, it's the relationship's fault, it's Mother's fault.

Cancerians are easily emotionally wounded and show it. They whine. They can be emotionally draining. Even the men can be old fussbudgets.

To help get them through a mood, make them their favorite cake and coffee and serve it *exactly the way they like it*. Then they will sit down and make little grunts, sighs and squeals of delight over it and it will help them to no end to pull out of the mood. Cancerians seem to believe that a nice bowl of soup and a bit of mothering can fix the world. Indeed, it often seems to shore up their world when it is caving in.

Cancerians like a lot of emotional support and comforting, lots of cuddles and cooing. Sometimes it can feel as if they are clinging so hard they might strangle you.

Another thing you may find is that Cancerians tend to be bossy—not in the lordly do-what-I-want Leo way, but more in the do-this-because-it-is-good-for-you, nagging-mother-hen way. You may find yourself wanting to shout at them, "Listen, if I want to do something that's bad for me like spend my own money, skip breakfast or put sugar in my coffee, that's my business. Bug off!"

They are shrewder and more dominating than they at first appear. Cancerians wish to dominate the relationship, but they see this as being *for your own good,* like a matriarch.

Cancerians often try to control relationships by making themselves *indispensable* in their partner's life. They will cook, iron, sew, tidy. After three months, they hope to hear: "I don't know how I ever coped without you." After six months, they hope to hear: "I would never be able to cope without you."

They will respond, "You won't have to."

But all this mothering has a price. Cancerians tend to make a one-way contract—a unilateral agreement—in their head: they will mother you and in return you will be domestically and emotionally obedient. The price is: you must not ask for more independence than they were planning to give you. They are terrified of their chicks leaving the nest—and that includes you.

If you try to exert your independence, you will be subjected to Cancerian torture tactics: sulking, brooding, nagging, whining, slander, gossip.

They don't believe in your right to independence and privacy. They believe in their divine right to meddle. They justify this with the all-purpose excuse: "But I worry about you."

To get the most out of a relationship with a Cancerian you must totally embrace the domestic life. Cancerians invented the saying, "Be it ever so humble, there's no place like home." To them, home is a combination mental refuge, spiritual sanctuary and psychic womb. They usually put most of their money into their house.

Make sure that when your Cancerian comes home you provide a few quiet moments for them just to savor this return to the womb.

You may have some trouble motivating them to go out. You need to present going out as an extension of domestic bliss. The hotel is a "home away from home." The restaurant has food "just like Mother used to make." Overseas vacations may be limited to visiting relatives. Domestic vacations involve a Winnebago—where the Cancerian can take their home with them, like a Crab.

Cancerians are very child-oriented. They will generally want to discuss children from a brutally early stage of the relationship. You must not suggest that you don't ever want children—unless you're ready to terminate the relationship. If the Cancerian does have children, they can sometimes focus on them so exclusively that their partner feels neglected and forgotten.

Dogs, cats and horses are often Cancerian child-substitutes. If you are not an animal lover, forget it. They will expect you to sleep with their cats in the bed. Be prepared. You may have to sit on the floor to watch TV because the cats have taken possession of the sofa. Never dislocate a cat so you can have a seat.

Remember: you won't just be in a relationship with them. You will also be in a relationship with their mother. Even if the mother is dead or lives in another country, you will hear so much about her that you may feel she lives next door. Pull out all the stops to get the mother to like you.

Pull out all the stops to get their animals to like you too. If the animals don't take a shine to you, your Cancerian partner is likely to become suspicious of your character.

A final warning: Cancer rules the stomach, so they might go on and on about bowel regularity, burping, flatulence, indigestion. Some Cancers are hypochondriacs.

If you can cater to the Cancerian need to cling to domestic safety—if you can cater to their need to be mothered and if you yourself don't mind being mothered—then you can get a lot of warmth, comfort and security out of your relationship with a Cancerian.

However, if you want to expand your horizons and extend your mind, if you want adventure, foreign travel, independence, you could be severely disappointed. See Sagittarius instead.

Must-Do's

Always, always compliment their cooking. Always ask for a second helping. Be a serious eater.

Love sitting in their living room and fluffing the pillows, petting the cats, etc.

Enjoy their domestic comforts. Say, "I love coming to your place. I always feel at home. You make me feel so welcome."

Ask after their family.

No-No's

Never ever say anything against their mother, your mother or mother-hood in general.

Never let them know if you hate children.

Never say you don't want children.

Never criticize the bad habits of their pets.
Never make a mess in their kitchen.

How to End a Relationship with a Cancer

■ ■ ■

How to end a relationship with a Cancer?

Carefully.

You can expect big emotional scenes. You've become a part of the domestic furniture. They will see your departure as removing part of their house, part of their security blanket.

Wean yourself away slowly. Continue to adore their cooking, continue to take the dogs for walks, but slowly withdraw from physical contact.

A less desirable but sometimes necessary tactic is to tell them suddenly. However, first upgrade your health insurance and wear protective clothing for the occasion. Then allow them to take it all out on you. Let them hit you, throw things at you, flail away. (Warning: This solution is not recommended if they do weight training.)

This will be a great emotional release for them. Afterward they will feel sufficient guilt about what they have done to be contrite and amenable even after the breakup.

Another tactic is to accept an overseas posting where there are nasty epidemics—dengue fever, Delhi belly, malaria, etc. Cancerians, with their tendency to hypochondria and hypersensitive stomachs, are unlikely to pursue you.

Or be hypochondriacally creative and develop an allergy to one of their pets. An allergy to cat hair is perfect. They'll never give up the cats for you.

They're often obsessed with having children, so you could confess that there is something that disqualifies you from ever being a parent. Break down and confess that you've had a vasectomy or tubal ligation. Confess to a hereditary illness in the family—insanity, perhaps—something that has a fifty percent chance of surfacing in your offspring. Tell them you're sterile. If all else fails, tell them you can't stand the thought of having children.

This will generally disqualify you as a partner.

Cancerians at Their Best

■ ■ ■

Cancers will nurture you, coddle you, feed you and protect you. They'll always be there for you with tea and sympathy. You can look forward to a lifetime of affection from a responsive, intuitive and devoted partner. Your friends will love to visit your home so that they too can bask in an atmosphere that sings with soothing, healing, openhearted vibrations.

Cancerians at Their Worst

■ ■ ■

Cancers can be emotional vampires who will drain you through their mood swings and sulkiness. They can be possessive and jealous, and even become hysterical if they fear you want more independence than they planned to give you. They tend to blame their partner for their problems and can be professional worriers who are obsessed with food and money. They will smother you, burst into tears at the drop of a hat and act helpless and childish. You will grow bone-weary of their "martyr" persona and be bored brainless by the way they cling to their past and their home, refusing to go out, travel or change in any way. They will also refuse to let your friends visit the home, seeing this as an invasion of their sanctuary. You will long for escape from the gilded cage of the Cancerian home.

Sexy Cancerians

■ ■ ■

Princess Diana, Ernest Hemingway, Lena Horne, Leslie Caron, George Sanders, Gina Lollobrigida, Yul Brynner, Ginger Rogers, Diahann Carroll, Henry VIII, Julius Caesar, Harrison Ford, Gustav Mahler, Linda Ronstadt, Sylvester Stallone, Robin Williams, Tom Hanks.

Unsexy Cancerians

■ ■ ■

Mitch Miller, Ringo Starr, Phyllis Diller, Red Skelton, Rose Kennedy, Louis Armstrong, Merv Griffin, Nancy Reagan, Meryl Streep, Donald Sutherland, Bill Cosby.

LEO
♌

July 24th to August 23rd

∎∎∎

True democracy is government

of the people, for the

people, by me.

The Lure of a Leo

■ ■ ■

With a champagne glass in one hand, they toss back their glorious mane of hair and flash a confident smile. They make large theatrical gestures as they animatedly share their latest triumph with you. They tell a joke and give it their seal of approval by laughing heartily as they lift their glass for another pour.

Within five minutes after meeting you, they get your phone number and then sweep grandly away for more champagne, more pâté de foie gras, more caviar, more conversation, more, more, more.

You've just been swept along—or bypassed—by the leonine center of the party.

Leos are the glamour kings and queens of the Zodiac. They are the life and soul of the party—and insist on being so. They need to be center stage: the bigger the stage, the bigger the audience, the better. They want to tell the best jokes, get the biggest laughs, win the most admiration. But who would deny these natural showmen and -women a bit of vanity and arrogance when they are fundamentally warmhearted, hospitable and romantic?

If you want a fun time with someone in pursuit of the good things in life, if you like going out—premieres at the theater, top restaurants, dancing, good wines—Leo will help you enjoy it all the more.

If you enjoy spending money, well, Leos will help you do more of that too. Leos are big-time operators. They want to devour life whole *now*. They want the best life has to offer and they want it right away. They want to eat it, wear it, see it *now*.

So it's simple: all you have to do is convince them that you are one of the good things in life and they'll want to devour you whole too—*now*.

How to Interest a Leo

■ ■ ■

Key tactic: Appear inordinately confident.

You cannot act too confident for a Leo. Don't hesitate to ask for their phone number within three minutes of meeting them. You must seem coolly confident and in control. You need to have an air of certainty—certainty that they will feel attracted to you, that they will enjoy talking to you and, of course, will want to get to know you better.

Other Sun signs might see this as brash, even rude. Leos won't, provided you handle it with panache.

Leos aren't backward about coming forward. You can ask them out literally within minutes of being introduced. They'll be impressed by your boldness and your air of authority.

Key tip number one: If you want to vroom, groom.

Before you can get undressed, you have to dress up. For the first date, turn yourself out impeccably. You don't need to look trendy, but your clothes should reek of quality. They will secretly inspect the label on your jacket as you drape it over the chair.

Key tip number two: To get the best out of a Leo, your credit cards definitely need to be in good shape. Be prepared to spend and live the high life. Never forget that they love the best that life has to offer.

To get a Leo's attention, tell them you love nothing more than going out and having a great time; you adore lavish dinners, dancing and the theater. On the first few dates, you must impress on them that you are seriously dedicated to *la dolce vita*. You love enjoying yourself and seeing other people enjoy themselves.

More than any other sign, they will notice not being shown the big time. They will take note of any reluctance to put your hand in your pocket. It's their way of determining that you value them. For a Leo, generosity is next to godliness. When the time is right the best of Leos will return your gesture—often two- or threefold.

Never quibble about the price of something in front of a Leo. They will see you as petty and vulgar. They themselves may well quibble about prices—but don't you dare.

Above all: never come across as in any way miserly or a killjoy.

Leos' Achilles' heel is their hair. Male Leos often have a fetish for beards and mustaches, which will disappear and reappear with the seasons or their moods. Some are veritable Samsons and believe their virility lies in a bushy beard or thick, shiny hair.

Leo women love to have their hair done. When a Leo feels depressed, her first recourse is to call her hairdresser, who doubles as therapist. (Many hairdressers depend on coiffure-obsessed Leo women for a substantial part of their income.) Woe betide if the Leo's haircut turns out badly; she can become almost suicidal. If she has a new haircut, tell her how *wonderful* it is. If it's a disaster, don't say, "No, no, it's great. It'll look even better in a week."

You must never fail to flatter Leos about their hair or beard. And never give a Leo a small compliment. None of this understated "Oh, your hair looks nice." No, no, no. The compliment has to be *huge.* "Your hair is fabulous. Where do you get it done? It looks absolutely fantastic." *Sotto voce*, tell them, "Your hair drives me crazy. I want to run naked through your hair."

Leos cannot get enough compliments: on their hair, clothes, eyes, teeth, anything you can think of. Unlike Aries, they won't see this as the pathetic fawning of a lapdog. They will see it as their due, as an astute observation on your part. *Yes, I am wonderful, aren't I? Here is someone astute enough to recognize quality.*

They love good wines. Rush to get them a glass and be there with refills. (There could, of course, be fringe benefits later in the evening.) They love the loosening effect of alcohol. Leos don't mind getting a bit tipsy but insist on doing it with the best vintages and in good company. For them, alcohol is a fun drug. They expect you to join them. If you're a teetotaler, perhaps Leo is not for you. Consider a Virgo instead.

On all levels, Leos want their mate to be their match—in vitality, fun, glamour, passion, decadence.

Leos like a bit of a gamble, so take them to the races, where they can not only bet on the horses but dress up at the same time. They like backgammon, mah-jongg, and cards. They play to win. If you can find an inconspicuous way to let them win, they'll be on a high (which may pay off for you later).

They are impressed by people who are informed about the arts. Try to find out what their particular artistic interest is and bone up on it.

They are not fastidious about details. They won't care too much if your house is messy. They won't notice the dust on the objets d'art—so long as you have the objets.

Suggested opening lines: "I *love* your hair." "There's something about a man with a beard. Do you have it professionally trimmed?"

What to talk about: The latest shows, cultural events, large-scale fun escapades you've had, exotic vacations you've enjoyed and the collectibles you brought back. (Leo is one sign you can actually invite upstairs to see your etchings—so get some.) Tell them the latest jokes—or get them to tell you a selection of theirs.

Where to take them: Grand events, French restaurants, premieres, vineyards, fashion shows, gallery openings, Persian carpet showrooms, antique shops, luxury resorts, shopping, out-of-state shopping or, even better, shopping overseas (especially if you can afford first-class tickets). Leos would rather have a weekend at a five-star hotel than three weeks camping in idyllic surroundings.

What to give them: They love to deck themselves out with expensive jewelry, the best perfumes and colognes, anything from Saks or Bergdorf Goodman. They are not shy about letting you know what presents they would like, so keep notes on any dropped hints. You will be rated as mean and undesirable if you fail to deliver the goods. Fork them over and you could be rewarded. Don't and you may be a has-been before you have been.

How to Seduce a Leo

■ ■ ■

It's simple, really: They want the best, so convince them that you are the best.

Leos are impressed by confidence, by the worldly I-know-what-I'm-doing-and-where-this-is-going approach. Act as if you are in command of the situation.

Once you are sure the groundwork is well and truly laid, and that the next thing to be laid is them, you should not have too much trouble with that part. Leos are seldom shy or coy.

But don't let the time get overripe. Leos are a pretty lustful lot. Two weeks is a long courtship for your typical Leo.

Leos are at their very best at the beginning of a relationship. They positively glow in the drama, passion and rituals of courtship. They have colossal nerve and don't generally experience the doubt and fear of rejection most people go through at the beginning of a relationship.

Key tip: For Leos, a good aphrodisiac is having a lot of money spent on them.

The key word is "lavish." Lavish praise on them. Lavish dinners with them. Lavish presents for them.

It's not that the Leo wants to bankrupt you. But they do want you to indulge them within your means. You're being tested. Leos know that people spend money on things they value. They want to be sure you realize that they are the most valuable thing in your life. And just maybe they are. You've probably made worse investments.

Frankly, the more you spend, the more likely you are to get them into bed. This leads us to . . .

Seduction 1: The Five-Star Seduction or *La Séduction de Luxe*

This is to be attempted only with clean credit cards.

You take them for a disgustingly lavish meal in the formal restaurant of your local Hilton or some other five-star hotel.

After the lobster *à l'impériale*, you say, "The maître d' has arranged for dessert to be served privately upstairs. Shall we go now?"

(Some advice to men attempting to seduce Leo women: At this stage, you may end up with the remainder of the bottle of wine poured over your head. This expression of public outrage is a favorite sexual fantasy of all Fire sign women. All eyes are on you—this is now a public performance.

Remember, Leos love boldness and style. Employ both now. If she doesn't immediately storm off after dousing you, all is not lost. Take her by the wrist, pull her toward you and say, "I always knew you had real fire in you. Shall we go now?")

Upstairs will be found the archetypal Leo seduction: the king-size bed, the French champagne on ice, flowers, chocolates. Leo heaven.

Mutual heaven.

The ultimate variation on this is to provide the same indulgence in Paris, New York or London.

Jet overseas on business. Phone to say you miss them. Say you've bought a first-class ticket for them to join you for a week. How could they resist?

Seduction 2: A Streetcar Named Desire

This is a more mobile version of the Five-Star Seduction. You hire a chauffeur-driven stretch limousine for a few hours. Champagne, chocolates and caviar await your Leo in the rear of the limousine. The soundproof, opaque window is up between you and the driver, of course. You have arranged that he will take you on a *long* ride somewhere.

This is certainly a way to get the Leo motor purring. A good opportunity to shift their gear, floor the accelerator and move into overdrive.

Definitely worth considering for the more daring Leo.

Seduction 3: The One-Star Seduction or The Intimate Liqueur

If your budget doesn't run to the above, don't despair of winning the generous-hearted Leo. Try the same seduction at home.

Suggest that they come back to your place to share the fifty-year-old port you've been saving for a special occasion. Have suitable treats waiting: handmade chocolates, pastries, deluxe ice cream, strawberries.

When you get them back to your place, wait on them hand and foot, see to their every comfort and move confidently from hand-feeding them to having them eating out of your hand.

Seduction 4: The No-Star Seduction

One crude but nevertheless effective piece of advice is: get them drinking. Leo is a Sun sign for whom alcohol is a definite leg-opener or at least a zipper-loosener.

Leos certainly love glamour, but they can at times be basic and raunchy. A little medicinal alcohol helps to move them swiftly from the graceful and glamorous to the wicked and wanton.

Seduction 5: The Flower Shop

Leos love to be the center of attention. They also adore grand, over-the-top theatrical gestures.

The day after your first date, have a minimum of six dozen roses delivered to their office. It must make a show. They'll bask in the puzzled and envious glances of their colleagues. Almost certainly they will call you to acknowledge your tribute. When they do, invite them to either the Five-Star or One-Star Seduction. You may, with luck, receive an invitation to dine at their place.

If you haven't heard from them within twenty-four hours, send them another four dozen roses with a note saying, "Dinner at my place 8 P.M." If Leo doesn't phone you to accept or postpone, or if they don't turn up, forget it. They don't want you. Move on.

Seduction 6: The Tasteful Dirty Weekend

This is really a seduction by implicit mutual agreement and consists of inviting Mr. or Ms. Leo for a weekend away.

Leos require a certain amount of official courtly behavior. You know you have a dirty weekend in mind and so do they, but you don't say, "Let's go away for a dirty weekend."

No, no, no, no, no.

You say, "Would you like to come away for the weekend? I know this absolutely charming bed-and-breakfast with this wonderful atmosphere in the vineyard district. There are wine-tastings all around. I'd love you to come."

Leo will know what other tastings are being suggested besides wine.

Leos are so open and lacking in deviousness that it would be a rare one indeed who would agree to go away with you and not sample all you have to offer. They would feel guilty about exploiting you.

You will, of course, ensure that you are booked into a single suite with only one double bed and champagne waiting on ice. There should be no problem.

Seduction 7: The Bacchanalia

This is the Leo seduction par excellence—pull-out-all-the-stops, over-the-top, Leo-style.

The idea is to re-create the ambience of a Roman orgy: a Felliniesque overindulgence in wine, food (etc.!)—all just for two.

You invite Mr. or Ms. Leo to your place for dinner.

The soon-to-be-seduced Leo arrives at your door, expecting to be wined and dined but definitely not suspecting the Bacchanalia you have prepared.

Open the door dressed in a casual, off-the-shoulder, semiformal toga. They will be laughing with delight as you thrust the first of many inhibition-loosening glasses into their hand and point them in the direction of the bedroom, where their own toga is laid out ready for them to slip into.

Have them recline on the divan and ottomans near a table laden with wine, grapes, candles, smoked salmon, oysters, caviar, figs, cheeses, pistachios, strawberries, sorbets, etc.

From there it's simple—keep them drinking, keep their glass full, serve them grapes. Lavish them with attention.

Pretty soon there will be room for two on the divan. A quick flip of the toga and it's *Et tu, Brute.*

Seduction 8: The Surprise Formal Dinner

A less theatrical version of the Bacchanalia is the Surprise Formal Dinner.

Send the Leo a formally printed invitation to a dinner party: Black tie. RSVP.

They will think it's a dinner party for twelve to twenty people.

But it's not. It's just for the two of you.

When they arrive, you will be dressed to kill—of course. And there will be crystal, silverware, candelabra, roses everywhere. If your culinary skills fall short of haute cuisine, have your affair catered.

When Leo asks, "Am I the first to arrive?" say meaningfully, "My dear, tonight, all this is just for you."

If they ask what's the occasion, reply: "I'm selfish. I just wanted you all to myself for the evening."

If they stay on for the first course, they will probably still be there for breakfast.

Seduction 9: The Cecil B. DeMille

This seduction taps into the Leo desire for self-adornment, theatricality, megaromance, role-playing and ritualized mating behavior.

The difference between this and the Bacchanalia and the Surprise Formal Dinner is that those should come as a delightful surprise, whereas in this seduction the object of your passions participates in the staging and plays along from the very beginning.

Suggest to your Leo that you have long fantasized about staging a dinner for two in the style of *Gone With the Wind*: Rhett Butler, Scarlett O'Hara, mint juleps and Southern chivalry. Ask if they're game.

A good costume rental shop should be able to provide all the paraphernalia. You will cook the Southern fried chicken and pecan pie.

Hopefully, theatrical Leo will get so caught up in their role opposite your Scarlett or Rhett that they will melt into your arms by sheer force of surrogate passion.

Part of the alluring delight of this seduction is the sheer fantasy thrill of ripping off voluminous petticoats, unzipping long leather boots, unbuttoning bodices.

Of course, it doesn't have to be Scarlett and Rhett. It could be any number of *femme fatale/homme fatal* historical couplings. Consider:

Cleopatra and Marc Antony

The geisha girl and the samurai

The sultan and the new girl in the harem

The Egyptian high priest and the temple virgin

The French courtesan and the musketeer

The Hawaiian princess and the buccaneer

Anything else you think you can get away with

Seduction 10: Hey, Big Spender

"I shop therefore I am" is the Leo motto. Leos love to shop—whether they buy or not. See if you can exploit this obsession for a sexual seduction. Go shopping with the Leo.

The basic idea is for the man to buy Ms. Leo some sexy, extraordinarily expensive lingerie, "On the condition, of course, that you let me take it off you later tonight." Be suave, but be brazen. Remember: Leos respect boldness.

The female variation is to go shopping with Mr. Leo and ask his opinion on some sexy lingerie. Whisper in his ear, "If you buy me this for Christmas, I'll let you take it off me." How could any red-blooded Leo refuse? Who cares if it's only September? He could still fill your stockings.

Other good Leo seductions:

The Challenge (see Aries)

The Dare (Aries)

The Tom Jones (Taurus)

The Romeo and Juliet Balcony Scene (Cancer)

The Declaration of Love (Cancer)

The Return of the Old Flame (Libra)

The Gold-Plated Seduction (Libra)

The Passport to Unscheduled Delights (Sagittarius)

The Seduce-Me (Capricorn)

Seduction by Lethargy (Pisces)

Sex with a Leo

■ ■ ■

Leo is the bossiest sign of the Zodiac. The female Leo will want to order you around all over town. However, once the bedroom door closes, she wants a real he-man. In the bedroom, her mate must ooze confidence and assume total control. Leo women despise wimps. Never *ask* if it's all right to do such-and-such. Just do it. It's Me-Tarzan-You-Jane time. (Don't drag her to the bed by her hair, though—remember the hair obsession!)

The key to handling a relationship with a Leo female is to come across as Clark Kent most of the time—going along with whatever she wants but making sure she is fully aware that you-know-who with the flowing cape is there as soon as you drop your mild-mannered clothes.

Leo men like to be in control—in and out of the bedroom. However, always remember that Leos like their partners to match them—in strength, assertiveness, passion, confidence and glamour quotient.

Once you've got them into bed, you have to keep the good things in life coming. Keep associating sex with the best: good taste, art, decadence, luxury, indulgence.

Leos are naturally passionate—and they're usually pretty physical, so you may need to keep your champagne glass in one hand and your bottle of vitamins in the other.

Leos are natural showpeople and are proud of their ability to give a good performance in the bedroom. Unfortunately, this self-consciousness can make them spectators of their own sexual performance. You can play on this Leo desire to perform to enhance the sexual ambience. Place mirrors on the walls and even the ceiling.

A variation on this is to take advantage of the Leo desire to dress up. You can both get dressed up for sex—perhaps black tie or fancy dress. Make love with your clothes on. Or, before a cocktail party, make a grab for Ms. Leo from behind just as she is putting the finishing touches on her makeup in front of a mirror.

Leos are exhibitionists. Once at the cocktail party, feel them up discreetly. Public-performance sex can often be a secret Leo fantasy.

Leos love touching and hugging—in public too. If you are naturally shy about displaying public affection—like a Capricorn, for instance—you might have something to sort out with your Leo partner.

Leos like to think they can satisfy their partner better than anyone else ever has. Challenge them to do so. Subtly mention particular positions or achievements of past love encounters (frequency, endurance, technique). Leo will take note and endeavor to exceed.

Leos like to dominate so much—why not go whole hog? Let them live out their fantasy. Become their Sex Robot for a session. Do only what they want, when they tell you.

A favorite fantasy of Leos is having sex with famous people—either present-day or historical. Use this penchant to create a sexual fantasy role-play.

Leos like to be *adored*. To get the best out of a sexual relationship with a Leo, make it very obvious that you do adore them. The best way to convince a Leo of this is to spend money on them. Buy them silk underwear. Get them that expensive watch they so much want. Inundate them with frequent gifts of flowers.

How to Handle a Relationship with a Leo

■ ■ ■

The key to handling Leos is simple: Let them think they are in charge.

They don't actually have to be in control. The real strings could be in the hands of a quiet Capricorn or Scorpio. But *they must have the illusion of power*. If given a choice between being a puppet *on* the throne and being the real power *behind* the throne, the Leo will take the throne every time.

Consider their symbol—Leo, the Lion, king of beasts. This aptly sums up their attitude. They believe that obedience, praise and the royal high life are their due.

If you want a smooth relationship with a Leo, let them think they are in control while you quietly guide them to the choice you want them to make.

You may have to forgo getting your own way quite a bit, even when justice and reason are on your side.

They so love to organize others—why not let them? Allow them to display their executive abilities. Provided your bank account is in good order, let your Leo make the dinner reservations and the vacation plans—along with just about everything else.

A childish willfulness about Leos will surface from time to time that can be quite wearing. You have to go where *they* want, eat at the restaurant *they* want, listen to the music *they* want. During a bout of this instant-gratification superdominance mode, Leos expect other people to adapt immediately and without dissent.

The worst of Leos can be very poor at expressing gratitude for gifts and favors that they perceive as their royal due. The words "please" and "thank you" do not come naturally to their lips.

Leos believe in generosity. The best Leos are very generous indeed. But be warned: they also believe in being on the receiving end of generosity. Regrettably, much Leo "generosity" is really a down payment on return favors. Many Leos keep a running account in their head (my generosity vs. their generosity); they expect, or indeed demand, that your generosity to them exceeds theirs to you. If it doesn't, you will be perceived as unloving or mean. They will add up all their favors to you, but their memory may be less acute when it comes to things you have done for them.

What can we say? Royalty demands tribute.

But royalty does not need to apologize. If they get something wrong and there is no denying it, Leos may say, "Oh, yes, I made a bit of a miscalcula-tion" and quickly change the topic. You can't expect royalty to apologize to their subjects!

They can, at times, be insufferably self-righteous and pompous. Not to mention totally lacking in humility.

They cover up feelings of vulnerability with bossiness. The more emo-tionally vulnerable they feel, the more dictatorial they are likely to act. It can be pretty hard to spot the emotional vulnerability behind the barrage of orders they are hurling at you.

However, a Leo can be a benevolent ruler. Make them feel appreciated and adored and they will favor you by ruling with a gracious, lordly hand. For instance, if they know your finances are genuinely tight, they will be the first to help you out.

Leos love to give royal advice to people about how to run their lives. They can be the worst sort of amateur therapists, dealing out unsolicited advice to friends and strangers alike. Their own lives and finances may be a total mess, but that won't stop a Leo telling other people what they should be doing to fix up their lives. If the two favorite words of Leos are "I want . . . ," the next two favorites are "You should . . ."

At their very worst, Leos can come across as hypocritical and hypercritical—as if no one could, in the long run, ever be good enough for them.

Leos have very long memories for *other* people's faults and mistakes. Be prepared for them to trot out yours during an argument. Leos may even criticize you in public. They are quite capable of picking holes in your dress sense, your lack of generosity, the way they treated them yesterday, last week, last month, six years ago—all in front of other people. The more negative Leo may even bait you in public for the sheer joy of staging a drama in front of an audience. This is the Leo holding court. They want to make their royal proclamations in public.

But don't dare criticize them in public (or in private, for that matter).

If you are sensitive to public exposure, like a Pisces, Virgo or Capricorn, you need to plaster a sickly smile on your face while they hold forth on your inadequacies. Later take them aside and explain that the next time they try that, you will catch a taxi home, never to return.

Leos generally love going to and giving parties, for here they have a captive audience. Let them hold the stage. There are advantages for you. Afterward, you should be in for a good time—they'll be feeling so high. Most Leos like sex after a party.

Not uncommonly, Leos become instant experts on any subject. They will read half a chapter of a book on nutrition and lecture anyone and everyone on diet. They will give you a sermon on the dangers of cholesterol, and two days later you'll surprise them tucking into a greasy hamburger while simultaneously scolding you about the evils of sugar. Next time you open their fridge, you'll discover their secret cache of fudge and cheesecake.

Try to understand this: *The king makes the law; the king is above the law.* It's up to the king's subjects to hear and obey. You can't expect the kingly Leo to obey these laws—they make them up. This is not logic—it's Leo logic.

The golden rule of all Leos is: *Do as I say, not as I do.*

Key tactic: Allow them to express themselves in this big-time bossy way but *never* come across as a wimp.

At the right time, you have to display your own true grit. They want you to obey them but they also want you to be their match. At those times when Ms. Superwoman Leo or Mr. Superman Leo is not coping, you have to weigh in as Mr. or Ms. Wonderful yourself.

In short, allow them to have their way as much as possible but maintain your individuality and strength at all costs. As the Leo is bossing you around, try to remind yourself that they are basically bighearted and loyal.

All the astrological textbooks will tell you that loyalty is the greatest Leo virtue. And indeed it is. But in the Leo mind, loyalty does not equate with truthfulness. They will expect total, undivided loyalty from you. In return, your Leo will give you loyalty—with a secret escape clause filed away at the back of their head. Their loyalty will be contingent upon your providing total satisfaction in and out of the sack. If you don't, your efforts will be "supplemented" by someone you'll never know about.

This will be justified on the grounds that what you don't know won't hurt you . . . or them.

Leos must be well serviced by a package of lust, romance and passion, all wrapped up in flair, chic and glamour. Only then can you be sure they're not shopping elsewhere. Always remember: Leos are great shoppers—in more ways than one.

They have a fine flair for decadence and grandiosity. The danger is that they often don't know when to stop. And because they see themselves as advice givers rather than advice receivers, it can be very tricky to let them know when they've had enough—enough alcohol, enough pastry, enough oysters, enough nights out, enough already. Only the specter of a swelling waistline or bulging thighs, collapsing health and the threat of the diseases of high living are likely to spur the Leo to curb their legendary appetites.

Must-Do's

Be prepared to lavish them with expensive treats.

Compliment them on their hair.

Be prepared to go out. If you're a stay-at-home by nature, see Cancer, Taurus or Pisces.

Be prepared to entertain at home.

Make sure your hair looks immaculate and learn how to achieve casual chic. They want to look glamorous standing next to you.

If you're aiming to acquire a visiting Leo woman, buy a good hairdryer for her to use when she's in residence.

Have good wines on hand—and extra credit cards.

No-No's

Never criticize a Leo. They expect to be able to criticize you but they don't want this behavior to be imitated.

Never be the first to leave a party.

Never go bankrupt!

How to End a Relationship with a Leo

■ ■ ■

You could try the frank approach and aim to keep them on as friends.

Leos are proud, so they are not likely to beg you to stay. They are not likely to sob and scream in front of you. They will generally reserve the waterworks for the privacy of their own home.

Remember that Leos are good at criticizing others, so they may take the opportunity of the breakup to give you a lot of blunt advice. Steel yourself for an encyclopedic rundown on your every inadequacy and every time in the last ten years you messed up, blew it or failed . . . in their eyes.

Leo may well agree that there are a lot of good things between the two of you, and that you should remain friends. Certainly Leos are worth keeping in your address book. They are admirably loyal and can be the sort who will get together with an old flame every six or twelve months for a dirty weekend—provided it's done with style and good taste. This is definitely a partner you can appeal to on the grounds of "once more for old times' sake." It is not unknown for Leos to keep old lovers going on a *Same Time, Next Year* basis for two decades or more.

But if you really want to terminate things forever, turn stingy and scruffy. Wear old clothes with stains and holes. Refuse to go out, especially anywhere that costs more than six dollars a person. All you want to do is stay at home, watch videos and eat McDonald's. The affair is over.

Leos at Their Best

■ ■ ■

Leos will give your life an injection of fun, playfulness and glamour. They will make you feel that life is to be savored and that when you're with them, you have a right to the good times. You will feel very special indeed being romanced by this loyal, bighearted, high-spirited, dramatic lover.

Leos at Their Worst

■ ■ ■

You'll feel as if you're having a relationship with a spoiled child. You'll find yourself constantly pandering to their laziness, self-indulgence and prima donna personality. Their egos will demand a constant diet of instant obedience, flattery and kowtowing. They, in turn, will be force-feeding you an unpalatable diet of royal decrees, patronizing comments and unsolicited, often hypocritical advice.

Sexy Leos

■ ■ ■

Mick Jagger, Jacqueline Onassis, Mata Hari, Mae West, Robert Redford, Neil Armstrong, Carl Jung, Arnold Schwarzenegger, Madonna, Coco Chanel, Melanie Griffith, Whitney Houston, Gene Kelly, Patrick Swayze, Peter O'Toole, Robert De Niro.

Unsexy Leos

■ ■ ■

Benito Mussolini, Dustin Hoffman, George Bernard Shaw, Alfred Hitchcock, Cecil B. DeMille, Annie Oakley, Napoleon, Fidel Castro, Lucille Ball, Roman Polanski, Andy Warhol, Sean Penn.

VIRGO
♍

August 24th to September 23rd

■ ■ ■

Hey, hold on, cut that out,

now stop that . . . I thought when you said

you wanted to do something together, you

meant tidy up the kitchen.

The Lure of a Virgo

■ ■ ■

They look so neat and clean.

Their manners are so perfect.

They seem so caring and modest and considerate.

They're so . . . well . . . nice.

Perhaps you want someone in your life who is genuinely nice, someone who is genuinely helpful, someone who is genuinely sensitive, someone who is, well, genuine. Then consider Mr. or Ms. Virgo.

If you want a proper gentleman or lady in public, someone who will never embarrass you, a Virgo will usually fit the bill.

If you like a safe, secure, predictable life, well, a Virgo would be the last to complain that you never whisked them away on a spur-of-the-moment escapade.

They can also help you pull the practical and domestic side of your life into shape—not to mention encouraging you to get serious about health and exercise, look after your body and do your bit for the environment.

And they have their physical attractions: they tend to keep their waistlines and are often lean-limbed, with youthful, glowing skin. But their greatest attraction is their smile. When a Virgo smiles, his or her face is transformed and a lovely, appealing inner boy or girl comes shining out and lights up the room.

A final attraction (if you can call it that) is that Virgo is unlikely to wear you out sexually and leave you wasted, sore and spent with insatiable sexual demands.

How to Interest a Virgo

■ ■ ■

Loyalty, steadfastness, honesty, dependability, responsibility: these are what Virgo is looking for.

Key tip: A Virgo needs to trust you.

Impress them that you are honorable and can be counted on—that you don't have terrible moods or unpredictable quirks, that you are even-tempered, equitable and constant. Come across as positively wholesome. They need to be certain they will never be confronted with any of the wild or even mildly rippled backwaters of your psyche. They don't want any pebbles thrown into the smooth pond of their lives—and certainly no boulders.

A Virgo expects you to be dependable and orderly. Never be dirty, unkempt or (shudder!) smelly. They will note and rate the cleanliness of your hair, your socks, your underwear. They are capable of detecting stains usually invisible to the naked eye. You must be punctual and your deodorant must never let you down.

Only when your most admirable qualities have been firmly established in their mind can you move on to romance and intimacy.

Virgos have a very well-developed work ethic, so you need to impress them with your dedication to your job. Especially emphasize that you regard your work as making a contribution to society. Don't tell them you work as a garbageman; tell them you are in the recycling industry. Don't tell them you work for a wood-chipping company; tell them you work in resource management. Don't tell them you are a prison warden; tell them you work in social rehabilitation. If you can't think of a way in which your job actually helps others, moan about how frustrated you are because you could actually do other people a lot of good if only the bosses wouldn't stop you from doing what needs to be done. Virgo will probably be able to identify with this.

All this is indispensable groundwork because when the time comes to get down to the sexual nitty-gritty, your Virgo needs to trust you 110 percent. They need to be convinced of your sense of duty and responsibility.

To match them, you'll have to project your most altruistic, caring, genuine, orderly, modest front. Let's face it, it could be a lot of work keeping up with all this goodness.

Virgos have neat, precise, ordered lives. They want someone who will fit in with this neatness, precision and order. This is why many Virgos end up with other Virgos—or opt for the single life.

Key tip number two: Never be the cause of "mess" in any of its wicked manifestations. Cleanliness is godliness. You must convince Virgo that not only will you not mess up their life—you will actually help raise neatness and organization to new heights. Insist on washing the dishes; volunteer to clean the bathroom. Remain vigilant for any opportunity to prove yourself a grade-A wiper, stacker or scrubber. This will impress them.

Don't invite them back to your own place unless it's spotless.

Key tip number three: Avoid ostentation. Virgos don't expect to be ostentatiously flattered or wined and dined just for the sake of display. That comes under the heading of "phony." They don't want phoniness. They want genuine . . . er . . . genuineness.

Suggested opening line: "Can I get you a napkin?"

What to talk about: Health, fitness, diet, "natural" products, work—they're happy to discuss their work or your work. Tell them about the child you are supporting in a Third World country, any relative or friend who works for the underprivileged. Mention that you are a big supporter of Greenpeace and grow your own medicinal herbs.

Where to take them: Macrobiotic restaurants, walks in parks and in the woods, cycling, scenic restaurants in the mountains, picnics, weekends at health spas, historic buildings with wonderful gardens, public lectures.

What to give them: Health books, juice extractors, handmade wooden bowls, pottery, perfume-free no-animal-testing detergents and cosmetics, loofahs and back brushes, things for the garden, herbs in terra-cotta pots, herbal teas, herbariums, potpourris, English country-style wooden furniture, flowers—including dried ones.

How to Seduce a Virgo

■ ■ ■

Key tip number one: Don't freak them out or stun them in any way during the seductive process.

No shock tactics. Most Virgos will feel threatened rather than excited if you try to sweep them off their feet. There must be no alarming moments.

"If it were done when 'tis done, then 'twere well it were done slowly." It would be a grave mistake to try to pounce on an archetypal Virgo.

If you freak them out, all your previous efforts will have been in vain. They will retreat into prissy and prudish mode and your solid groundwork will turn to mud.

Do not jump this person in a parking lot, behind a bush or especially at work. None of that. Work is taken very seriously. Modesty and propriety demand that the venue be lock-sure, triple-bolted, superprivate.

Don't expect your archetypal Virgo to be overcome by a surge of raw lust because this is your first time together and they just can't wait. Nor should you expect to be delighted by a delicious lack of inhibition. They often need long foreplay. In fact, they may well need eight-, nine-, or tenplay.

There is hardly a hint of the devil in your archetypal Virgo, which is why spontaneously jumping them is contraindicated. A certain amount of patience is necessary. A spirit of urgency will tend to put them off. Virgos believe in considering things—and then considering them some more. Then sleeping on them and considering them again.

Key tip number two: Never ever present sex as an illicit thrill.

It would be a terminal mistake to try to excite a Virgoan by playing up the wicked we-shouldn't-really-do-this-so-we-must-do-it-*now* illicit lure of sex. Virgoan thinking would be, "If we shouldn't really do this, we most certainly won't. Why have you even suggested it, you degraded animal?"

Virgos are very self-critical. They are terrible moralizers, so you have to tease them along a bit to convince them that what they are about to do is not only terribly moral, but good for their health because it's natural.

Key tip number three: Support their sexual egos.

Virgoan egos are often more than a bit behind their actual worth. They often need bolstering—especially in seeing themselves as sexually desirable.

Gently and with extreme diplomacy express your appreciation of their physical appeal. Support the building of confidence on all levels of their life—their career, their social activities, their talents—including those performed in a horizontal position.

This can have long-term sexual benefits for you. It's worth memorizing this equation:

Reinforcement → Confidence → "I'm sexy" → "I like sex"

A final warning: don't necessarily expect a Virgo to pick up on the sexual vibes you put out. Virgos can be sexually obtuse. They can lack talent in sexual banter. Many people carry torches for Virgos for years: they go out with them, lunch with them, drink endless cups of herbal tea with them, have deep conversations with them and, in all this time, it never occurs to the Virgo that this person has the hots for them.

Seduction 1: The True Confession

Honesty is a good tactic in the seduction of a Virgo.

Confess that you are sexually attracted to them. They may be shocked (or pretend to be shocked), they may even blush, but *they will respect your honesty.*

This acknowledgment of their sexual attractiveness will also help to increase their sexual self-esteem, which is, as we said, important for Virgos.

Perhaps it may be best to make this confession in a safe public place where they know you won't jump them. Now retreat for a reasonable period, hours or days, depending on your Virgo, and give them time to assimilate this disturbing news. Return to politely test the waters. If the temperature is right, take the plunge.

Proceed to the Cuddle Litmus Test (Pisces), or proceed to . . .

Seduction 2: The Slow-Motion Seduction

Key tactic: Ease along the guilty part of your Virgo.

Bear in mind that guilt can be a big issue with Virgos—especially guilt about sex. The adult part of them senses where the two of you are going, but the guilty inner child may still be quietly freaking out. Try easing them along, making each step feel very safe, as if nothing is going to happen—certainly nothing at all untoward. "Let's go back to my place for a cup of coffee . . . yes, I have decaf . . . Why don't we sit on the couch." (After much kissing and slowly, slowly, slowly fondling) "We'd be much more comfortable lying down . . . Let me rub your neck for you . . . your back . . . oh, my belt's tight after all that food, I'll just loosen it . . . You must be hot . . . can I help you with your shirt . . . your skin feels so nice . . . let's just lie here and hug for a while."

Seduction 3: The Slap-and-Tickle

One helpful tactic for the seduction of Virgos is to unleash the playful child that is buried under all those parental injunctions against sex. You need to create a bona fide excuse for them to be silly, have fun and let it all hang out.

Tickling could work. If you can get them giggling, you may well be on the way to more adult forms of play.

See if you can engage them in childish physical games—tag, water fights, mud fights. Take them to the swings and the merry-go-round. Lots of potential for back-to-back, front-to-front, pelvis-to-pelvis contact here. Double up on the swings, head for the seesaw, use your imagination. Consider a trip to an amusement park. Consider the possibilities of dark tunnel rides.

Seduction 4: Pig-Out in the Park (with Reduced Fats and Sugars)

Like Taurus, Virgo is an Earth sign. As such, sex in the great outdoors can be quite a stimulating idea. See Pig-Out in the Park (Taurus). However, modify the menu *à la* Virgo. Pack your picnic basket at the organic foods store.

Seduction 5: The Clean Weekend

The idea here is to invite your Virgo away for a weekend—not a dirty one but a clean one. You must, if pressed, be able to state clearly that you don't intend to hit on them—even though you do.

Possible scenarios include inviting them to join a party at a friend's vacation home, inviting them to go camping with a group, taking them away to a country inn with "separate bedrooms, of course."

Your "chaperoning" friends can be forewarned to disappear at the lift of an eyebrow. Many things are possible. At least you will have gotten your Virgo away from work, duties, responsibilities, chores. You may have the opportunity to try some of the other seductions outlined here.

Even if you don't succeed in getting lost in the garden of earthly delights, you'll have a fighting chance of putting in some good spadework and planting the seeds of pleasures to come.

Seduction 6: The I-Need-You

Virgos, perhaps more than any other sign, need to feel needed.

Tell them how much you need them in every way. Talk sincerely about how much you respect them, how you need them to be part of your life, how you need them to want you, how you want them to need you, how you need them to need you the way you need them. They may well yield in response to this professed need (even if only just to shut you up).

Searingly passionate sex might not be the result, but it could be a good starting point. Practice makes perfect.

Seduction 7: The Masters-and-Johnson

Virgos often see sex as another skill they need to learn in order to have a neat, "normal," healthy life.

This suggests a possible avenue of seduction: holding out the carrot of sexual education. Formulate a plan based on the age, experience and background of the particular Virgo.

Quote Chairman Mao: "There is no correct theory without practice."

If you have found yourself a Virgoan woman who confesses to sexual hangups, you might engage her in a highly theoretical discussion of possible courses of action. Buy her a copy of the brilliant book *Nice Girls Do* by Irene Kassorla. Lend her your annotated copy. Offer yourself as a therapeutic assistant.

Seduction 8: The It's-Good-for-You

This is the last resort for seduction of a Virgo.

If you reach an impasse where their urge to do the deed is being paralyzed by the equal and opposite force of their inhibitions, it may help to emphasize how necessary a good sex life is for proper health. Talk about Chinese medicine and how sex is necessary to properly balance your yin and yang. Discuss its beneficial effects on the thymus gland. Drop in some talk of Wilhelm Reich and how the orgasm is the major way that the body throws off stress. Mention how doctors now believe that correct hormonal function depends on having a decent sex life, how sex stimulates the production of endorphins, which have a deep natural regulating effect on the brain . . . and that sex improves sleep, digestion and performance at work.

It could help.

Seduction 9: The Mrs. Robinson

Middle-aged Virgos have often had a chance to work through the sexual repression of their youth. They can then be almost desperate to make up for lost time. In this mode, Virgos have been known to suddenly throw themselves at the most inappropriate people.

The tramp within the lady is now prepared to embrace all manner of sexual peccadilloes.

If you think you have spotted a Virgoan Lady Chatterley, look through the Scorpio seductions for some ideas to tempt her.

Other good Virgo seductions:

Seduction by Curiosity (see Gemini)

The Intimate Evening for Two (Cancer)

The Declaration of Love (Cancer)

The Stray Dog (Cancer)

The Polite Withdrawal (Cancer)

Seduction by Assumption (Libra)

The Relationships Workshop (Libra)

The Discreet Overture (Capricorn)

The Cuddle Litmus Test (Pisces)

Whispers in the Dark (Pisces)

Sex with a Virgo

■ ■ ■

The symbol of Virgo is a virgin woman. There is a good reason for this, as many people in relationships with Virgos soon find out.

It seems to be a karmic challenge for people born under this sign to deal with childhood sexual repression and overcome a distaste for bodily connection. They need to learn that sex is to be enjoyed as one of the good things in life, even if it is sticky, sweaty and smelly—not to mention squishy, squelchy and sloshy.

All too often their relationships are moral, caring and sincere but lack sexual spark. They involve a meeting of the minds but not the gonads.

Virgos are often sensitive souls, conservative by nature, not natural rebels. In consequence, as children they are particularly vulnerable to parental injunctions against sexuality. The archetypal Virgo genuinely wants to be good; if they are told as children that sex is bad, they will tend to believe it, and the result is a bundle of repressed impulses. They lack that spark of the devil and the rebel that helps other signs to get over childhood conditioning against sexuality. To make it worse, they are often masters of self-denial.

The most repressed Virgos can be surprised to hear that it is sexually exciting to arouse another person. They have to learn that it is a turn-on to turn on someone else.

Deep inside, Virgos carry around a mental report card which, in descending order of importance, rates the various aspects of their life. It goes something like this:

1. Work   A–
2. Health   B+
3. Home   B–
4. Positive impact on the community   B
5. Hobby   C+

The trick is first to convince a Virgo that the category "Sex" should be on the report card at all, and second to see if you can move it higher up the list, because they will tend to put it at the bottom, somewhere below watering the garden and just above turning over the compost heap. One way to get them to give sex more consideration is to suggest that their sex life is significantly below the national average.

But many Virgos cannot see why one would expend time and effort on dealing with hangups about sex. Better off putting the time into their job, securing their future, painting the house.

Virgoans have a need to justify everything in life—especially sexual activity. They could be the sign most likely to say: "I couldn't have sex with anyone I didn't love." You may have to help provide them with justifications for sexual activity.

Virgos are very impressed by logical, rational arguments and by physical health. If you can present logical, rational reasons why people who have strong sex drives and fulfilling sex lives are physically, spiritually and mentally healthier, you may get their attention.

What often leads them to try out sex in the first place is curiosity. They see themselves as learners and they earnestly desire to be good at everything they do. In consequence, they often acquire technical sexual expertise before discovering real lust, raunchiness and true sexual urges.

While they'd rather not take the initiative in sex, nevertheless they may be quite concerned that you are taking charge the whole time.

Virgos may need a lot of gentle leading in sex. Virgo is not a Sun sign that sees sex as a way to discharge anxieties or escape from them. Anxiety acts like ice on their sexual libido. They need to feel their life is in order: that they've done the wash, stacked the dishes, put the garbage out, written the reports for work. Finally, when they feel they are entitled to some self-indulgence, they can relax and allow the temperature of their libido to rise. Chores first; pleasure second.

Key tip: Keep it squeaky clean.

They may expect you to shower before sex, after sex and between rounds. They generally do not want to approach a body that has any odors. Virgos know bacteria. They notice odors.

Look clean and smell clean when you arrive on the doorstep. If your hair is still slightly damp, great. They'll know you've showered within the hour.

They embarrass easily, so talking plainly might be a turnoff. Don't call a fuck a fuck; don't even call it "having sex"; call it "making love."

They generally require long, patient foreplay. Even longer if that hidden cache of naughtiness and wickedness you're trying to root out is buried deep—as it often is.

One danger is that you may find that your own desire for sex starts to wane because it takes so much hard work to get them going. You may start to have doubts about whether it's worth it yourself. So don't initiate sex when you are tired. Address yourself to seducing your Virgo partner only when you are feeling not only sexual but patient and persevering as well.

Don't ever expect a Virgo to catch a slightly later bus to work so they can have sex with you in the morning. As to the idea of taking a day off work just to engage in hanky-panky, *well!*

After work, they are often too tired—or their head is still buzzing with life in the office. After meals, they may be too full to do it. After alcohol, too dizzy. On the weekend, too involved with fixing up the house, chores, shopping, exercise, etc.

This is not a Sun sign devoid of sexuality. Think about this: Sophia Loren, Raquel Welch and Sean Connery are all Virgos.

There is a sexy earth goddess inside every Virgo woman waiting to be released. There is a sexy, earthy beast inside every Virgo man waiting to be unleashed.

When the sexual barricades start to fall and the Bastille no longer needs to be constantly stormed, *voilà*, the French Revolution. You may have a sexual frenzy on your hands with a person desperate to make up for lost time. You may find the Ice Maiden has shortened her skirts, exposed her cleavage, changed her hair, put on provocative makeup and become a born-again Mrs. Robinson. (Or the male equivalent.)

The rewards of a relationship with a sexually awakened Virgo are great indeed.

How to Handle a Relationship with a Virgo

■ ■ ■

Virgos are usually very easy to get along with because they don't have overbearing egos. They are fair and caring. If you can give these gifts back to them, if you can refrain from disturbing their orderly lives, you'll have the boon of a very calm, decent friend—for Virgo always expects a lover to be a friend first and a passion second.

Key tactic: The most important thing is not to dislocate the orderliness of Virgo's life. They want a neat life with neat relationships.

The art is to convince them that you not only dovetail into their existing routine but improve it. You not only don't mess up their place, you make it tidier. You not only don't distract them from their work, you make it easier for them to manage their home and so enjoy their work more. Ensure that you add to all aspects of their existence.

One danger is that you may feel you will never be the most important part of their life—probably because you won't be. Often their work is. It gives them status and security. Accordingly, you must never set yourself up in competition with the job. Never complain about the time or concern they give their job.

Virgos invented the phrase: "A place for everything and everything in its place." This includes you, by the way. Cleaning and tidying up is a form of therapy for Virgos. Virgo fundamentalists seem to be on a mission to stamp out dirt and deception. They believe that vacuuming and tidying can save the world.

Always remember: *Virgos will not put up with a slob for the sake of passion.*

Allow them to further your education in all aspects of home economics. Learn to hide your disorder. If you plan a visiting relationship with a Virgo, have a separate closet that is all yours where you can shove your mess. If you are sharing a place, better to have a separate room for all your own things and occasionally for you—one where you can close the door and hide your clutter. Indeed, it is often better if you have separate bedrooms so their bedroom can be maintained in their own rigid fashion. In extreme cases, you may even need to consider adjoining apartments or houses.

The worst of Virgos are nitpicking and critical in the extreme. They hide their vulnerability under a mask of perfectionism. This type of Virgo is impossible to please—mainly because they don't want to be pleased. If you met their impossibly high standards, they would have nothing and no one to blame for their inner tensions and angers. Then they would have to start looking inside and realize that instead of being the neat person of their self-image, they harbor raging angers and vulnerabilities buried since early childhood.

Virgos are impressed by logical, rational arguments. They are left cold by emotional manipulation, anger and hysterics—especially in public. "I won't be spoken to like that . . . Talk to me when you come back to your senses . . . Just get control of yourself . . . Don't be so childish."

Key tip: No outrageous behavior in public, ever.

Virgos are sensitive souls. They often require a great deal of emotional support. Think twice—or three times—before you offer any criticism, because they are extremely self-critical. Give feedback gently. Say as many positive, complimentary things as you can.

Virgos are most often genuinely nice people. If you can lift your neatness rating to their requirements, they are often easy to live with and like.

Must-Do's

Bathe frequently.

Be patient.

Share the cleaning.

Put things back where they belong.

Bring them an occasional bunch of flowers.

No-No's

Never leave the bathroom messy.

Never draw attention to yourself or them in public. Don't pinch their butt in front of other people. Even holding hands could be borderline.

Don't put your elbows on the table. Fold your napkin at the end of the meal.

Never raise your voice.

How to End a Relationship with a Virgo

■ ■ ■

The key words here are "honesty" and "openness."

Virgos usually hate a scene and are not vengeful. It's unlikely that they will try to take you to the cleaners either emotionally or financially.

It's probably best just to tell them it's simply not working out for you anymore. Tell them they are one of the nicest people you've ever met but somehow, well, the chemistry isn't there. There isn't that passionate connection between the two of you anymore. You wish them all the best—they really deserve the right person in their life; unfortunately it's not you.

Generally, with Virgos, it's up to *you* to act ethically toward *them*.

One advantage of an affair with a Virgo is that they are generally very decent afterward. Their egos are often vulnerable, however, so try to leave their self-image in at least as good a state as you found it.

All this notwithstanding, a major warning is that guilt is a Virgo tool of trade. You could be cast in the role of the man with the match opposite their Joan of Arc. You may have to deal with the biggest guilt trip laid on you since your mother caught you playing doctors and nurses with the kids next door.

Virgos at Their Best

■ ■ ■

You won't believe your luck in having found such a genuinely caring, dependable, supportive partner. You'll be able to relax and feel secure with someone who is loyal, monogamous, responsible and fair. You'll feel encouraged to join them in their admirable quest to be healthy, wealthy and wise. They'll help you create a well-ordered existence: a neat home, healthful food, regular hours. And as an added bonus, they remain youthful well into middle age.

Virgos at Their Worst

■ ■ ■

You'll feel you're in a relationship with a cross between a schoolmarm and a junior Boy Scout. Frequently nitpicking, prudish, undemonstrative, repressed and self-righteous, they can often find sex distasteful and not worth the effort. You will end up with a wobbly sexual ego yourself due to having to make all the sexual overtures and finding them met with lack of interest, yet you will feel guilty about becoming angry and frustrated with someone so wholesome and nice. You will increasingly come to think that there must be something wrong with you—a suspicion that will be reinforced by the way they pick at you all the time. You'll experience lust deprivation and chronic hunger pangs for wild sexual spontaneity.

Sexy Virgos

■ ■ ■

Sean Connery, Raquel Welch, Sophia Loren, Charles Boyer, Yvonne de Carlo, Claudette Colbert, Lauren Bacall, Anne Bancroft, Greta Garbo, Twiggy, Jeremy Irons, D. H. Lawrence, Richard Gere, Jacqueline Bisset, Charlie Sheen, Michael Keaton.

Unsexy Virgos

■ ■ ■

Leonard Bernstein, Joseph Kennedy, Lyndon B. Johnson, Elliott Gould, Raymond Massey, Peter Falk, Maurice Chevalier, Mother Teresa, Larry Hagman, Buddy Holly, Stephen King, Bill Murray, Lily Tomlin, Frankie Avalon.

LIBRA

September 24th to October 23rd

...

Do you take this person to be your

lawfully wedded spouse, to have, to hold,

to cherish, in sickness and in health,

forsaking all others until somebody

better comes along?

—Libran Wedding Vow

The Lure of a Libra

■ ■ ■

Cleopatra, Adonis, Helen of Troy, Queen Guinevere, Brigitte Bardot, Superman (i.e., Christopher Reeve), James Bond (i.e., Roger Moore). Librans all.

Librans are so often the classic, well-proportioned beauties of the Zodiac.

These handsome show ponies are always well groomed, *très soignés*. They like to preen and pose for any passing judge, showing off their sleek form to the best advantage. Librans are masters at exploiting their natural good looks. Peacock-like, they dress to display. If necessary (and often it's not), they will work hard to mold, maintain and enhance their figures and features. The slightest hint of flab will have them running to the nearest gym or Weight Watchers meeting. The female Libran is prepared to virtually starve herself to keep the figure she had when she was eighteen and still be able to fit into that size 10.

Ms. Libra is a natural couturière and can whip up a designer-quality outfit in an evening. Librans know style and frequently end up working in the fashion industry—often as models. If you are looking for a very chic, very stylish woman to decorate your arm, a woman to make your friends apoplectic with jealousy, a woman who is part ingenue, part femme fatale and part love goddess, Ms. Libra could be for you.

If you are a woman of refined tastes who has had her fill of scruffy men perpetually in need of a haircut and with holes in their underpants, if you are after a chic yet masculine man—part boyish charmer, part Adonis and part ladykiller—then Mr. Libra could offer the touch of class you crave.

If you want a partner prepared to share your interests, Libra could definitely be the one for you. They are the chameleons of the Zodiac and will assume your interests and hobbies.

Libra could also be perfect if you're feeling lonely and want close, clingy togetherness with someone who'll listen to all your past relationship angst. They like nothing more than to hear how you suffered in relationships before you found them. Of course, in turn, you will have to listen to their litany of past pains.

This sign rules partnership and marriage. So if you're in a real hurry to get married (provided you're not counting on it lasting forever), Libra is probably your best bet.

They're handsome, svelte and accommodating, but there is something very important you ought to know about the psychology of the Libran. Libra is perhaps the most difficult sign to break from. The end could be fraught with tumultuous scenes and mini—nervous breakdowns. The emotionally immature Libran is obsessive about having a partner in life. Moreover, Librans in general are a very poor choice for a secret affair, as they like to wear a relationship like a Cartier watch—as a status symbol.

The symbol of Libra is the Scales. Librans seem to hold in balance—or imbalance—the elements of the two signs they fall between, the emotional restraint of Virgo and the hot intensity of Scorpio. They can oscillate dangerously between the two. However, the emotionally mature Libran who has got the balancing act together is true gold. They understand the art of compromise, they believe in give and take and they want nothing more than to live in a harmonious relationship.

How to Interest a Libra

■ ■ ■

One difficulty in actually obtaining a Libran in the first place is that they are almost always in a relationship. They so hate to be seen as unattached that often they refuse to see themselves as totally single. They may still be sort of seeing Such-and-such while sort of going out with So-and-so. Accordingly, if you meet a Libran you have the hots for, and they are already technically "in a relationship," consider presenting yourself as a prospect anyway.

This is the sign you are most likely to have to compete for. However, it is also the sign about which you can feel least morally squeamish when it comes to tossing your hat in the ring with a number of hats already lying there. Libra always has an eye out for an improved version of their current partner.

Key tactic number one: Flattery will get you everywhere.

You must find the right moments to compliment them on their appearance. Tell Ms. Libra she looks stunning, that she is the best-dressed woman there. If Ms. Libra tells you she made the dress herself, be astounded to the point of disbelief. Say you assumed she bought it in Paris or New York.

Admire Mr. Libra's taste in shirts, his haircut, his earring. Ask him how often he works out at the gym. If he doesn't, be amazed that he can look so great without working out every day.

While administering these compliments, you yourself must be at your most elegant. If in any doubt, rush home, grab the iron, raid your wardrobe and return looking great before approaching the Libran object of your desires.

Librans insist on having a partner who is refined. They have to believe that you understand fine and beautiful things—especially when it comes to your dress sense. The thongs-and-T-shirt brigade need not apply. A Libran can detect thirty percent polyester at fifty paces.

You may need to work on your etiquette and study up on which wine goes with which dish. If you know the difference between *sauce béarnaise* and *sauce béchamel,* they will be dreadfully impressed.

Key tactic number two: Immediately start talking about relationships.

Remember that Librans are into togetherness. Their relationship is the most important thing in their lives. The first thing a Libran wants to know about you is: "Are you in a relationship?"

Never simply answer yes or no. It's not that simple—at least not to a Libran.

Choose from the following list:

"I'm sort of seeing someone but it's not working out."

"I'm sort of seeing someone but I don't know where it's headed."

"I'm sort of dating a couple of people but it's nothing really serious."

"I was sort of seeing someone but I found out they were married."

"I sort of just met somebody but I know it's not going to work out."

At this stage, to improve your prospects, talk about how much a relationship means to you, how being in a relationship is the most important thing in your life, how you want to share everything in your life with a partner, how you need a fulfilling relationship to be a fulfilled person and have a fulfilling life, etc., ad nauseam.

You are now a potential partnership prospect.

Now pose one or all of the following questions:

"Are you in a relationship?"

"Are you waiting for someone?"

"Are you free tomorrow evening?"

Key tactic number three: Present yourself as a demi-god or -goddess of desirability.

Librans thrive on derived status. Aries (the opposite sign to Libra) wants to be the star. Libra wants to be married to the star—or at least be photographed with them.

If they can see you're Hot Property, they'll want you to become their property. How you appear to be Hot Property is up to you. Perhaps you are beautiful or handsome. Perhaps you're rich. Perhaps other people are chasing you. Perhaps you are talented and heading for the big time. Perhaps you are in the big time. Or perhaps you have the talent for appearing to be one of these things when you're not.

One warning here is that if you do succeed in becoming this Adonis or Aphrodite of desirability, the Libran mind will immediately leap to thoughts of marriage.

One final tip (tacky but true): the recently divorced Libran is a pushover. Even more so if they are separated but not yet divorced.

Suggested opening line: "Are you waiting for someone?"

What to talk about: Relationships, fashion, who's getting married to whom, who's getting unmarried, who's doing what to whom, who's happy and who's unhappy, who's seeing a therapist, Hollywood gossip about which star is doing what to whom, what went wrong with Charles and Di, who's sleeping with Di, who's sleeping with Charles.

Where to take them: The ballet, balls, elegant stores, elegant restaurants with impeccable service where the presentation of the food is as important as the taste, perhaps Japanese, the lobby or bars of elegant five-star hotels where they can sip drinks and be seen, back to your place for advice on interior decoration—your drapes, your cushion covers, your bed linens.

What to give them (making sure it's beautifully wrapped): Mirrors, books on relationships and interior design, silk scarves, ties, roses, crystal vases, expensive jewelry, perfume, fine leather goods, gift certificates for top department stores, clothes storage systems, the most expensive sewing machine on the market.

How to Seduce a Libra

■ ■ ■

Librans receive plenty of dates and invitations—and they are not generally reluctant to exploit their attractiveness in an apparently cynical fashion by acting the temptress/tempter and playing hard to get. In this sense, Librans can be perceived as terrible prickteasers or pussyteasers. This could be a bit unfair to them. In their eyes, they are simply presenting themselves at their best in case Mr. Right or Ms. Right happens to walk into the room. Librans are great relationship shoppers and are always in the market for a better model than their current one.

The fact that they have gone on a few dates with you does not mean you have been placed in the Mr. or Ms. Right category—you may not even be in the Mr. or Ms. *Possible* category. So be sensitive to the vibes. The fact that you are drippingly hormonal does not mean they want you in the same way. You may be a fill-in—a temporary dinner date as they continue their search for Mr. or Ms. Perfect.

Librans fear rejection. In consequence, they tend to be passive in matters of passion and aim to be pursued rather than pursue. They actively wait for the right person to come their way and then try to draw in a potential prospect using their physical appeal.

Librans are the Venus flytrap of the Zodiac. Their good looks and Marlene Dietrich aloofness can drive would-be lovers wild with the dual desire to place them on a pedestal and ravish them on the spot.

Don't give in to the second impulse. Direct tactics make Librans uncomfortable. They are amazingly adept at defusing direct questions like "Do you like me?"

Classic Librans like to hold on to this courtship stage for a long time—they enjoy playing the tease while being pampered and idolized. They feel powerful and in control when playing hard to get. Libran women in particular like to drive men to a frenzy, then retreat as if in fear, pulling away from a horny male showing signs of rampant sexual desperation.

The more desperate you are for them, the cooler you must appear. They don't like the idea of being overwhelmed by animalistic passion. This is not a Sun sign to try to impress with the earth-shaking magnitude of your lust. They expect decorum.

At this stage, they require endless attention—even to the point of fawning. The women especially will expect the full courtship bit: doors opened for them, constant solicitous questioning about their welfare, flowers, expensive gifts, hand-holding.

As they are tempting and tantalizing you, they themselves are deeply involved in a process of evaluating you—and reevaluating you. This continuing assessment can be a very protracted business. Librans are renowned for taking a long time to make up their minds.

Key tip: The seduction process must be geared around making it easy for them to decide to have a relationship with you.

Or, better still, easy for you to make the decision for them.
Which leads us to . . .

Seduction 1: Seduction by Assumption

The power of the unspoken word.

The key here is to act as if they have invited you back to their place for coffee. You just naturally accompany them to the door. You just naturally follow them inside. You just naturally take their hand and draw them to you. You just naturally lead them to the bedroom. You just naturally remove your jacket and drape it carefully over a chair. You just naturally commence kissing and undressing them.

Calm confidence. Certainty. No urgency. *Allegro non troppo*.

The point of this is that, if they don't want you, it forces them to make a decision in the negative. They have to get together their identity enough to decide one way or the other.

Should you be rejected outright—"I'm just not sexually attracted to you"—well, there are other fish in the sea. At least you can stop wasting your time on being strung along by the vacillating Libran.

Should you be postponed—"I'm not sure if I'm ready for this yet"—you may proceed to Seduction 2.

Seduction 2: The Relationships Workshop or The Rhetorical Seduction

The aim here is to get them to admit that they do feel attracted to you.

You can hold this Relationship Workshop anywhere—candlelit dinner at your place, coffee at their place, a walk along a beach. The strategy is to see whether you can whip up some enthusiasm on their part.

Let us assume that you are taking this slowly and, after a respectable length of time—say two or three dates—you park the car at a suitably romantic spot: the sun setting, the moon rising, the stars appearing. Now look earnestly at them and say, "I need to know where our relationship is heading. I need to know how you feel about me."

The trick now is to guide the discussion in such a way that they don't have to express their own enthusiasm. What you are after is guided consent. You know they want you. You know they won't tell you they want you. Therefore, you must tell them that you know you both want it—but subtly, carefully, delicately.

A good idea is to make statements and ask rhetorical questions. Ideally all they have to do is nod. "I feel this special energy between us. Don't you feel that? I feel that this relationship could be going somewhere. I feel it's time to take our relationship to another level. Don't you? All relationships are a risk but the way I feel about you, I want to take those risks. Don't you?"

If you can get a nod at this stage, move in then and there for some physical preliminaries, break away, allow a moment or two of deep and meaningful eye contact, start the car and drive them back to your place. See Seduction by Assumption.

Seduction 3: The Sickeningly Sincere Candlelit Dinner

A good seduction scenario is to entertain your Libran with an elegant, private meal at your home: several small and exquisite courses, your best silverware, red roses everywhere.

All other aspects of your home must look immaculate. You yourself must eat slowly, displaying impeccable manners, tending to their every pleasure. If you normally chow down (like a good Taurean, for instance), snack before they arrive.

As the meal progresses, compliment them on how they look. (Flattery will get you everywhere, remember.) Draw them out so that they start thinking and talking—not about sex, but about relationships, of course.

Emphasize that you want to build a relationship of real significance. You might get them talking about their past relationships—or you could talk about yours. (See tips under the Relationships Workshop.)

Serve them coffee on the couch, sit close and move into deeper, more personal talk. Tell them you feel very glad they have come into your life. Say that even though you know this relationship is only beginning, you just know it is going somewhere significant. "I find you very attractive. I feel this could be a very significant relationship. I feel this could have a real future. I feel that this is the most important relationship I've had for a long time. You're like nobody else I've ever met."

Don't blow it by moving too quickly, but it might be worth heading toward the remark, "Don't you think lovemaking is the absolute foundation of a good relationship between a man and a woman?"

As you move into more intimate contact, be solicitous of their feelings. Never be too eager, but when the "moment de pounce" arrives be suavely dominant. Seduce with sophistication.

A key tip for this and all seductions of Librans: Conceal your physical flaws. And allow them the chance to conceal theirs.

Librans are very fussy about physical appearances—their own and their partner's. Accordingly you are well advised to cover up any parts of you that fail the trim, taut and terrific test.

Lights out—or one candle—could be the solution. That way they won't start rating your physical flaws—or be too self-conscious about any portion of their anatomy that is in less than professional model condition.

Seduction 4: The Sugar Daddy or Sugar Mama

This seduction preys on the Libran tendency to keep one eye open for a better-placed lover.

Libran women are secretly impressed by the bank account and the savoir faire of an older man with a good position in society: style, status and security all in one package. You need not be as wealthy as they like to think you are, but timely mutterings about gold shares, property deals and mergers will slip from your lips between mouthfuls of pistachioed turkey ballottine.

You must be well off enough to dress well and provide the essential string of tasteful little gifts. You could have a bit more dash than cash, but you must have *some* cash. Your Libran must be left with the impression that you are definitely able to take care of them: you're solid, wise, experienced. You have a Gold Card personality.

This is a seduction to be undertaken at your leisure and pleasure. It is unlikely to yield fast results, but with solid, regular work on your part and assuming no better prospects present themselves to your Libra, within a few weeks you should be all right.

This seduction is best used in pursuit of a lengthier relationship with a Libran. It allows them time to marinate. Suave, polished, urbane is the way to come across.

Seduction 5: The Gold-Plated Seduction

This is an archetypal short-circuit seduction for Libra provided you're loaded.

This is a seduction by royal tribute: Sheba bringing tribute to Solomon or Caesar bringing tribute to Cleopatra.

Head straight for the nearest Cartier's, Neiman Marcus, Tiffany's, etc. Seek advice from some sales assistant with good taste. You are after something solid, classic and loaded with platinum, twenty-two-karat gold, diamonds, emeralds, etc. Some possibilities: diamond earrings, a Rolex, a string of pearls, a gold bracelet. Have it professionally gift-wrapped, of course.

Present it that evening over dinner at your local equivalent of the Ritz. Proceed to Seduction by Assumption.

Seduction 6: Seduction by Potential (The Poor Man's Seduction)

This seduction is to be attempted only by impoverished but terribly refined intellectuals. Sophisticated, in-depth intellectual discussions can be a way to make a large impression on a Libran and can constitute a form of foreplay. Libra, like Gemini and Aquarius, is an Air sign and all Air signs are susceptible to seduction via foreplay of the cerebral cortex.

At this stage and we mean *at this stage,* you may not be able to live up to the normal Libran requirements, but you will soon because you have heaps of potential. Ideally, you are completing a degree in some disgustingly profitable field and are due to be snapped up by a multinational corporation and fast-tracked into their senior executive ranks.

You may happen to mention—briefly, tastefully, only once (fear not, they will take note)—that the other people you will be working with are taking home a minimum of a hundred grand a year.

Say you will need new suits. What do they think about Gianni Versace? Do they prefer Giorgio Armani? Would they help you shop for your new wardrobe?

This seduction relies on the fact that Librans don't want you to be the one that got away.

Proceed to the Sickeningly Sincere Candlelit Dinner and emphasize in the course of conversation that you are looking for someone to "build a life with."

Seduction 7: Seduction by Competition

A key tip for getting a Libran sexually interested is to come across as Hot Property.

If you're not actually a star, if you're not as delicious as Mel Gibson or as delectable as Michelle Pfeiffer, if you're not rich or famous . . . never mind. There is a simple technique for appearing to be Hot Property: make it known that many members of the opposite sex are in pursuit of you.

If the Libran sees others pursuing you, this will convince them you are desirable; therefore they will desire you. Libran logic at work. They want someone everyone else wants.

Librans like others to compete for their favors and, in turn, they see a potential partner as more valuable if they have to compete for him or her.

If you aren't actually being pursued by a horde of hunks or a battalion of beauties, don't despair—all you need is the *appearance* of being pursued. For this you can use techniques such as the Return of the Old Flame, the Phantom Lover or the Hot Hunk.

There is another plus to using Seduction by Competition. Librans are terrible vacillators, and this includes deciding whether to jump into bed with you. If they feel they are in competition with another person, they may leap into bed with you a lot sooner for fear of losing you to another and so having you become the one that got away.

Seduction by Competition (i): The Return of the Old Flame.

One way to accelerate the Libran seduction process is to tell them about an old flame who is about to return from overseas. You may talk of Stefan or Jacqueline, who phoned to say they'll be back next week and wants to have a serious talk with you. Wonder aloud what this ex-boy/girlfriend could possibly want to talk about. If the Libran doesn't immediately suggest that they might be interested in getting back together, mention the possibility yourself. Make no comment about what your thoughts on the matter might be. Or consider saying, "Yeah, so he/she's good-looking and rich, but I don't know . . . I want someone who understands the importance of a relationship. Then again, maybe they've changed."

Your value and the urgency of the situation have now skyrocketed in the Libran's mind. Proceed to the Sickeningly Sincere Candlelit Dinner.

Seduction by Competition (ii): The Phantom Lover.

Here you increase your desirability in the eyes of the Libran by creating a smokescreen of phantom lovers who are eager to sample your charms. Send yourself flowers when and where the Libran will take note. Ensure that the Libran is there when you hear certain messages on your answering machine. Have the Libran continually catching you on the phone turning down a date. Perhaps you could receive unsigned love letters from someone promising you the earth and too shy to reveal their identity—yet. Ask the Libran if it was he or she who sent them.

Seduction by Competition (iii): The Hot Hunk or Blond Bombshell Technique.

You arrive at a party where you know your Libran target will be. Draped over your arm is this most exquisite enhancement to your appeal and desirability: the quintessential Blond Bombshell or Hot Hunk. Arrive an hour late and make a grand entrance. Jaws must drop as you enter the room with BB or HH at your side.

Where you find them is your own business. In the absence of a friend, neighbor, cousin or old classmate who fills the bill, phone an escort agency.

Your desirability to the Libran has jumped exponentially. You must be highly desirable because you have such a highly desirable person with you. Therefore, they desire you. Once again, this is Libran logic.

Congratulations, you're now Hot Property. Move in fast. Proceed to Seduction by Flattery, followed quickly by Seduction by Assumption.

Seduction by Competition (iv): Seduction by Social Expectation. Librans have been known to take a lover simply because "everybody else is doing it." If all their other friends are having affairs and they aren't, they will be tempted to begin one simply to keep up with the Joneses.

How you pull this one off will depend on their social milieu. If you can impress on the Libran that their friends are engaging in something they are missing out on—you will have gotten their attention. If you can further convince them that their friends will be jealous of their having gotten *you,* you will be halfway home.

Seduction 8: Seduction by Flattery

All Libran seductions should be complemented by Seduction by Flattery. In this method, you focus specifically on the narcissist inside every Libran.

Stage-One Flattery (at first meeting)

"You've got fabulous hair."

"You look stunning in that outfit."

"Haven't I seen you before somewhere? Do you ever lunch at the Russian Tea Room?"

"Are you a model? Haven't I seen you in a magazine somewhere?"

"Are you dressed by Bijan?"

"I couldn't help noticing your [some item of clothing]."

"I couldn't help noticing your dress. Is it a ———?"

"Have you ever been told you look a bit like Brigitte Bardot/Catherine Deneuve/Sharon Stone/Michelle Pfeiffer/Elle MacPherson?"

"Something about you strongly reminds me of Sean Connery/Kevin Costner/Patrick Swayze/Clint Eastwood/Robert Redford/Mel Gibson."

Stage-Two Flattery (more intimate—one-on-one)

"You've got a fabulous figure."

"How often do you work out?"

"You've got stunning eyes."

"You've got great legs."

"I love your shoulders."

Stage-Three Flattery (between first and second base)

"You drive me crazy."

"You're absolutely gorgeous."

"I've never met a woman/man like you."

"You're the woman/man I've been looking for all my life."

"I can't believe we found each other."

"You've got skin like silk." (Your hand should be covering a fairly wide territory by this stage.)

"Did you know that you've been driving me wild with desire for weeks?" At this stage, you can express more than verbal appreciation.

Proceed to Seduction by Assumption.

The time lapse between Stage One and Stage Three could be months, or days, or even hours, depending on your Libran and whether the stars are with you.

Seduction 9: The Libran Wedding Fantasy

Plan this seduction for the night after a wedding—not your own, someone else's. This will have Libra's romantic juices flowing. The whole wedding atmosphere is a major form of foreplay for a Libran. Indeed, you may not have to wait until *after* the wedding—remember *The Godfather*. There's more than one use for an organ loft.

Other good Libran seductions:

Seduction on the Battlefield (intellectual battle only—see Aries)

The Polite Withdrawal (Cancer)

The Romantic Movie Move (Cancer)

The Declaration of Love (Cancer)

The Five-Star Seduction (Leo)

The Flower Shop (Leo)

The Surprise Formal Dinner (Leo)

The I-Need-You (Virgo)

Whispers in the Dark (Pisces)

Portents of Passion (Pisces)

Sex with a Libra

Librans like to make an art form of sex. They want the vibes, ambience, mood, setting, lighting all to be right. It sounds good but let's face it, it could be a lot of work arranging all this every time you want a bonk.

They also like a lot of verbal-intellectual foreplay before getting down to it. Librans often require the investment of a lot of time and effort for a comparatively small amount of passion.

They want to create an idyll of love and beauty and sex combined. They are also often hung up on wanting to appear beautiful during sex, so make sure the lighting is low-key and flattering. For the same reason, forget about morning sex—Librans will want their hair done and makeup on first.

This obsession with physical self-assessment during sex causes some Libran women to hold back rather than abandon themselves to lust and passion. Many of them are unable to go with the wild, spontaneous, animalistic side of sex, and in consequence, they may become disillusioned with it all.

In their desperation to stay in a relationship, Librans can be too accommodating of the wishes of their partner. In doing so, they can neglect their own sexual needs and come to secretly resent sex and their partner. They can become depressed because they are subjugating their own feelings for the sake of the other.

On the other hand, if you are prepared to lay the groundwork to help them discover what *they* really like, you could have a wonderful sexual relationship with someone who really wants to please.

Typical Librans have a whole fantasy thing about marriage. If you are going to do a sexual role-play with a Libran, the best one might be the virgin bride on the wedding night. Other good sexual role-plays for Librans are Guinevere and Lancelot, the pirate and the harem, the lord of the manor with the right to deflower the local village maidens, or the madam (or pimp) who arranges a girl (boy) for you who then doesn't turn up, so that they have to fill in themselves.

Librans can be into exhibitionism—given the right lighting. This is one sign that might be very turned on by creating a (tasteful!) video of sexual union.

How to Handle a Relationship with a Libra

■ ■ ■

Be prepared to put a lot of time into a Libran relationship. They are often obsessed with how much time you spend on them. Virtually all time spent away from them will be regarded as an indication that you do not love them anymore. If you hanker after freedom, a lot of time to yourself, time for your friends, a spontaneous relationship that isn't analyzed to death, Libra is unlikely to make you happy.

Librans are not keen on the "open-door" household. They don't want your old school friends dropping in at 11 p.m.

They like you to spend money on them because it proves your relationship with them is your first priority.

Librans often have a very poor self-image in the absence of a relationship. They hide their lack of self-esteem under style, conceal their vulnerability under expensive labels. They continually rate themselves against the looks of others; they are more interested in *Cosmo*-consciousness than cosmic consciousness. At their worst, they confuse impressing others with fulfillment and choose image at the expense of inner development. Their biggest insult isn't "shallow" or "selfish" but "can't accessorize." They are often in touch with how they look but sadly out of touch with how they feel. This can result in repressed hostility and depression because they aren't true to their deeper, more spiritual needs.

They want you to believe they are your perfect mate. They mistakenly think this means that they have to share every one of your hobbies, friends, interests. Chameleonlike, they will change their clothes, their makeup, their eating habits and their religion to fit in with their partner. If their current significant other is agnostic, they will be too; if their subsequent partner is Christian, they'll be born again. If their current mate is a sophisticated gourmet, they'll spend hours poring over *Larousse Gastronomique*. If the sophisticate is replaced by a health-obsessed vegan, they'll be sprouting mung beans and alfalfa on every kitchen windowsill.

Librans are not so much loyal as desperate to have a relationship with someone so as to feel whole. They are relationship addicts who above all else fear loneliness. Marriage is the meaning of life.

The emotionally immature Libran is obsessive about having a partner at all costs—preferably a better partner than they already have! So beware. They will be clinging to you while keeping one eye open for a brighter prospect.

Librans are notorious for overlapping relationships. From the point of view of their partners, the Libran might be called unfaithful—but the Libran won't see it that way. Memorize the following irregular verb: *She is a slut; you are an unfaithful bastard; I have overlapping relationships.*

It is not atypical for the partner of a Libran to be blithely content in an apparently stable relationship and suddenly be informed that it's over. Librans are not likely to dump you simply because of some inadequacy in you or the relationship. It is far more likely that they will discard you in favor of some other prospect they have been secretly sizing up for months and whom they have finally decided exceeds you in quality.

Librans are notorious for taking a long time to make up their minds, for endlessly weighing the alternatives. "Is she *really* right for me? There *could* be someone perfect out there."

The Libran idea of commitment is to commit to you until death do us part—or until someone distinctly better comes along.

There are certain danger signals to be alert to: they gradually start paying less attention to you, or there is a sudden spate of self-improvement—dieting, new hairstyle, shopping for new makeup and clothes. If you spot these signals, chances are you have started to slip down the Libran scale and they are weighing the merits of someone else.

Consider this quintessential Libran woman, known to one of the authors. If a friend happened to drop in on her out of the blue, she would be casually lounging around in a leather catsuit with perfect hair and makeup. She worked part-time as a model. She was a divorcée who lived with a professional gardener who would drive her children to school, pick them up, do the shopping and cook for them all. If he even looked sideways at another woman, she would go into paroxysms of jealousy. Meanwhile, she would accept lunch and dinner invitations from other men, even be flown to another state to advise a man on his interior decoration. She kept shopping around until she met an older man who, in the first few days of their acquaintance, chose Libran Seduction 5 and bought her $2,000 earrings. She left the gardener and moved on.

So you've been warned.

She may look sweet in a bodice but there is a Boadicea inside every Libran woman. He may look tall, dark and handsome but there is still a pugnacious Napoleon inside every Libran man. Beware the iron fist in the velvet glove—the acid tongue behind the sweet mouth—the Fury lurking underneath the Pollyanna or Peter Pan persona.

Librans can play the sweet little girl or little boy and bend over backward to please you, but there is more to them than that. They adopt that persona to get what they want. If the act doesn't work, they can drop it in a flash and the inner Harpy will come screeching out.

They can be manipulative—they are relationship strategists and their chief tactic is domination through niceness. They repress their own anger and plaster it over with a saccharine facade to achieve their main goal, which is simply to stay in a relationship. They are prepared to subjugate their feelings, their needs, their identity to keep the relationship going.

Librans will do almost anything to keep the appearance of harmony—even if there are torrents of venom under the surface. They will paper over cracks in the relationship with social clichés—apparently concerned about your welfare but actually seething with hidden angers, which can burst out at any time.

The biggest eruption is bound to occur if you break up with them. This is when you may well watch your beautiful butterfly transform itself into a vampire bat.

Librans love to get married. They love the image of two perfect beings merging in an aesthetically perfect ceremony. Librans often want the marriage ceremony more than the marriage: the connubials rather than the commitment. They are also the greatest divorcers in the Zodiac—all part of their endless quest for Mr. or Ms. Ideal.

You may feel that you are forever trying to measure up to this image of Mr. or Ms. Right they are carrying around in their head. Librans have great difficulty in accepting people the way they are. "I love the person I was going to mold you into . . . I love the person you were going to become . . . I love the image I had of you."

At their worst, Librans can vacillate endlessly in making decisions—turning things over and over and over in their mind, never able to make a commitment to a course of action until fate intervenes and makes it for them. Or until you intervene and make the decision on their behalf—and the danger here is that then you will have to accept the blame. It will become your responsibility should things go wrong. Librans like to avoid responsibility.

Indeed, Librans sometimes want their partner to take over responsibility for their life as a whole—providing for them, pampering them. Librans can be very self-indulgent. The women in particular were often "Daddy's Little Princess" and seek to re-create that relationship with other men.

They believe in equality in relationships but also believe that some are more equal than others, specifically they deserve "more equal" treatment because of their good looks and nice personality. You may be the one chosen to provide them with this more equal treatment.

Must-Do's

Be prepared to talk about the ins and outs of relationships nonstop.
Give tasteful gifts regularly.
Study *Vogue*—develop style.
Be aware that they are capable of shopping around for someone else behind your back.

No-No's

Never ever forget their birthday, the anniversary of the day you met and what music was playing at the time, the first time you kissed and what music was playing at the time, the first time you went to bed and what music was playing at the time.

Never turn up for a social occasion looking anything but immaculate.

Never fart, burp, snort, guffaw or speak loudly at social gatherings (or in private if you can avoid it).

How to End a Relationship with a Libra

■ ■ ■

Libra is perhaps the most difficult Sun sign to end a relationship with. Screaming, psychodramas, recriminations, nervous breakdowns and attempted suicides are par for the course.

They will always want to know why, why, why. "Didn't I always make love to you whenever you wanted it, didn't I learn golf to please you, didn't I this, didn't I that?"

Trying to nurse them through the trauma of the breakup by hand-holding and tender loving care may make it even worse. It may be better simply to run away. Be a bitch or a bastard and just clear out overnight and let them have their nervous breakdown. You may exercise a modicum of compassion by calling up their best friend or mother so they can rush over with appropriate medication and sympathy.

If you are financially involved with a Libran, a breakup can be a disaster of the first order. In their mind, they have adapted their whole life to fit around you—taken up your hobbies, adopted your interests, accommodated your brand of sex—and for this they believe *you owe them.* Commonly Librans will conclude that you have been "just using them all along from day one" and paint themselves as victims in the relationship. As such, Librans often expect financial recompense on a large scale.

A further special warning. Librans (the male ones especially) specialize in always being just about to divorce their wives. They may keep an ever-expectant mistress dangling for ten, fifteen, twenty years while they are just "waiting for the right time to make the break," "waiting until the children are old enough," "waiting until the wife can handle it," "waiting until she gets over her heart bypass."

A Libran will almost never break up a relationship unless they've got someone lined up to replace you—no matter how unsatisfactory the relationship is. So a possible breakup facilitator may be to lend them some assistance and line up your replacement. This is certainly the safest tactic.

Remember, Librans are generally attractive to the other sex and are always putting out the vibes. They can't stand to be out of a relationship for any length of time. Accordingly, a good tactic is to have a legitimate reason to be out of town for a few weeks. Chances are a friend of yours has been lusting after them anyway. Perhaps you could arrange for them to keep your Libran company for a few evenings. Libran nature abhors a relationship vacuum. With any luck, after an absence of a few weeks, you will return to be devastated when you learn that your partner has taken up with your friend. Oh, how sad.

This scenario has worked for one of the authors, and it may well work for you too—in fact, while the author was away, the Libran tried out not one but two of the author's friends. Mind you, this didn't stop the Libran from abusing the author for subsequently taking up with another. That's Libra for you. Which brings us to the final warning: Librans can be very possessive even after a relationship has ended. They are allowed to begin a new relationship but won't be amused if you do. They will almost never like any woman or man that you have a subsequent relationship with. They can leave you for another and never forgive you for it.

Librans at Their Best

■ ■ ■

Librans are a class act that will bring beauty and harmony into your life. The ideal social animal, they will smooth the waters for you domestically and socially. They will bend over backward to create a convivial, welcoming atmosphere wherever they are. You will be the envy of your friends with this svelte, cordial, concerned, popular partner. They will help you create a home environment that is tasteful, elegant, harmonious. They are experts at both giving and receiving attention and compliments. They will always be concerned with maintaining peace, equality and fairness in your relationship.

Librans at Their Worst

■ ■ ■

You won't understand how you let their sheer physical appeal suck you into a relationship with such a shallow creature who is lazy, self-indulgent and more concerned with appearance than reality. You yourself will be judged according to the value of your wristwatch and the cut of your clothes rather than your qualities as a person. Their anger and hostility will be repressed and disguised under a layer of cloying sweetness.

One of your agonies will be the way they agonize over decisions—churning things over and over until you make the decision for them out of sheer impatience. (Anything that then goes wrong will of course be your fault!)

They will expect gratitude—emotional and financial—simply because they have favored you by being in a relationship with you. Meanwhile, they will be secretly shopping around for some new, improved version to replace you. By contrast, if your approval rating is high, they will endeavor to rush you to the altar at the first opportunity.

Sexy Librans

■ ■ ■

Brigitte Bardot, Christopher Reeve, John Lennon, Groucho Marx, Charlton Heston, Roger Moore, Carole Lombard, Katherine Mansfield, Marcello Mastroianni, George Peppard, Susan Sarandon, Bruce Springsteen, Michael Douglas, Sylvia Kristel, Sigourney Weaver, Angie Dickinson, Johnny Mathis, Sting, Catherine Deneuve.

Unsexy Librans

■ ■ ■

Julie Andrews, Mahatma Gandhi, Buster Keaton, Eleanor Roosevelt, Oscar Wilde, Friedrich Nietzsche, Dizzy Gillespie, Mickey Rooney, Chuck Berry, Johnny Carson, Jimmy Carter, Annette Funicello, Jesse Jackson, Oliver North, Luciano Pavarotti, Meatloaf, Walter Matthau, Nana Mouskouri, Martina Navratilova.

SCORPIO

October 24th to November 22nd

...

It's dirty, it's disgusting,

it's degenerate—I love it.

The Lure of a Scorpio

■ ■ ■

Who is that?

And why are they staring at you?

And those eyes—those mysterious, brooding, come-hither, harem eyes seem to be drawing you in. You could be so easily sucked into the vortex of their sexual magnetism.

Take one step toward those cobra eyes and you risk becoming enmeshed in the Scorpionic web.

Scorpio continues to provoke you with look, gesture and word. If Scorpio can make you blush, squirm or flinch, it's a triumph. It is as if they are getting a thrill from titillating you in public. Their dress, too, speaks of passion.

Be warned, for this Scorpio you have just met is not superficial. Even a fling is not likely to be taken lightly. This is not frivolous fun. It's deadly earnest.

Much is promised. But how much will be delivered?

If your previous relationships have been lacking in lust, if you feel yourself drawn to the dark side of the erotic, Scorpio could be the partner you are after—for, more than any other sign, they hold out the promise of plummeting to the mysterious depths of the sexual underworld.

How to Interest a Scorpio

■ ■ ■

Key tactic: Scorpios are interested in everything dark, hidden and mysterious. So the trick is to present yourself as precisely that: dark, hidden and mysterious.

Start wearing dark glasses—especially at night. If you are a man trying to attract a Scorpionic woman, sport a permanent two-day growth and develop a Jack Nicholson persona. If you're a woman trying to attract a Scorpionic male, play the vamp—black miniskirts, black tops with oozing cleavage, musky perfume and provocative makeup. Dark colors signal a sense of mystery to Scorpios. Invest in a wardrobe of black clothes with a dash of whorehouse red.

Scorpios want to feel that you find them captivating. Scorpios love to stare at people. Stare back. Practice this in your bathroom mirror—staring intensely. See if you can add a glint of wickedness.

Try telling your Scorpio that there is something about them which intrigues you but you can't quite put a finger on it . . . yet. Or say that the first time you saw them, you just knew you had been in a past life together. Or, if this is too much for you, tell them that they are exactly like someone you had a wild dream about two months ago. (If *this* is too much for you, so is the Scorpio—find another Sun sign.)

If they press you for details about this past life (or dream), smile enigmatically. "Oh, I'll need to know you a lot better before I can talk about that one."

Tell them a psychic told you that you had a past life as (choose from the following list): a Tibetan monk who used to slip down to the local village to break his vow of celibacy, an Indian medicine man killed in a fight with the chief for control of the tribe, the right-hand man of Alexander the Great, a slaveowner in the South who took sexual advantage of his/her possessions, an Egyptian temple dancer who was seduced by the pharaoh, a Chicago gangster's moll who ratted on her man to the police, a sacred prostitute in an Atlantean temple who killed the head priest after he ravished her.

Even if your Scorpio doesn't believe in reincarnation—or simply doesn't believe your story—they will still be interested and see you as interesting.

They are fascinated by power, so it is a good idea to emphasize anything in your current life that demonstrates you exercise power over others. For instance, you may be an elementary school teacher. If they ask you what your job is, you don't say, "I'm an elementary school teacher." You say, "I shape and manipulate young minds. I get a real buzz from it." Don't say you're an accountant; say, "I organize the management of huge amounts of money." If this makes them suspect that you may be involved in laundering lucre for shady concerns—so much the better. Don't say you're a computer programmer; say, "I control information for a multinational company." No need to elaborate too much on your career. Remember, you have to appear mysterious.

If they ask you what you do, another good tactic is to just raise an eyebrow, lower your voice, smile ever so slightly and whisper, "Everything." That should get their interest.

They adore people close to a source of political and financial power. Drop the names of a few political figures or business magnates you know (or your close friends know). Tell them about any big killings you have made in business.

The ideal way to keep a Scorpio interested is to create conversations that are a mixture of psychology, sex and power.

Talk about Freud.

They love a hint of the wicked—they won't be attracted to you if they don't think you're wicked enough. They want to see that unmistakable glint in your eye.

To get them really interested, perhaps you could drop some mention of sexual mysteries or secret techniques that you might have tried—tantric sex, Taoist sex or sex magic. Guaranteed to intrigue them.

Suggested opening line: "I feel as if I've met you before. Did you have a past incarnation in the West during the Indian massacres?"

What to talk about: Big money, politics, the stock market, investments, sex, psychology, power—all aspects of power, any sort of mystical or psychic experience you've had, Freud, Jung, hypnosis, death, near-death experiences, your past lives.

Where to take them: Power lunches, executive breakfasts, your astrologer, tarot card readings, cathedrals, sleazy bars, psychic channelers, horror movies, the bedroom!

What to give them: Whodunits, true crime books, books on the occult, crystals, books on sex and psychology, tarot cards, runes, astrology books, books on investments, vibrators, books on ancient Egypt or Atlantis or reincarnation, black or red sexy lingerie, textured condoms!

How to Seduce a Scorpio

■ ■ ■

Sex for a Scorpio is often a power play. Tenderness, yes. Kisses, yes. But you must radiate mastery and confidence. Never appear uncertain that you will reach your sexual destination.

There is a sexual provocateur inside every Scorpio male and a pro-vocatrice inside every Scorpio woman. This can be a difficult sign to read. When push comes to shove and the panties are down, they may like to be taken forcefully. On the other hand, you could end up being charged with sexual harassment. Be careful. Better to err on the side of caution.

Typical Scorpios can go from passive to active very rapidly. Initial reluc-tance and outright apathy can be transformed into lightning arousal. You may get a shock when the seemingly cool Scorpio suddenly cuts off your would-be seduction by grabbing you where you'd most like to be grabbed.

Scorpios are into power. Some Scorpios hold back from the initial en-counter to gain more power in the situation. They want to be certain the other person is completely in their thrall. They may even try to exercise power through use of "rules": I don't go to bed on the first date, I don't enter the woman the first time. Watch for this. Remember it. At some later stage, shock and impress them by saying, "I have rules," and then impose some of your own about what they can and can't do.

The biggest danger is being attracted to a Scorpio who is going through a period of celibacy. Scorpios have been known to impose celibacy on them-selves for many years. Many feel guilt about sex, which they transform into a "saint" mentality, as if abstinence makes them more powerful or more spiritually pure. Consider Mahatma Gandhi—a Libran but with Scorpio rising and Mars, Venus and Mercury in Scorpio. He swore off sex and to prove the strength of his will slept next to virgins! Scorpios have strong wills and can turn their willpower to strangling off their sexual desire.

If you meet a celibate Scorpio, it's not necessarily a matter for total despair. They can alternate—abruptly—between whore and madonna, saint and sinner, priest and pervert. If anything can tip them from absti-nence to orgy, it will be the seductions outlined below.

There are other dangers with this sign too. Scorpios tend to equate sex with power. Your Scorpio may interpret your desire to get them into bed as an attempt to gain control over them. They may resist it for this reason—even though they want you badly. They may also withhold sex just for the delicious power thrill it gives them. They may withhold sex because sex alone is not enough—they want to plunge into the vortex of sexual obsession, all-consuming love, monogamy, twin-soul togetherness and dramatic instant marriage.

You have to watch what you're getting into with a Scorpio. But if you successfully seduce one, the rewards can be orgiastic. And when you do, seduce to intrigue. Take them on a pile of silk cushions or a Persian carpet—forget the bed. Make love to them the first time in an unusual position.

Seduction 1: The Gothic Thriller

This is an excellent tactic for getting a Scorpio's serious attention—it may not get them into bed right away, but it will make such a provocative impression on their subconscious that they will never be able to forget you.

The important thing here is that they must come over to your place at night. How you get them there is your business. You may invite them over for a drink or for dinner. Perhaps you were supposed to pick them up for a date but your car suddenly broke down, and you have to call them to come over and pick you up.

When you see them coming, unlock the front door and make your way into the bedroom. When they knock on the door, call out, "Come in! It's unlocked!" When they enter, they won't see you. Call out, "I'm in the bedroom. Come in."

As they push open the door to the bedroom, they will see the quintessential Scorpionic bedroom fantasy come to life: purple candles, musky incense, wicked music. Perhaps organ music: Bach's *Toccata and Fugue in D minor, Carmina Burana* or "The Ride of the Valkyries," Gregorian chant, Madonna's *Erotica*, church hymns (perhaps "O Come, All Ye Faithful").

And, of course, there you are in the midst of all this: nude beneath a thin satin sheet. Perhaps you can think of an even more provocative way to display yourself.

Say nothing. Just reach out your hand to them.

They may not rise to the occasion. They may be overwhelmed. They may be in shock. They may flee. They may scream. But you will have made your mark on their subconscious. You will have held out the promise of dark, mysterious sensuality—of sex on the edge.

If they run, phone them and invite them right back. Ask whether they didn't like the music. Invite yourself over to their place.

No matter how they react, never apologize, and don't explain yourself either—remember, you have to appear mysterious. Just smile . . . and proceed to one of the other seductions. Or, if you dare, repeat the *exact* scenario so that they know what's coming.

Seduction 2: The Mutual Mental Masturbation Method

Now, this may come as something of a revelation. It is a secret Scorpios have long kept to themselves: Scorpios think about sex more than they actually do it.

They like to be mentally provoked—by their own imaginations or by another's. Sometimes they like this more than actual sex.

One way to get a Scorpio worked up is to play on this desire to be mentally titillated.

Mutual Mental Masturbation (i): The Dry Run. The idea here is to give them a verbal dry run of what you are planning to do once you get them back to your place. You might do this as you are driving home. Or you might combine this with the Vamp (see below) and whisper it to them in a public place. "The minute I get you alone, I'm going to pin you against the wall and start to undress you with my teeth. I'm going to take an hour just to undress you slowly, button by button. Then I'm going to lick every inch of your . . ." Etc.

Mutual Mental Masturbation (ii): Folie à Deux. Scorpios love to delve into the subconscious of others. They love sexual fantasies. Suddenly, in the middle of a conversation about something else, start to share your secret sexual fantasies with Mr. or Ms. Scorpio. Encourage them to share theirs. Keep trading fantasies. Cut them off in midsentence and demand that they come back to your place to act them out. Or take them on the spot.

Mutual Mental Masturbation (iii): The Dirty Phone Call. Try out either (i) or (ii) above or one of the Vamps (below) over the telephone. Or call up to share an erotic nightmare you just had. Tell them you are coming over. Arrive naked under a trench coat.

Seduction 3: The Vamp

The Vamp is a particularly good technique for women to use on Scorpio men. (Daring men might like to try out Vamps 3 and 4.) Like Mutual Mental Masturbation, it works on the Scorpionic desire to be sexually titillated. Suddenly and unexpectedly, turn into a combination of Mata Hari, Lolita and Marilyn Monroe.

Practice speaking breathily. And prepare for meltdown.

Vamp No. 1: The Secret Vamp. You are dining with your Scorpio man, perhaps with his friends or relatives—maybe even his parents. You are wearing a very short black dress—perhaps a veritable fig leaf of a miniskirt. You lean over to Mr. Scorpio and whisper in his ear, "I have no underpants on." Not just his ears will prick up.

If you've got the basic instinct for it, you might dare to tread closer to that furry line between the erotic and the vulgar. Having abandoned your underwear, find an appropriate place and time to cross and uncross your legs in the direction of your Scorpio man. (See the famous scene in the movie *Basic Instinct*.)

Vamp No. 2: The Happy Hooker. You arrange to meet Mr. Scorpio at a particular place. He is expecting you to be wearing normal attire. Instead you are decked out like a cross between a high-class socialite and a street hooker—with a decided emphasis on the latter: black skirt, black stockings, even fishnets, lots of makeup, dangerous cleavage. Before the shock wears off, make your demands: "It's not dinner I'm interested in eating tonight. Take me home." If you want to try an even more outrageous version of this, consider dressing up as a schoolgirl—except with sheer black stockings and heavy makeup.

Vamp No. 3: The Don't-Get-Excited-Please. You should try to pull this one off only if you have perfected the husky, breathless, seductive voice: evil and innocent at the same time. The idea is to use this voice to taunt your Scorpio with rhetorical questions. You can try this in public, at a restaurant table perhaps, at the movies, in their car, on your sofa. You may even place your hand on some soft part of their body and stroke it—the flesh above the elbow perhaps. Whisper breathily: "You're not excited, are you? I don't want you to get excited. Who knows what might happen if you got excited. I'm not ready. I'm not sure if I want to. You wouldn't make me, would you? That wouldn't be right. Oh, don't tell me you're getting excited. Don't get excited. Stop getting excited. Don't think about it. Think about something else. You don't want to make me do it, do you?"

If Mr. Scorpio is not desperate to claw the clothes off you after this, forget him.

Vamp No. 4: The Morticia Addams. Remember how Morticia Addams used to drive Gomez wild with desire by speaking French? Here the idea is to drive your Scorpionic man wild by talking to him about erotic delights in a foreign language. Of course, the precondition is that you know at least one foreign tongue. (Or at least a few phrases.) Again, you must speak to him in breathless Marilyn Monroe tones. French is good, of course. Or Italian, Spanish, almost any language in which you can sound erotic. (Cantonese and African dialects incorporating glottal stops are not recommended.) Lean over and whisper in his ear. When he asks what you said, don't provide a translation. Instead say, "Things I'd be too embarrassed to ask for in English."

Vamp No. 5: The Reverse Happy Hooker. This is a really Scorpionic one. The idea here is to offer to pay the Scorpio for sex.

Be overcome with lust—preferably in public. Lean toward them and speak urgently, *sotto voce:* "I have to have you. I want you so badly. I can't wait. I can't believe how badly I want you. How much do you normally charge? Whatever it costs. I just want you so bad, I'm melting. Tell me what I get for the money. Describe it to me. I have to hear."

Seduction 4: The Whip-Me-Chain-Me-Take-Me

This is the fast-track short-circuit Scorpio seduction. Say, "I want to be used and abused. Take me home."

Not generally recommended as the opener to a serious relationship. But if you are primarily interested in short-term sex and if you really do want to be sexually used, if you are ready to be on the receiving end of the full Scorpionic sexual treatment, this will get their immediate attention.

You may try adding a touch of class by combining this seduction with the Vamp.

Seduction 5: The Reverse Grab

If you are certain you have your Scorpio on the boil or you just feel daring, why not try the boldest seduction of them all: the Reverse Grab.

Instead of you grabbing them, the idea is to take one of their hands and place it on one of your erogenous zones.

You'll certainly make an impression—of some sort. If they swiftly withdraw their hand in shock, it failed. If they are noticeably slow to withdraw, proceed to Vamp them. If they don't withdraw their hand at all . . . well, if you need things explained from there, maybe you should consider crocheting as a hobby instead.

Seduction 6: The Striptease

Scorpios love to be titillated, so if you've got the body and the dancing ability, perform a striptease for them. Quintessentially Scorpionic. Play Joe Cocker singing "You Can Leave Your Hat On" and go for it.

Worthwhile variation: engage them in a game of strip poker.

Other good Scorpio seductions:

The Dare (see Aries)

The Initiation (Aries)

The Pretend Virgin (Aries)

The Tom Jones (Taurus)

The Public Provocation Proposition (Gemini)

Seduction by Competition (Libra)

The We-Shouldn't-Do-This-So-Let's (Aquarius)

The Freebie (Aquarius)

The Sexual Sorcerer/Sorceress (Pisces)

Portents of Passion (Pisces)

Sex with a Scorpio

■ ■ ■

Scorpios are generally fascinated by sex. They are fascinated by its connection with the subconscious. They are natural Freudians, believing that sex is the dominant drive in the universe.

Sex and power, money and power, sex and money are all deeply connected in the smoldering cauldron of the Scorpio psyche.

For Scorpios sex is never an end in itself. There is something else on their agenda: power. They will use sex to gain power and money. They will employ sex as a weapon in the continuing battle to dominate their partner; the more passive Scorpio will see sex as something the partner uses to control them and so may withdraw from sex to put an end to what they see as their partner's attempt at domination.

They fear dependency on another—including sexual dependency—and may withdraw from a lover if they feel themselves becoming too enthralled.

Scorpios test their lovers endlessly. Any sign of sexual shortcoming (for instance, if you are too tired to perform) is more likely to be met with sarcasm than sympathy. Scorpios are not noted for their understanding when it comes to such matters. They are known as the "demoralizers" of the Zodiac and can take an almost perverse pleasure in kicking you when you are down.

The Scorpionic idea of monogamy is you being faithful to them.

The word "moderation" does not appear in the Scorpionic dictionary. Scorpios can go instantaneously from whore to born-again virgin. They can circumcise sex out of their lives and withdraw to contemplate their psychosexual navel for months or years at a time and be unconcerned or surprised by your inability to do likewise. Or they will simply want to intellectualize sex, read about it, study it, do workshops on it, talk about it, imagine it— everything but do it.

When they are in the hands-on mode, Scorpios can embrace wild, sexual infatuations that can lead to sudden marriage. They are attracted to the sexual underground: rough trade, prostitution, clandestine affairs. They like hard talk and taunting. They want you to be demanding during sex. They are intrigued by video porn, sex magazines, Eastern sexual esoterica, sex aids, bondage, leather, S&M, discipline, cross-dressing—even if they don't want to get into any of these things themselves. They are interested in the dark, transformational side of sex—sex on the edge of social and moral confines (or even beyond that edge). They are attracted to dangerous sexual venues: churches, red-light districts, public bathrooms, their parents' bedroom, graveyards at night. They are attracted to sexual role-playing that involves virgins, money, corruption, the breaking of religious vows.

And they are hard to satisfy.

The key tip for keeping a Scorpio sexually interested in you is: *Think wicked.*

How to Handle a Relationship with a Scorpio

■ ■ ■

The female praying mantis lures the male to her. It's not just sex she has on her mind: she wants to make a meal of the male. The hypnotized male can't help himself—even though he knows he will be devoured in the process. This is a good metaphor for what can happen to you with a Scorpio: you can feel irresistibly drawn to them even though you sense the emotional H-bomb on the horizon.

This is called PMS—the Praying Mantis Syndrome. Would-be lovers of Scorpios need to be aware that Scorpios can emotionally and psychically devour you, your self-esteem, your energies, your willpower and maybe even your bank account as they are screwing the life out of you.

Scorpios at their worst take a perverse pleasure in applying the sting in their tail. It can actually irritate them to see you happy and carefree. They see this as wallowing in shallow pleasure, and will try to drop a rock into your ocean of calm—just to stir up a few waves.

It can be a serious error to visit a Scorpio for comfort when you are feeling vulnerable—best to stay home alone or visit your mother or pat your dog or drop in on a Piscean. Every sign has its dark side. It's best you know now about the delicious little buzz a Scorpio gets from twisting the knife. Scorpios are not natural comforters and secretly find it difficult to respect someone who has allowed life to get the better of them. Scorpio is the sign that rules destruction, and Scorpios find it hard not to join in when they see something being destroyed—even if it is you.

So beware the tail of the Scorpion. It can sting you unexpectedly in the Achilles' heel you didn't even know you had. . . . And they are quite prepared to do it in public.

You are well advised to prepare your sardonic replies and sarcastic repartee. A good selection of drop-dead lines can go a long way. If they have been spreading comments that you're a "nice girl but hopeless in bed," resist acting the discreet lady; instead shrug and say, "What can you do with a huge ego attached to a little willy?" If they make a remark about your tits being small, offhandedly comment, "I can always get saline implants for my breasts, pity he can't get one for his dick."

That sort of subtle thing.

They are into power for the sake of power. The desire for power with a Scorpio is enormous, even compulsive. Scorpios find it difficult to be fair in love. They can be arrogant, dictatorial, Machiavellian. They invented the axiom "The end justifies the means." Cobralike, they can hypnotize you and psych you out while they doggedly stick to a point they know is wrong. They can manipulate you with secrets that aren't: they may refuse to tell you what they did last Saturday night, when all they did was sit at home and brood. They cover up insecurity with disdain and mystery.

They see hidden motives in everything and can be outright paranoid. They can see your desire for intimacy as an attempt to get a hold over them by learning their weak points. If they feel themselves getting too attached to you, they may withdraw because they fear dependency—as if this would place them in the position of weakness. For these reasons, there is often a deep inner core of loneliness inside a Scorpio. You may never be sure how much of them is really invested in the relationship. They secretly protect their own interests and may, for instance, have a secret cache of money that they see as their escape route.

They want total freedom to do whatever they want but will go into paroxysms of jealousy if you even look sideways at another person. Not only must you not cheat with other people, you must not even consider it. Scorpios can get jealous not only about what you do but also about what you think. They will want to know your thoughts and quite probably will intuit them. They want to have deed and title over your mind as well as your body.

To maintain their interest, you must keep a certain amount of your mystique intact. Scorpios love to pry into and expose your innermost secrets—this is one way they get power over you. But they don't want to expose their secrets to you; this would place them in your power.

You are well advised not to reveal any truth about your past or any vulnerable corners of your psyche, unless they already have: tit for tat. You show me yours and I'll show you mine.

You have to play counterspy to their spy. You have to stay one step ahead of them but be shrewd enough not to rub their nose in it.

Scorpios harbor a deep suspicion that no one else could be as deep or complex as they are. You must maintain your mystique to convince them otherwise.

Scorpios can be positively obsessive—about almost anything, but especially about themselves. They are often their own worst psychiatrists.

Some Scorpios go through periods of self-destruction and regeneration. They have been known to drink and smoke for days on end, watching movies until 4 a.m. and surviving on frozen pizzas and chocolate bars. Then they suddenly pull themselves together, shower, dress to the nines and walk out to face the world as if nothing has happened. Friends who have been fearing the worst and leaving desperate messages on their answering machines ask, "Where have you been? Are you all right?" They answer, "I'm fine. What are you talking about?"

You must patiently indulge these black periods of obsession and self-destruction, and not get caught up in the maelstrom yourself.

Scorpios are not noted for their objectivity. If they experience a period of depression, it is because they are so deep and intense. If you go through something similar, it is because you are weak, wishy-washy and wimpy.

They want peace but in fact live on the edge of compulsive excess. Scorpio is a strong-willed sign, and Scorpios can use their willpower to resist change. Like its opposite, Taurus, Scorpio is a fixed sign, and like Taurus, it is better advised to embrace change. Scorpio rules death and rebirth, and often a crucial death or birth brings about a fundamental upheaval in a Scorpio life.

As a Scorpio's partner, you are well advised to help them find a vent for their scheming and pursuit of power outside the relationship. They need to find a creative focus for this inner drivenness or they will find a destructive focus—which could well be you. Often psychically powerful, Scorpio needs to be encouraged to find a truly spiritual outlet for these psychic gifts.

Key tip: Learn to cope with extremes.

Always be reading a book or taking a course involving exploration of the subconscious—rebirthing, past-life regressions, Jungian psychology, all that. Always give the impression that you are probing, delving, investigating—preferably into realms they don't know too much about. That should make you look deep and keep them interested in you.

You'll never be bored with a Scorpio—but you'll never be comfortable either. It is easy to be fascinated by Scorpios but often difficult to like them. They can be regular bitches or bastards.

To really get the most out of a relationship with a Scorpio, you have to be a combination of Count Dracula, Carl Jung and Madonna.

Must-Do's

Maintain an aura of mystery.

Develop an interest in psychology, especially Jung or Freud or Stanislav Grof.

Encourage them to find a focus for their scheming outside of their relationship with you.

Stand up for yourself—don't allow yourself to be dominated.

Allow them periods of brooding but don't get caught up and don't accept the blame.

Take martial arts classes!

No-No's

Looking sideways at another person.

A shared bank account.

Acting like a wimp—keep your weaknesses to yourself.

Plain white underwear.

Telling them anything you don't want the IRS, the police, the CIA, your relatives or the public at large to know—otherwise, should you break up, the consequences could be a touch apocalyptic.

How to End a Relationship with a Scorpio

■ ■ ■

There was a female character in a television series who discovered that her boyfriend was out of town cheating on her. She got into his apartment, threw all his clothes on the floor, hosed down the entire apartment—clothes, carpets, furniture, everything. Then she threw watercress seeds everywhere, closed the windows and doors and turned the heat up full blast. When the boyfriend returned from his dirty weekend, every one of his possessions was sprouting two inches of watercress shoots.

This woman was a Scorpio. No doubt about it.

How to end a relationship with a Scorpio? With a lawyer, rottweiler and psychic at your side.

Scorpios have a fully justified reputation for jealousy and are notorious for seeking revenge. This won't be something trivial like having a screaming match with a jilted Aries in public; we are talking about a deep-seated need to sting you with their tail and inject the venom.

The jilted Scorpio wants you to suffer. If they are intelligent and creative, it gets worse: they may wait some time to exact their vengeance. You'll know it when it happens, but it will be impossible to foresee.

In any relationship with a Scorpio, you should be looking toward protecting yourself legally and psychically.

With a Libran, you could try fobbing your lover off on someone else; this is not an effective *sayonara* for a Scorpio. You could set them up with some gorgeous alternative whom they might even start sexually exploring—but they will probably want to keep you dangling.

One tactic may be simply to run away: go underground, move to a secret address—preferably overseas.

Another possibility is to play on Scorpio's fascination with the mystical. You could get hold of a "tame" psychic or astrologer and bribe them. Then you send your Scorpionic partner to this mystic who will tell them that they are just about to meet the perfect partner who will make them blissfully happy forever after—adding that this will never happen if they don't immediately ditch their current relationship (i.e., you). If they don't, the psychic will suggest, they will end up penniless and alone. That might just about do it.

If you do decide to leave a Scorpio, rush to the nearest astrologer and psychic to seek the best time to make the break.

Above all, protect your financial interests and change the locks. Scorpios are quite capable of taking the afternoon off work to clean out your house, including quite a few of your favorite possessions—the ones they leave unsmashed, that is.

Scorpios at Their Best

■ ■ ■

You'll feel as if you are the costar in a dark and racy real-life version of 9½ Weeks. Intense, passionate, lusty Scorpio will take you to the outer limits of sexual indulgence. Loyal, shrewd, resourceful Scorpio will stand by you in tough times. You will be able to rely on their strong will, self-control and insight. You will never be bored with this deep, magnetic and enigmatic lover. They will never tire of being your partner in inner exploration and the search for the spiritual path.

Scorpios at Their Worst

■ ■ ■

You'll feel like a costar in the real-life version of The Exorcist—you will alternate between trying to exorcise the possessed and feeling possessed yourself. Manipulative, power-obsessed, jealous, sarcastic, secretive, vindictive, ruthless, Scorpio may abandon you overnight and never be heard from again or turn up after six months and expect you to understand their regular need to withdraw, brood and be alone. They may also withdraw for months at a time from sex. They are capable of manipulating with everything you can imagine—sex (or the withholding of sex), money, sarcasm, tantrums, even threats of suicide. When Scorpios are at their worst, you will feel like a fly in a spider's web.

Sexy Scorpios

■ ■ ■

Grace Kelly, Pablo Picasso, Charles Atlas, Marie Antoinette, Burt Lancaster, Richard Burton, St. Augustine, Goldie Hawn, Cleo Laine, Jodie Foster, Calvin Klein, Kevin Kline, Vivien Leigh, Bo Derek, Demi Moore, Winona Ryder, Jamie Lee Curtis.

Unsexy Scorpios

■ ■ ■

Billy Graham, Roy Rogers, Spiro Agnew, Jonathan Winters, Indira Gandhi, Martin Luther, Prince Charles, Ed Asner, Roseanne Barr, Walter Cronkite, Rodney Dangerfield, Danny DeVito, Charles Manson, Sally Field, Richard Dreyfuss.

SAGITTARIUS

♐

November 23rd to December 21st

∎ ∎ ∎

Without the negative, we would have no capacity to

differentiate the positive, so that the negative is a

necessary precondition to the existence of the positive

and our perception of it. So it follows absolutely that one

is compelled to take a positive view of the negative. Ipso

facto, the negative is positive due to its positive effect

in allowing us to discriminate the positive from the

negative. Therefore, the negative is positive. So

stop whining, shut up and think positive.

—The Sage, I. Tarius

The Lure of a Sagittarius

■ ■ ■

Do you want a bed partner with a lust for life—including a lust for lust?

Are you looking for someone to share your own thirst for adventure, for parties, for dancing, for travel, for truth, for more, ever more out of life?

Do you value independence above all else and want someone to share this independence with?

Then look no further than Mr. or Ms. Sagittarius.

In all senses of the word, they are *seekers*. They seek good times, fun, action, movement and life in abundance.

They are also great seekers of truth. They are known as the philosophers of the Zodiac. The more evolved Sagittarian is a truly independent thinker—interested in anything and everything. They are tolerant and broad-minded. Mind you, by a bizarre twist of Sagittarian logic, they are totally intolerant of people whom they regard as intolerant.

Sagittarians pride themselves on thinking positively and insist that the people around them do likewise: forward, ever forward in the pursuit of adventure, good times and the money that pays for them. Life is to be seized by the balls.

Forward, ever forward, too, in the pursuit of truth, liberty and justice for all (i.e., for all people who think positively, as Sagittarians).

Anyone the least bit negative is not a suitable bedfellow for a Sagittarian and, indeed, may be regarded as second-rate all around.

Sagittarians' love of impulsiveness and physical adventure means that sex is always on the menu.

If you're a man who's been hankering for a latter-day Amazon with a social conscience, Ms. Sagittarius could be for you. If you're a woman who's been hankering for a man with a high sex drive and IQ to match, a man in pursuit of the good things in life with ambitious plans to get them, Mr. Sagittarius could be for you.

But be warned, this "seeking" quality of Sagittarians can extend to their sex lives as well. Notoriously, the Sagittarian can suffer from (or enjoy, depending on your point of view) the Don Juan complex—or the Donna Juan complex. They are the spiritual, geographical and sexual gypsies of the Zodiac.

How to Interest a Sagittarius

■ ■ ■

Key tactic: Come across as if you've overdosed on positive affirmation tapes.

Sagittarius is ruled by Jupiter, the largest planet in the Solar System. In accordance with this grand scale, Sagittarians want a partner who thinks big. To catch a Sagittarian, it is a good idea to present yourself as an entrepreneurial type: someone with big goals and ambitious plans for achieving them.

Sagittarius is the sign of travel and foreign cultures. So talk about your experiences in exotic places. If you've spent a few months in an ashram, a night in a pyramid or a weekend in Zanzibar, great. Blow it up out of all proportion.

If you haven't traveled much *yet* (say "yet"—thinking positively), talk about any hobby that shows your transcultural awareness: Tai Chi lessons, Egyptian belly dancing, Thai cooking, American Indian sweat lodges, whatever. Especially mention any foreign languages you know: an ideal tactic would be to talk about the language you are currently learning for your next overseas jaunt. Hint at expeditions to Bhutan, Tibet, Tunisia.

Bring them back to your place to show them photos of your travels. Sagittarius is one of the few signs you could seriously invite over to watch the two-hour video of your trip up the Nile.

Sagittarians will always be possessed by some cause. They are great ones for jumping on bandwagons. (Mind you, they jump from one bandwagon to another pretty frequently.) Find out what their current cause is and be equally fanatical about it. Join Greenpeace. Do not dare question *any* aspect of the current cause. For instance, if it's saving every tree in the world, don't dare say, "Well, we do need some trees for houses and furniture." This will put them right off. You must adopt the cause single-mindedly and mindlessly. You must be totally committed and totally positive.

Sagittarians love to feel they got a bargain on something. They love the atmosphere of markets and thrift shops. Picking up something exotic or rare for a song gives them a sense of triumph. (Not to mention being able to put their savings toward their next foreign expedition or entrepreneurial scheme.) One good way to interest them is to help them get a bargain on something they want or to swap notes about how to get the best deals in travel.

They usually come across as friendly. They are easy to make overtures to. If they are interested in you, they won't be shy, so directness is recommended. Forget coy. Ask them for a date at the first meeting.

A good way in is to suggest an ethnic nosh. "Do you like Thai food? I know a great place. How about tonight?"

Say "tonight" rather than "tomorrow" because they respect impulsiveness and because they're probably busy tomorrow night. Already you are someone who "goes with the flow." This is one aspect of thinking positively.

And if the restaurant is cheap, they won't think you're cheap. They'll think you're savvy. They like their dating partners to be *au fait* with where the interesting restaurants, places and people are.

Another good opening line is: "Come up and see my etchings"—if you made the etchings yourself. Sagittarians are impressed by talent—artistic, business, intellectual. They expect that sexual talent will accompany these other talents.

Sagittarians tend to overschedule their lives. If their diary isn't jam-packed, they feel that life is passing them by. You too should come across as having a full timetable. "Oh, that night's difficult. No, no, I can reschedule that. Yes, okay, we can do that night." This is important evidence that you are enthusiastic. Expect Sagittarius to have to schedule you in and don't be put off if you must wait a week before they can find time for your first date.

Suggested opening line: "Let's get out of this place and go dancing."

What to talk about: Travel, foreign cultures, meditation, philosophy, positive thinking and self-improvement classes, global consciousness, entrepreneurial schemes, politics, religion, Taoism, feminism, spiritualism, environmentalism, capitalism, Marxism, racism, sexism—just about any ism you can think of.

Where to take them: Meditation classes, bookshops, ethnic restaurants, fund-raisers for refugees, free films on Himalayan adventures, camping, bungee-jumping, horseback riding, Hare Krishna restaurants, flea markets, a lecture by a visiting Tibetan lama. Sagittarians have such broad interests, you can take them just about anywhere.

What to give them: Glossy travel books, art books, books on the latest intellectual fad, luggage, camera equipment, gift certificates for a parasailing or parachuting course, something useful and portable they can take when traveling, ethnic objets d'art—a Tibetan prayer wheel, Moroccan lamp, batiks. Many Sagittarians have a favorite mode of transport—a motorcycle, a superior car, a horse. See if you can give a present to suit.

How to Seduce a Sagittarius

■ ■ ■

Key tip: Come on hot and strong from the beginning.

Sagittarians are not that interested in long overtures. Sagittarius is a Fire sign and is more likely to be impressed by forthrightness.

Remember that they appreciate impulsiveness. Indeed, Sagittarians have a reputation for making love to strangers—especially strangers from foreign countries. The archetypal Sagittarian has no inhibitions about making love on the first date or indeed at the first encounter.

Once you've ascertained that you've got their interest and have been short-listed on their sexual agenda, move in quickly and with assurance. If you're not confident, they will take this as a sign of a negative attitude and will go off you before they've ever got on you.

Indeed, whether man or woman, if interested, Sagittarius is usually prepared to do the pursuing. Guilt or shame about sex is foreign to them. One-night stands or quick affairs in foreign locales are all options on their sexual menu. Sex is their sport, exercise, hobby and quasireligious celebration of the life force, all rolled into one.

No need to think: "First we establish a relationship and then sex can rear its head." For Sagittarians, sex is the door into the relationship, not vice versa.

So be direct in your approach. This leads us to . . .

Seduction 1: The Grab

Make a wordless but unmistakable move—waist-grabbing, a cuddle with wandering hands, bottom-fondling. While their hands are occupied making coffee, come up behind them and grab their breasts—or aim lower. This will show whether your chances are good from the start.

If their eyes widen in startled pleasure, yours will later, too. (See also the Outrageous Move, Aries.)

If they don't discourage you, keep going and see what develops.

This one is simple and superdirect: no props, no planning, no expense. Jump in, try something obvious and if you don't get flattened or thrown out on your ear, you're on.

Seduction 2: The Stop-I-Can't-Wait

Sagittarians respect lust.

Lust is equated with life force. Sagittarians reach boiling point at a lower temperature than other Sun signs. Your lust can set theirs off.

Impress them with the overwhelming nature of your lust. "Pull the car over! I have to have you right now." "I can't wait until we get back to your place. Let's find a bush somewhere."

Or just try urgently pulling them into an improvised venue. Perhaps a darkened doorway at night. (For other possible places, see Seduction 5.)

Seduction 3: The Egomaniacal Sales Pitch

This is one sign on whom you could use this revolting line: "If you don't give me a try, you'll never know what you're missing."

This is marginally more creative than simply telling them you're a good lay. It pays to advertise—with Sagittarians, anyway. Offer to provide references.

Above all else, Sagittarians *hate* to think they may have missed out on anything exciting. If you can convince them that you are a truly top-notch experience, they will be achingly tempted.

Like other Fire sign females, Sagittarian women harbor a deep suspicion that the size of a male's genitals is in direct proportion to the size of his ego.

Similarly, the male Sagittarian equates brashness with sexual expertise. So come across as inordinately confident of your sexual prowess, secure in the knowledge that you can move the earth for them.

Seduction 4: The I'm-Available

This seduction will work best if you happen to be sleeping somewhere in close proximity to the Sagittarian—in an adjoining motel room, the same block of apartments, on the same street, in adjoining train compartments, neighboring tents, whatever.

The essence of this seduction is simply to tell the Sagittarian you are available for sex anytime, anyplace, any position.

Tell them in the evening, "I want you. When you want me, let me know. I'm available. I'm ready when you are." If appropriate, administer a passionate kiss and a hot look and walk away. Back to your own bed.

It's quite possible the Sagittarian will follow you immediately.

If not, don't worry. Just go to sleep and save your strength. The Sagittarian may not be able to sleep. They may be tossing and turning all night, worried that there is this great experience waiting next door. They may well beat down your door in the middle of the night or early the next morning.

If not, arrive with croissants the next morning; ask how they slept. If they don't confess to lust straightaway, consider the Outrageous Move (see Aries).

Seduction 5: The Passport to Unscheduled Delights

The essence of this seduction is to cash in on the justifiably legendary Sagittarian proclivity for picking up people while traveling. They are into the one-city stand.

They like to make love en route.

They are also the sexual vagrants of the star chart. They don't need a five-star hotel to get hot. A tent will do. Sometimes not even a tent is necessary. A rock, a pool, the leaf litter on a rain forest floor.

A typical Sagittarian fantasy is to have an affair stretched over three continents—bicycling across Asia Minor, in a villa on the Mediterranean, under the stars at Ayers Rock.

Sex with a Sagittarian can be a moving experience.

The precondition of this seduction is that at least one of you must be on the way to somewhere else.

The Passport to Unscheduled Delights (i): The Emmanuelle Classic.

Yes, the classic boink: Emmanuelle meets Boeing. The lavatory of a 747. The standard way to join the Mile-High Club. Yes, it's been done. But it's worth doing again.

The Passport to Unscheduled Delights (ii): The Airline Blanket.

Slightly more interesting than the lavatory is what can be done under an airline blanket. Suggested procedure: having ascertained that you're seated next to an attractive Sagittarian, first be solicitous of their comfort. Ask them which seat they'd like—offer them the window. Suggest they'd be more comfortable with the armrest raised. Now you are elbow to elbow, thigh to thigh. Buy them a drink or two. Ask the attendant for a blanket (note: *a* blanket). Place it over yourself—and look for an opportunity to get them under it too. Wait until they are nodding off, perhaps. They awake to find that you have solicitously tucked them in under the blanket with you. Start with the relatively unalarming. Hold their hand. Stroke their arm. Move to the thigh. We leave the rest to you.

The Passport to Unscheduled Delights (iii): Making the Connection.

While waiting for a connection, why not try to make another sort of connection? If you've got a two- or three-hour stopover, many international airports have hotels attached where you can take a room for a few hours. It could be one of the best investments you've ever made if you have the right Sagittarian. But if half an hour is all you've got, consider the advantages of the lavatory for the handicapped. Extra space. Often unisex. Sagittarius is not averse to the quickie.

The Passport to Unscheduled Delights (iv): The Orient Express.

Consider the possibilities of the sleeping compartment on a train. You are likely to meet Sagittarius in the dining car or bar. Consider offering them a quiet drink back in your compartment—or perhaps you have some amazing exotic knickknack or book you know they'd be interested in. Perhaps you have some other amazing thing they'd be interested in as well.

The Passport to Unscheduled Delights (v): Musical Tents. This is one to try on a camping trip. Sneak into their tent and say, "Shhh! It's all right. It's only me." Try Seduction by Assumption (see Libra). Or, if you really need an excuse, perhaps your tent could collapse in the middle of the night—or spring a leak.

Seduction 6: The Tarzan-and-Jane

The Tarzan-and-Jane Seduction taps into the animal half of the half-man/half-beast Sagittarian: back to primordial, raw lust in the outdoors. Sagittarians are big believers in the great outdoors and find fresh-air sex quite a turn-on.

This is a seduction to try only if you are fit. Maybe you'll have to go into training. You must endure extended physical exertion and still rise to the occasion. It is not necessary to dress in loincloths and swing from vines, but you must get those muscles rippling. For Sagittarians, physical exertion is a form of foreplay. They love to feel their own muscles working and love to see sweat dripping off bodies of the opposite sex.

The Tarzan-and-Jane (i): The Peak Experience. Take your Sagittarian on a mountain-conquering expedition—preferably a small mountain. Impress them with your joy in exertion, nature, exercise, leeches. Once you've reached the top of the hill, spontaneously rip off your shirt to let your skin breathe and feel the sun against your flesh. Take them by the hand, find the nearest flat piece of land and plant your flag on the peak.

Sagittarians hate to miss an opportunity to prove that the life force is pumping through their veins. They would hate to miss out on being able to tell others how they were mounted on the mount.

The Tarzan-and-Jane (ii): Jungle Beasts. If mountain expeditions are a bit much for your quadriceps, consider a walk in a rain forest. Ponder the possibilities of the trunk of a tree, or a lush bed of fallen leaves. Or check the map beforehand for the location of a suitable alligator-free pool. Spontaneously rip your clothes off, plunge in and call out, "Last one in is a wimp."

The Tarzan-and-Jane (iii): Après-ski. Four hours of hard skiing, back to the chalet and light their fire.

The Tarzan-and-Jane (iv): Horseback Riding. This is an archetypal Sagittarian seduction tapping straight into the symbol of Sagittarius: half man, half horse.

Horseback riding is a major form of sexual arousal for many Sagittarians—especially the women. So arrange some horseback riding somewhere off the beaten track. Once far enough into the woods, transfer to the Stop-I-Can't-Wait.

Another alternative is to have your horse go lame so that you must mount their horse behind them. Your hands are going to have to hang on to something. Take it from there. See what can be achieved on the back of a horse.

The modern variation on this is the Harley-Davidson Seduction: wild and free on the highway of life. Sagittarian heaven.

The Tarzan-and-Jane (v): From Here to Eternity. Suggest a stroll along a remote moonlit beach. Gaze at the moon. Hold hands. Lead them to a group of boulders. Or do the Burt Lancaster bit and pull them down into the surf at the edge of the sea. Take it from there.

The Tarzan-and-Jane (vi): Body Heat. Sagittarians are often crazy about tennis and similar physical competition. See if you can turn this into a love match. The ideal scenario is for you to either *just* win or *just* lose a tight match and then take them for a private sauna afterward. If you can manifest extreme lust under these hothouse conditions, they will find it hard to resist your serve.

The Tarzan-and-Jane (vii): The Wet T-Shirt. Contrive to fall into a body of water wearing minimal clothing and no underwear. Have them help pull you out. Shiver and move close to draw on their body heat. Take it from there.

The Tarzan-and-Jane (viii): Seduction by the Stars! A somewhat less athletic version of the Tarzan-and-Jane is to take your Sagittarian nature-lover stargazing. This is especially good if you can point out the constellations. The ideal place for this would be at the edge of the desert, lying on the sand. But almost anywhere would do. Suggest that you both lie down to gaze silently at the stars. Stare wordlessly. Synchronize your breathing. Reach for their hand. Reach for it all. There's more than one way to put stars in their eyes.

Seduction 7: The Intellectual Tarzan-and-Jane

Somewhat easier than jumping from vine to vine and beating your chest is to jump from idea to idea and beat your ideological chest. Ideological solidity and intellectual enthusiasm are equated in the Sagittarian mind with sexual prowess and can-do.

The Intellectual Tarzan-and-Jane (i): The Ideologically Sound Seduction. This is the seduction to save for the archetypal Sagittarian ideologue. The best scenario is a combination of warm fire and heated discussion. This is not seduction by battle. You basically have to be on the same side as they. You may be presenting a different perspective but your arguments must be ideologically sound (i.e., you agree with them). You must come across as *passionate* about your beliefs and suitably politicized. When minds converge, bodies must follow.

The Intellectual Tarzan-and-Jane (ii): The Demonstration of Affection. Attend a demonstration for their current cause. March shoulder to shoulder, placard to placard, comrade to comrade and, hopefully later, pelvis to pelvis.

Seduction 8: Jungle Drums (or Dirty Dancing)

Perhaps more than any other sign, body-oriented Sagittarius finds dancing a form of foreplay. This includes almost any form of dancing: rock, disco, the tango, the lambada, square dancing, whatever. Get them dancing; watch for the smile, the glint in the eye. Switch to the Grab. Try pulling them close and try the Stop-I-Can't-Wait. Tell them you simply have to have them right now and lead them off the dance floor to the nearest car/hayloft/lockable room/darkened doorway/patch of bushes.

Or you may try a tamer version of this seduction by getting them dancing back at your place.

Seduction 9: The Loose End

This seduction relies on catching the Sagittarian in a rare uncommitted moment. Perhaps, after repeated phone calls, you reach them late at night or on a Sunday morning, when they actually don't have anything scheduled and aren't on their way out the door. Sagittarians hate that.

Immediately tell them you are on your way over with a bottle of wine and a pizza or some other goodies. They so hate being bored and feeling they are missing out on something in life. Offer to fill their schedule.

Proceed to the Grab or the Intellectual Tarzan-and-Jane seduction.

Other good Sagittarian seductions:

The Pounce (see Aries)

The Outrageous Move (Aries)

The Instant Seduction (Gemini)

The Wild Escapade (Gemini)

The Public Provocation Proposition (Gemini)

The Five-Star Seduction (Leo)

A Streetcar Named Desire (Leo)

The Reverse Grab (Scorpio)

The Seduce-Me (Capricorn)

Seduction by Humor (Aquarius)

Sex with a Sagittarius

■ ■ ■

Buy your vitamin pills now.

Sagittarians can test your stamina. You could be expected to go rock climbing all day and make love half the night.

Or they may expect you to sit around in spiritual meditation all day and then want you to move straight from the lotus position to all sorts of other positions. The quick switch from the sacred to the profane, from the mission to the missionary, is normal for a Sagittarian.

The symbol of Sagittarius is the centaur: half human, half beast; half spiritual, half physical. That is why an ardent discussion of the Neo-Platonists can be a form of Sagittarian foreplay. And it's why boinking like alley cats is the natural Sagittarian complement to an evening of yoga.

One problem that can intrude into the bedroom is the legendary Sagittarian foot-in-mouth disease. And we're not talking about toe-sucking here—though this pastime is not to be ruled out. We're talking about a brutal, clumsy frankness that can deflate the most bloated gonads. "Gee, it's odd how you really tall guys can have such small pricks . . . er, just as well I don't like big pricks."

Or consider the Sagittarian male in action. "Isn't it strange how you women with big hips often have small tits. It must be convenient not having to wear a bra."

Try to remind yourself that the Sagittarian does not mean to hurt. It is just that the mouth frequently opens before the brain.

Honesty minus diplomacy = brutality

If you are a bit insecure about your sexual technique, equipment, excess fat, small breasts, thunder thighs, flabby bottom, receding hairline, spare tire . . . just put them out of your mind and do the Sagittarian thing: think positively. Concentrate on giving a superlative performance in the sack and this will put a soft-focus filter on any physical imperfections.

One problem with dating Sagittarians can be their tendency to jam-pack their lives. You may feel that you are slotted into the small gaps between their foreign language classes, their friends and their hobbies. If you are having trouble pinning down an overscheduled Sagittarian, try pinning them down—literally. Catch them in the fifteen minutes between appointments, corner them in the parking lot and go for it. Or call them up and say, "I can't wait until Thursday. I want you now. Get your ass over here in twenty minutes."

Weekends away are generally a good idea with Sagittarians; they won't be constantly rushing from one thing to another as they try to schedule you in for an hour on Sunday afternoon.

A typical Sagittarian progression in a relationship is: sex, companionship, more sex, affection, more sex, finally love.

How to Handle a Relationship with a Sagittarius

■ ■ ■

Sagittarians set the rules in their relationships: "This is how I run my life; if you can't handle it, too bad—go elsewhere."

They want a partner who is a fellow adventurer rather than an iron-clad commitment. They are not interested in slowing down their ever-on-the-go lifestyle to make more room for intimate sharing. Indeed, they can be frightened of true intimacy. Often they choose constant activity at the expense of forging emotional bonds.

The way to get the most out of a relationship with a Sagittarian is to *participate* . . . in all their adventures, classes, socializing—but do not expect much in the way of domestic or personal support.

Sagittarians have ways and means of forcing you to enjoy yourself. Always remember: they don't like people who slow them down. They are quite capable of dragging you around the foothills of Nepal or for a two-week trek across the African savannah while you dream of inner-spring mattresses, hot running water and Hershey bars. They see themselves as tough—so don't dare complain that you haven't had a bath for a week. Only wimps complain.

Key tip: Above all else, you must always think positive.

The Sagittarian is the original subscriber to the belief in the power of positive thinking. And, indeed, this is the sign for whom unquestioned optimism is most likely to work . . . sometimes. At other times, it will cost them small fortunes, large fortunes, their health, your health, their sanity, your sanity.

Like the other Fire signs, Leo and Aries, when Sagittarians are emotionally high, they forget there was ever a time in their lives when they were down or depressed. When up like this, they can be insufferable: "I've found the meaning of life and I can't believe you haven't." They're right; you're confused. And don't attempt to offer them any advice like "Slow down . . . tread carefully . . . one step at a time." This will be read as stupid negative thinking. When high on life, they lack all humility and are completely intolerant of opinions different from their own. They can have all the compassion and sensitivity of a runaway cement truck.

Sagittarians have an admirable curiosity. Many become professional students. They are versatile and broad in their interests—which can lead them to intellectual sloppiness and the championing of causes selected on the basis of intuition rather than thorough consideration.

As their partner, you must always appear to be energetic and full of love for life—except when they want to moan and get sympathy. In time, you'll probably learn that your Sagittarian partner is better at being sympathized with than sympathizing. Sagittarians have "real problems"; other people are just whining. If you are depressed, it's because you keep harping on those negative thoughts they already told you to get rid of. But if they are depressed, expect fire and brimstone. They have *real* cause for depression.

Even the rare chronically depressed Sagittarian hates to be around other people who are "negative." Generally, negative Sagittarians are those who feel trapped (e.g., by a marriage or a job) and are therefore unable to be all the things a Sagittarian values most—free, independent, impulsive, on the move.

Not only do they have a low tolerance for anyone who is sick or depressed, they deny physical failings and illnesses in themselves and expect others to do the same. Often they cannot give even themselves sympathy. They try to be tough and carry on with a bad case of flu—which ends up turning into bronchitis, pneumonia and a near-death experience (which, as everyone knows, can be very positive!). They simply don't seem to realize that rest and nurturing of the body is not a sign of weakness but of good sense.

"Crusading" is the right adjective for many Sagittarians. Remember that the Crusaders went off for years on a fruitless fight, leaving their loved ones to suffer and cope in their absence. This could be what you are up against.

Sagittarians are genuine in their crusading causes: they will put themselves on the line for something they believe in. This is one of their most admirable traits. They will adapt their whole life around their current cause or intellectual fascination and seek to win converts to it.

Sometimes this crusader self-image takes a turn toward the search for higher truth and the meaning of life, and they see themselves as mystic warriors.

Sagittarians are great talkers and, when in full flight, they won't pause for a millisecond between sentences. They are as likely to interrupt you as a

Gemini and have ways of preventing your getting a word in edgewise. You'll simply have to wait until they run out of steam. As you are listening to them thump the Bible over their current cause, it may occur to you that there is an inherent contradiction between their espousal of revolution, radicalism, anarchism and Indian gurus—and their basically bourgeois lifestyle.

You will occasionally be tempted to share this insight with them. And you can get away with it too, *as long as you do it with humor*. Sagittarians admire a sense of humor. Take the wind out of their sails in a clever way and they'll think you've got a good brain.

Sagittarius is the Sun sign most noted for being able to put both feet in their mouth at once. There is a positive and a negative side to this. They may be tactless, but at least they speak their mind so that you know where you stand. They tell you the truth—at least as they see it. The downside is that if your ego's a bit frail, it is likely to get a bruising. If you complain, the Sagittarian may be mystified. "Don't you want to hear the truth?" They never meant to hurt you, you know, and may be quite shocked that you are upset.

As for discretion, forget it. If you share your secrets with them, all their friends are likely to know within a week. Your reluctantly revealed true confessions will be remodeled into a saga, which they'll relate to people they scarcely know. Your only consolation is that this is rarely done maliciously. When they realize they've blabbed, they usually try to cover up and so make it worse. So this is perhaps not a good sign with which to have an affair if discretion is important. Sagittarians are quite capable of giving you a sexual rating and airing it to all and sundry.

Arguments with Sagittarians are best mended in bed. Unlike some signs, they don't need to feel good before they can become sexually aroused. Sexual arousal will *make* them happy. It will reimmerse them in the life force; a good roll in the hay will make them see you in a far more positive light—despite the fact that you obviously do not think positively enough because you have a different opinion from theirs.

When it comes to money, the Sagittarian likes to think big and talk big. There is a very real danger of overshooting the mark—overestimating their energies, underestimating expenses, overestimating the market, underestimating the time a scheme will take to pay off. More than any other Sun sign, they think the cosmos owes them the good things in life. They are ruled by Jupiter, the planet of good fortune, so they think the high life is their birthright. This can lead to falling face-first into the financial mire. You may be the one to bring a more cautious perspective to their grandiose plans.

Finally, this is the sign of the Don Juan and Donna Juan, so you might have to put up with their wandering eyes—and other wandering parts of their anatomy as well. Sagittarius is probably not a good sign to become involved with if you get jealous easily. It can be important to accompany them when they travel overseas—or you'll never know who they had a cultural experience with. They are inclined to go native in more ways than one. Generally Sagittarians feel no guilt about shacking up with another lover in the absence of their main squeeze.

Must-Do's

Be perpetually enthusiastic. Beat your chest. Come across as their fantasy Amazon or Tarzan.

Have your passport, backpack and sex organs always on standby.

Be involved in some cause or spiritual movement.

No-No's

Never whine about any difficulties you are going through.

Never show signs of emotional insecurity, physical debility or weakness of will.

Never ever criticize any of their causes.

Never pour cold water on their current grandiose plan.

How to End a Relationship with a Sagittarius

■ ■ ■

The direct approach is suggested for the overture, but it is not highly recommended for the finale.

When a relationship comes to an end, the Sagittarian horn-blower comes out—the entire street will know that you have used them, abused them, led them on, loved them and left them.

As with all Fire signs (the others are Leo and Aries), breaking up with this sign can be a delicate matter. The main thing is not to leave them for another person.

Or, if you are going off with someone else, for your sake don't tell them. Instead supply a plausible alternative explanation as to why the relationship had to end. Perhaps you can say you simply couldn't keep up with them physically or sexually; you need a quieter life; you simply couldn't pedal your bike fast enough to keep up with life in their fast lane; you could no longer hoist the mainsail on demand.

Better still, engineer their loss of interest in you.

Key tip: Lack of drive, verve, fire or enthusiasm in any aspect of life will put them off.

The easiest way to discourage a Sagittarian is to develop a major depression or have a nervous breakdown. This is called the power of negative thinking. Because they can't stand to be around negativity or what they perceive as emotional weakness, they will often develop an aversion to you without even knowing why. They conceive of themselves as being aware, caring people, but if you get depressed (perhaps for a quite understandable reason—for instance, the loss of a job) they will unconsciously want to see you less.

Another tactic is to become a chronic whiner—they abhor whining in anyone besides themselves.

Tell them you always get ill when you go away from home, you can only sleep in your own bed, all you want to do is nest into your own little domestic refuge for the rest of your life. Stop wanting to go anywhere. They'll hate that.

Lose enthusiasm for *everything*. Tell them you've stopped caring about the starving millions, ceased to be concerned about the environment, that you couldn't care less about dolphins . . . that you've reached a total state of existential apathy.

Lose interest in sex. Tell them your spiritual guru has advised you to become celibate for six months. That should do it.

Above all—appear lackluster. The minute they suspect you're weak, wimpy or washed up, you've had it.

Sagittarians at Their Best

■ ■ ■

You'll be on a pumped-up merry-go-round of passion, travel, parties, philosophical talks, sex, tennis matches, frank and honest interchanges, foreign language classes, street theater, sex, yoga classes, gallery hops, travel, more sex, more travel and Greenpeace demonstrations.

Sagittarians at Their Worst

■ ■ ■

You'll be screaming for the merry-go-round to stop. You'll wonder if you're in a relationship with them at all because they'll always be somewhere else—traveling, taking classes, visiting friends, etc., etc., etc. You'll feel that their feelings for you, like their time spent with you, are strictly scheduled and limited. You'll feel as if your relationship is going nowhere because they are always going somewhere else. When you most need them, they are guaranteed to either zoom off somewhere else or lose interest in you. Pompous, holier-than-thou Sagittarius will dismiss all your opinions and desires as inadequate and immoral compared to their grandiose ideals. You'll also find that all details of your private life have been spread far and wide, courtesy of the notorious Sagittarian big mouth. You'll find yourself craving a quieter, gentler, more caring, sharing existence with someone who is able to defer occasionally to your needs and listen to your opinions.

Sexy Sagittarians

■ ■ ■

Chris Evert, Steven Spielberg, Harpo Marx, Beethoven, Jeff Bridges, Maria Callas, Patty Duke, Jane Fonda, Billy Idol, Edith Piaf, Frank Sinatra, Tina Turner, Douglas Fairbanks, Jr., Dorothy Lamour, Kirk Douglas, John F. Kennedy, Jr., Bruce Lee.

Unsexy Sagittarians

■ ■ ■

Boris Karloff, Jimi Hendrix, Woody Allen, Walt Disney, Sammy Davis, Jr., Dick Van Dyke, Noël Coward, Margaret Mead, Winston Churchill, Dick Clark, Phil Donahue, Bette Midler, Ozzy Osbourne, Andy Williams.

CAPRICORN

December 22nd to January 20th

• • •

Are you happy to see me or is that a

résumé in your pocket?

The Lure of a Capricorn

■ ■ ■

Reliable, solid, practical, serious, disciplined, reserved, dignified, status-conscious, decent, sensible.

If you think this sounds boring, think again.

If you suspect that such an individual couldn't do much for your previously unsatisfied passions, please reconsider.

Capricorn is reputed to have the strongest sex drive in the Zodiac.

The symbol of Capricorn, the Goat, has long been portrayed as the horniest of beasts. The Greeks knew all about Capricorns. They made the satyr—half man, half goat—the personification of the all-voracious libido. The satyr was the being whose pleasurable duty it was to satisfy an entire herd of oversexed nymphs.

Pause here to reflect a moment on what you could be in for.

Do you need it?

Do you *really* need it?

Are you ready for it?

Can you handle it?

Then read on.

Overlibidinous they may be, but the proprietorial Capricorn will expect the restrained, well-mannered approach in public. However, once the bedroom door shuts, boy (or girl), are you in for a pleasant surprise.

If you want someone in your life who is upright, honorable and dependable, and yet who behind closed doors has a voracious sexual appetite, consider Mr. or Ms. Capricorn. They are unlikely to let you down—either in or out of the bedroom.

Like fine wines, Capricorns improve with age. They tend to be old when they are young and young when they're old. Often they are much better value after the age of twenty-eight—the age astrologers regard as the end of youth. They retain—or even increase—their sex drive as they mature, so if you feel you would benefit from an affair with an older, more experienced person, Capricorn is almost certainly the best choice. The only reason Capricorns are so numerous among the ranks of dirty old men is because they are the only ones who can still do it!

Capricorns believe that everything improves with practice. They are not naturally attracted to the one-night stand. That strikes a Capricorn as leaving the dinner table before the best dishes have been served. They want an affair that allows time for mutual sexual exploration. They want the promise of bigger and better things to come.

But here's the warning. Capricorns can appear dour and serious; they can't be described as romantic in the traditional sense of the word. They don't flirt. If you want hearts-and-roses courtship with a romantic fool, try an over-the-top Leo, a lovelorn Cancer or a dreamy Pisces. These signs are capable of the gooey romantic gestures a Capricorn would classify as silly and suitable only for gauche lovesick teenagers. Capricorns, more than any other sign, understand the value of time. Time spent on infantile flirting could be better directed toward advancing their careers. Their amours will not be permitted to interfere with the realization of their thirty-year plan for total success. On the other hand, lovers who understand the desire for success and even support it will be highly valued.

Capricorns can subjugate their romantic inclinations to their financial and career goals. Which brings us to an important warning: Beware the Capricorn gold digger. A minority of Capricorns fear not being able to fulfill their material needs by themselves. They suppress their true emotions and marry for money. They often go on to become sour, dictatorial matriarchs or patriarchs.

Capricorns have seriousness in their souls. They can be very serious about everything. Fortunately, that includes sex.

How to Interest a Capricorn

■ ■ ■

No trumpet-blowing. Capricorn knows that real achievers never blow their own horn. Wait for them to draw you out on your talents and successes. Capricorns are impressed above all by the self-made individual. Once they start to ask questions, emphasize what you have done for yourself in finding your own way in the world. Rich boys and rich girls who play at working fill them with ennui and contempt.

They hate sham, name-dropping and shallowness. Nor are they impressed by the gaudy. You think your trendy sports car impresses a Capricorn? If you own a sports car but you don't own your own home, Capricorn will not regard the flashy car as a turn-on; they will regard it as a sign that you are an idiot. You'd impress them far more with a reliable older car and a house you are paying off and renovating on weekends.

If you have money, great. But never come across as a nouveau riche spendthrift frittering away money to make an impression. That will not impress.

Capricorns have a high regard for quality and long-term investments. This is how they will assess you when they size you up as a sexual prospect. Capricorns are certainly capable of the short-term affair, but they want to know that the long-term effects of a short-term affair will be good. What would be the ultimate value in a wild fling that destroyed their long-term career prospects? Ridiculous. A waste of time and a threat to their precious reputation. What would be the use of a brief affair if it ended up with the other person hating you? Terribly silly idea.

Key tactic number one: You must convince the Capricorn that you are a mentally solid individual who, should the affair come to an end, will not engage in acts of vengeance, public screaming matches, nervous breakdowns, legal action or suicide attempts, but instead will behave discreetly, honorably, and truthfully and will ideally remain their friend.

Capricorn is a risk calculator. No matter how physically attracted they are to you, they will assess whether you are worth the risk. You have to convince them you are. If you're after spontaneous abandon with minimal thought for the consequences, find yourself a Gemini or Sagittarian.

Key tactic number two: Convince them that you are a person of genuine quality. Impress them with your honesty, your self-control, your consistency—all virtues highly esteemed by Capricorn.

Leave your outrageous clothing at the back of the closet. No T-shirts with suggestive slogans, no jeans that reveal anatomical details, nothing vulgar. Capricorns harbor a secret attraction to glamour—not flashiness or trendiness, but high-quality glam. If you can make a glamorous addition to their establishment image and have the genuine inner qualities they prize, Capricorn will be putty in your hands.

You must be perceived as good for their reputation. They want other people to see their partner as a person of outer and inner quality.

Remember that it is long-term reliability and quality they want—from possessions, from life and from you. Make it clear that you can take care of yourself, that you're not looking to be kept.

Capricorns see the sense in buying something that costs a lot but lasts a lifetime rather than something cheap that will be discarded in a few years. If the conversation turns to what you own, talk about the house you are paying off, the refrigerator that will work for decades, the antique table that will quadruple in value when you've restored it, your first editions, your antique jewelry.

All Capricorns want to make their mark on the world. Ask them about their career and where they plan to be in five years' time—or fifteen years' time. They're not interested in retirement. Retirement is for wimps. Achievers keep on achieving. Tell them you never intend to retire. A sure way to lose a Capricorn's interest is to talk longingly about giving up work for good.

Capricorns are circumspect with money. There are some whose frugality develops into arthritis of the purse finger. However, most Capricorns are not intrinsically mean. It's true they are not given to wildly spontaneous generosity and rarely splurge on themselves, but if you are valued, they will spend money on you . . . wisely and thoughtfully. The very big substantial plus of Capricorn gifts is that they are *gifts*. They are not down payments on return gifts or future favors.

Suggested opening line: "I couldn't help overhearing what you said about————. You've obviously got a good grasp on the issues. I spent three years working in this area. If you're interested we could lunch tomorrow and I could tell you about the latest research we've been doing in————."

What to talk about: In public, personal and intimate matters are strictly *verboten*. Instead, seek their opinion on the state of the world: business, politics, the effects of the latest government policy, the state of the economy. Don't try to engage them in hot debate. Most Capricorns can't see the sense in argument for argument's sake—save that for a Gemini. Ask their advice about something personal or professional. They will usually give level-headed advice culled from years of serious thought. Make it obvious that you value their opinions and you will have made a very deep impression. Remember: don't trot out your achievements until asked.

In private, after the relationship has started, you can talk about almost anything—especially sex.

Where to take them: Classy restaurants with quiet atmosphere and good service, antiques shops, historical estates, concerts, plays (especially comedies), musicals, evenings in front of the fire. Capricorns are usually open to new experiences, but avoid the weird, the wacky and the tacky.

What to give them: A Capricorn takes note when you have put thought or physical effort into a gift. Take extra care to obtain something for them that they really want. If they own something that has worn out after decades of use, buy them a new, significantly improved model—Capricorns are always looking for improvement in all aspects of life.

Just as good or even better: make them something. They appreciate the investment of time and work. Your rewards could be great indeed. Go for something practical and comfortable rather than purely decorative: hand-knit sweaters, bookcases, cushions, doorstops. Avoid chintz and froufrou. Go for functional, not fussy.

Consider presents associated with getting organized and with time: clocks (especially antiques), pocket watches, wristwatches, electronic organizers, diaries, answering machines, filing cabinets, desk organizers, briefcases, leather wallets and purses. Consider fine arts and collectibles—reproductions from museums and galleries, Victorian jewelry, an antique chair or cabinet. Consider fine things to wear: a silk tie, expensive black silk underwear. Capricorns look good in dark colors: black, dark blue, rich dark red.

How to Seduce a Capricorn

■ ■ ■

The two key words here are "privacy" and "discretion."

Forget backseats of cars, open fields, beaches at night—all too risky and exhibitionistic for Capricorns. You must get them behind closed doors—

preferably locked and bolted as well. Even a five-star hotel could be too public for some Capricorns. Good god, somebody might have seen them in the lobby. The desk clerk and the floor manager may be total strangers but they know what you're up to, and even that may make a Capricorn feel exposed.

Discretion strikes them as sensible. It may not work out—why should other people know about something that may not last? Why should other people know anyway? Discretion helps them protect their feelings and public image.

Some Capricorns find even the most minimal display of affection in public vulgar. Absolutely no public gropes, grabs, kissing or canoodling. It may even be wise to be circumspect about holding hands or putting an arm around the waist. It could be construed as bad taste.

They are attracted to success, sensitivity, sex.

Key tip: The most important thing for them to know about you is that you are 100 percent psychologically stable—not the least bit bonkers. It is crucial to appear emotionally together.

Do not gush over them. If you must gush, do it over something else. They don't like to be emoted over.

There must be no question marks about your sexuality and no quirky little corners in your erotic inclinations.

Controlled sexual energy is their top priority. They respect passion, but in their rational way, they regard passion without technique as chaos. Remember: Capricorns want quality in all things—including sex. Quality can only come with a combination of passion and control.

What they want is a well-mannered animal.

Capricorn women are rarely cockteasers—too dishonorable. Capricorn men are unlikely to be overcome by last-minute second thoughts, hesitations or misfiring equipment.

Remember that Capricorn is a highly sexed sign. Make no mistake. A cool controlled exterior they may have, but they understand passion and want it from you. Once discretion has been established and the spark is there, a veritable fireball of passion could be unleashed.

Because Capricorns most often had a less than fun-filled childhood, many an adult Capricorn is trying to make up for lost time. They are generally keen to get on with *it*. They don't usually need a lot of foreplay. When the stopper is taken out of their bottle, a sexual genie emerges who is eager to grant all sexual wishes. They are capable of sheer animal lust. Behind closed doors, Capricorn is the sexual surprise package of the Zodiac.

Seduction 1: The Discreet Overture

The Capricorn aura of restraint and self-sufficiency can present a forbidding aspect to would-be seducers. This can be one of the trickiest signs to make the initial overture to. Indeed, this can easily be the trickiest part in the whole Capricorn seduction process.

The right overture to the right Capricorn at the right time may be all it takes.

Key point: Discretion above all else.

If you're ready to make a move toward the Capricorn in your office, you must do it in such a way that absolutely none of your colleagues has the remotest clue. Discretion is everything. Do not prop yourself in their office doorway and flirt. Phone them—even if your office is just two doors away.

If they suspect you are likely to blab about it and that they risk becoming a hot topic of office gossip, you'll be dropped like a hot potato. Capricorn can freeze up faster and more permanently than any other sign. Instant glacial ice—forbidding and impenetrable.

Here are some suggested overtures:

Ask them to a business lunch to seek their opinion on something or in gratitude for some help they gave you. Pay them some honest compliments: "You've obviously got more brains than the rest of the office combined; I'm really impressed with you—on all levels." Confess it's not just their business briefs you're interested in.

Write them a note saying you have two tickets to the theater (preferably comedy)—would they care to join you? Or send a fax.

Call them and invite them out for a drink after work.

If you meet them at a party and find yourself too shy to ask Mr. or Ms.

Self-Contained Capricorn for a phone number, say your goodbyes and leave the party. Wait ten minutes, call back the party and ask to speak to Mr. or Ms. Capricorn. When they come to the phone, tell them how impressed you were with them. Confess to having been too shy to ask for their phone number in front of all those people. (Capricorns will understand this.) Swap numbers. Better still, ask them if they'd like to join you somewhere for a drink now.

Seduction 2: The Implicit Contract

While the overture to the Capricorn must be low-key, the rest of the seduction should be characterized by directness: a bullshit-free seduction.

Capricorns find the game-playing associated with the seductions of other signs more than a bit childish. They find so-called romantic moves vacuous, fatuous and embarrassingly juvenile.

Nevertheless, you should approach your Capricorn target with respect. In turn, they will respect you more if you don't pretend you're not after what you're after.

Key tip: Directness with decorum.

Accordingly, you should be looking to home in at the first sign that the time is right. Remember that Capricorn is highly sexed and quickly aroused and hates wasting time. This is a sign likely to understand and honor the implicit contract involved in questions like "Would you like to come back to my place for a cup of coffee?" The archetypal Capricorn understands that there is a sexual offer behind such a proposal and will not say yes obtusely. Capricorn is not a tease and is unlikely to drink and leave.

Other propositions worth considering:

"I have an excellent bottle of port back at my place. Should we go home and pop the cork?"

"I have a fabulous book on this subject back at my place which I really want to lend you; why not come back to my place and get it now?"

"How about inviting me back to your place for a cup of coffee?"

Seduction 3: The Explicit Contract

Naturally hormonal Capricorn can have a very businesslike approach to sex and may have trouble understanding the coochy-cooing that other signs require to become sexually aroused. Why do you need hearts and flowers? Why do you need to be wined and dined, flattered and romanced?

In fact, Capricorns can be so fed up with the hoopla many others need for sexual arousal that they may even have fantasies about businesslike sex, and encounters devoid of pseudoromance and social ritual.

This suggests seduction via the explicit contract: the businesslike proposal, one of the most direct of the direct methods. The prerequisites are preparedness on your part to forgo romantic lead-ins, willingness to be honest, and an ego strong enough to take it if they say, "Thanks but no thanks." The safety net here is that even should Capricorn turn you down, they so much value discretion and privacy themselves that they are unlikely to blow the whistle on you.

You might start this seduction by stating how attracted you are to them, followed immediately by a let's-give-it-a-go, no-obligation-to-commit proposition:

"Look, I'm only in the country/state for a few days [weeks, months]. I'm very attracted to you. You really turn me on. Let's go to bed. Even if it doesn't last forever, I think it could be great for both of us. We can still be friends afterward."

"Listen, both our lives are really hectic at the moment. Neither of us has time for an all-out relationship just now. But I'm very attracted to you and I think—I hope—you are to me. How about one night or day a week? Or one weekend a month. What do you say?"

"I'm really attracted to you. You drive me crazy. Why don't we go away together for a weekend? If the chemistry's there, we'll talk about what to do about it afterward. If it's not, hell, we'll still have a great weekend."

As with all Capricorn seductions, they want to know you are trustworthy and the aftermath will be benign. You have to convince them you will be discretion incarnate. If you can do this, you may well pull off Seduction by Businesslike Proposition.

Seduction 4: The Ultra-Private Seduction

With a Capricorn, it is often safest to plan the seduction at home. If it is your home, you must get rid of any other inhabitants for the night or the weekend.

You might like to make it clear that you are taking the phone off the hook so that you won't be disturbed. And switch off the beeper.

Total privacy and discretion. And the best of everything. Of course, you will have stocked up on all the goodies, wine and sweets they like. They will feel acknowledged and appreciated. If you are ignorant of their favorites, go for a top-quality selection. They will notice. Anything that has taken you time and care will earn you points. Fresh towels, linens, you may even consider ironing the sheets.

If you've gotten this far, it should be smooth sailing from here on.

Seduction 5: The Seduce-Me

The Seduce-Me is a reverse seduction in which you seduce the other person by inveigling them to seduce you.

This is a time-honored method among women. Since the beginning of time men have exulted in having seduced women who have actually seduced them.

Armed with the arcane knowledge that no matter how standoffish the Capricorn exterior, there is a time bomb ticking in their underwear, you can feel confident in lighting their fuse. Consider the following selections from the tinderbox:

Seduce-Me Seduction (i): The Veiled Hint: A veiled hint puts out the message that you're available and interested. "I haven't had a relationship for six months . . . I'm tired of dining alone . . . I want to break up this deep and meaningful relationship I'm having with my VCR . . . I can't hold hands with my stocks and bonds underneath the table . . . I want to snuggle up to something besides my teddy bear . . ."

Seduce-Me Seduction (ii): The Unveiled Hint. The advantage here is that you can pull out a blueprint of exactly how you'd like your jewels burgled. "I've always wanted to be ravished under a wisteria vine on a hot summer night . . . I just want someone to take me away for a weekend, somewhere quiet where my tensions and inhibitions can just melt away . . . I've never met a man/woman imaginative enough to . . . [fill in your fantasy]."

Seduce-Me Seduction (iii): Seduction by Seduction by the Stars. Buy a second copy of this book, circle the seduction you would most like to have performed on you, and send it to your Capricorn. In the front, write, "I'm a [whatever your Sun sign is]." You may also add, "I'm free Saturday."

A major warning with these Seduce-Me Seductions is that if you outline some specific seduction scenario and then get cold feet at the last moment and pull out, the Capricorn will label you unreliable, unstable, dishonorable and then you'll never get them in the sack.

Seduction 6: The Modified Vamp

Being naturally hormonal, Capricorn men are susceptible to being vamped (see the Vamp, Scorpio). The rider here is that this shouldn't be done in such a way as to bring attention to them in public. Unlike Scorpio, they won't be turned on by being vamped at their parents' place, for instance. Also they don't want to be vamped just for the sake of the wicked titillation of it—they will want to race you off on the spot, so make sure it's in private or somewhere private is at hand.

Seduction 7: The Marcel Marceau

Capricorns don't like a lot of chatter during sex—or before either. So why not try the silent seduction? One silent seduction is via touching and kissing. (See the Cuddle Litmus Test, Pisces.) You could also see what you can achieve by look and gesture alone.

Consider this progression: Gaze into their eyes. If they return your gaze, smile slightly. If they smile back, allow a glint to appear in your eyes. If their eyes answer you back, raise an eyebrow. If their smile broadens, tilt your head toward the door. If they respond by look or gesture, you're on.

A perfect Capricorn romance.

Seduction 8: The Disseminator

In general, Capricorns don't have the Aries fascination with initiation—the production-line deflowering of virgins. However, a typical Capricorn fantasy is the *training* of some (presumably young) sexual partner from the bottom up, as it were.

If you are interested in a Capricorn and need to further your sexual education, you can appeal to them to disseminate their knowledge. Come across as a willing student. Remember, you don't have to paint it in the most romantic light for Capricorn. They understand a businesslike approach to sex. You might even say, "Look, I really like you and am attracted to you. I don't know much about sex. I need someone to teach me."

And vice versa. If you have your sights on an inexperienced Capricorn, well, Capricorns are always eager to hone their skills. Suggest that you would like to be their sexual teacher—why don't the two of you put in some labwork? Definitely worth a shot.

Other good Capricorn seductions:

The Pounce (see Aries—but it must be in private)

The Tom Jones (Taurus)

The Instant Seduction (see Gemini—but not the Absolutely Instant variation unless you can ensure privacy)

The Fax of Love (Gemini)

The Wild Escapade (see Gemini—but only during annual vacations)

The Tasteful Dirty Weekend (Leo)

Seduction by Assumption (Libra)

The Stop-I-Can't-Wait (Sagittarius)

The I'm-Available (Sagittarius)

The Reassurance of Freedom (Aquarius)

Sex with a Capricorn

■ ■ ■

Once the bedroom door is shut and they can drop their public persona with their pants, Capricorn is unlikely to be shy.

Capricorns want all aspects of their lives to improve with time and practice—and that includes sex. They can't understand people who say, "Well, you can't expect it to be as good as it was in the beginning." Of course they can't understand. Capricorns expect it to get *better*. Capricorns believe *everything* improves with practice. Lots of practice. Lots and lots and lots of it.

At their best, they are highly educable, always willing to learn new things and usually very attentive to the needs of their partner. They aim to give satisfaction.

Capricorns have sexual appetites that can only be satisfied by regular banquets. They are most famous—or notorious—for their staying power.

They are keen to acquire a wide erotic repertoire and probably prepared to try out any position you can cope with.

The same cannot be said for venues, however. They are not at all into public sex—even sex in a secluded wilderness may be too public for many Capricorns.

Yet they are not puritanical and pride themselves on being reasonable. They are unlikely to think you're a fast girl or a Don Juan because you've clocked up a few sexual partners in the past.

For Capricorns, sex is the best and cheapest entertainment in town. They see sex and passion as normal. They are rarely interested in the deviant or the perverse. If you want to be severely spanked, find yourself a Scorpio. Anything beyond light bondage is almost certainly out. Partners who must have kinky gear or crazy scenarios in order to crack their whip fill Capricorns with distaste. While they are accommodating and willing to try out new things, naturally hormonal Capricorn will regard you as too strange to be desirable if your hormones can only be fired up through kink.

Nor do they usually want a running commentary during sex. Brief them about what you want at other times, and they will remember at debriefing sessions.

If you are not already convinced you know it all, if you are aware that there is more you would like to learn, an older Capricorn could be your best teacher. They are patient; they won't be put off by inexperience as long as you show an aptitude for learning.

Mind you, if you don't have a strong sex drive yourself and tend to lose sexual interest after the first few episodes, Capricorn may be too much for you to handle.

The thing most likely to interfere with your sex life is that terrible four-letter word: "work." Capricorns can be disgusting workaholics. At their worst, they inflate the importance of work out of all proportion. They tend to be overly aware that they have to work very hard in youth to reap rewards later on. This is a big recommendation for the older Capricorn, who is more likely to have the job scene in perspective. Especially in youth, Capricorns are the sign most likely to want to jump up straight after sex and go back to work.

Capricorns can also go through periods where they do not seem to have the energy for sex—usually because the energy is being diverted to work or family. It is also common for adult Capricorns to go through periods of sexual starvation.

For bouts of maximum protracted passion, get them away from it all. Your best bet is a vacation away from home. Capricorns tend to bring their work home with them, and they constantly see all the jobs that need doing around the house and feel obliged to do them promptly. Take them completely away from all responsibility.

Take them to a quiet spot—somewhere your Capricorn can focus on your charms. Capricorn is an Earth sign. Take them where they can get back to Mother Nature. Borrow a friend's cabin in the woods or cottage on the beach. No work to do at all. A good night's sleep, and let the naturally horny Capricorn nature take its course.

How to Handle a Relationship with a Capricorn

■ ■ ■

Capricorn is a sign of hidden depths. That stoic Capricorn with the efficient manner, the responsible attitude, the rational approach to life, the career, the ambitions—who would suspect the sexual beast under the business suit? Who would guess the grandiose dreamer behind the restrained facade?

And who would ever imagine that all this cool, rational, controlled exterior covers up a deeply unhappy childhood?

Capricorn's ruling planet is serious Saturn, the origin of the adjective "saturnine"—often used to describe Capricorns. They can be terribly dour and are prone to bouts of black depression, which they privately kick themselves for not being able to govern. It embarrasses a Capricorn to lose control. The causes of their black moods lie in childhood.

Depressions come about when a person's inner child feels in a no-win situation. Capricorns were so often in a no-win situation in childhood that it makes them vulnerable to depressions throughout their life. Probably more than any other Sun sign, Capricorns are likely to have had emotionally or even physically deprived childhoods. They are never ones to say, "Back to the good old days of childhood"—because most Capricorns didn't have childhoods they would want to return to.

The key to understanding your Capricorn partner is to realize that they were deeply aware as children that their childhood was unfair: perhaps they weren't appreciated by their mother or father, or their siblings got favored treatment, they were less loved, less looked after or had responsibilities placed on them that their siblings didn't have. They carry inside them deep psychological scars. "Life is unfair," they believe. "Other people don't appreciate me; I'm not lovable; other people are better off without me."

To have a rich relationship with a Capricorn, it is very important that they get the emotional support they didn't enjoy when they were young. Convince them that you are dependable, that when they need you—when they are ill or down and out—you will be there. Mother them when they need it. Help show them that it may be too late to have a happy childhood, but it's never too late to have a happy adulthood.

Key tip: Convince them that they are appreciated—that you see and value their virtues.

Capricorns need to be persuaded that they are appreciated by their current partner. This is one of the Sun signs most easily persuaded that they are being taken for granted. Always thank them. Tell them frequently how much they add to your life.

The injustices of their own childhoods often make them obsessed with being fair to others. This can be at their own emotional cost when they get involved with more manipulative signs. Injustice is also perhaps the major cause of Capricorn depressions—unjust treatment from loved ones or from life. They are deeply hurt by lying, the breaking of promises, the betrayal of trust.

Capricorn depressions can be frightening in their depth. They can plunge into complete existential despair: "What's the point of it all, the universe is unfair, God hates me." There is a deep well of sadness in the Capricorn soul. Capricorns know the meaning of loneliness. Many Capricorns have to learn how to be happy. This is why the second half of a Capricorn's life is typically much better than the first.

The bright side of Capricorn depressions (so to speak) is that they don't usually blame other people for them. They just endure them as best they can. If a Capricorn depression is really starting to get you down, you could try warning them that it is starting to depress *you*. Nine times out of ten, ultraresponsible Capricorn will somehow wrench themselves out of depression because they feel guilty about bringing you down.

However, in the end, if you really want your relationship with a Capricorn to last, *do not make them feel responsible for your emotions.* Say to them: "You're not responsible for my emotional reactions—I am. My feelings aren't your responsibility." A Capricorn will love you for that.

Key tip: Set yourself up as a refuge from their world of responsibilities.

For Capricorns in particular, their sexual relationship needs to be a source of joy—not drama.

Capricorns are ambivalent about intimacy. They crave it, yet they fear it. They fear being hurt and betrayed through trusting others.

Also they deeply fear hurting others. This is one reason they hesitate to let out their anger. They loathe losing their temper, and typically it will take an awful lot to make them do so. Then they will castigate themselves for losing control.

Prone to depression they are, but don't make the mistake of thinking that they are humorless—far from it. Capricorns have a dry, withering sense of humor. They love understated, telling delivery. They are often masters of satire and the drop-dead line. George Burns, Ted Danson, Cary Grant, Victor Borge, and Charles Addams (originator of "The Addams Family")— Capricorns all.

But it is vital to understand the difference between satire and ridicule. Capricorns might humorously satirize someone and accept others satirizing them. However, they won't ridicule other people so . . .

Key tip: Never ever ridicule a Capricorn.

Capricorns hate to be humiliated, especially in public. Never speak deprecatingly about them behind their backs. It is the quickest way to be dropped like a ton of bricks and frozen by the Capricorn ice.

They are also severely underimpressed by displays of anger and by nagging.

Key tip: Never nag a Capricorn.

They heard you. If you want to influence them, present your thoughts in a rational manner and give them time to consider. They will give the matter fair thought. They won't forget.

Because of their sense of fair play and objectivity, the best of Capricorns are prepared to work on themselves to make a relationship succeed.

It is only because they are trying to protect themselves from possible hurts that they come across as emotionally cold or unapproachable. They cover up their vulnerabilities with cool cynicism. It can often be hard to win the trust of a Capricorn and get them to open up. You'll never find a Capricorn with their heart on their sleeve. That's for Cancer, their opposite sign.

Try to understand that under that Mount Rushmore exterior often beats the heart of a true romantic. Remember the adage: "Cynicism is the last refuge of the true romantic." Capricorns are often badly hurt in early love relationships. Indeed, they very rarely find their true love early in life. It is a big mistake to think that the well-controlled Capricorn is not sensitive. If you criticize a Capricorn they will often take it very hard and get very depressed over it. They take criticism seriously and, if they decide it is justified, will aim to do something about it. This is a warning. Be reasonable. Don't ask for what you don't want.

All Capricorns have secret dreams and long-term ambitions. If they share their secret ambitions with you, it is a sign that they trust you and have faith in you. You must never belittle their ambition or suggest that it is out of their reach. They are like the plodding tortoise who somehow always overtakes the apparently brilliant hare. Above all, you must never reveal their secret dreams to other people. They will never trust you again and the relationship will start to wither from that moment—or be terminated forthwith.

As their childhoods were so often unfair and out of their control, Capricorns try to win in life by being in control. They try to create certainty, order and structure in an uncertain universe. They hate to feel powerless or dependent on others. They hate the feeling that anyone else is calling the shots. They try to control life by planning, self-discipline, hard work, the accumulation of knowledge, power and money—seeking honor and success in the external world to compensate for the lack of love, justice and attention in their childhoods.

They have quite a puritanical, self-critical streak, and although they want sex and money they often beat themselves up in the pursuit of them.

The best of Capricorns have a character born from adversities faced and overcome. They are often courageous, persistent, self-disciplined, noble, dignified.

Capricorns are born with a strong sense of purpose in life and a desire to leave their mark on the planet. Many a Capricorn has worked out their ideal life path before graduating cum laude from kindergarten. Unfortunately, many sell out on this dream and get trapped by their desire for security in an unsatisfying job.

Capricorn is not, by any stretch of the imagination, a lucky sign. Capricorns tend to pay for every mistake and they generally have to work for everything they get in life. This includes their self-esteem: they are not naturally confident; their self-confidence develops from decades of effort.

They can become envious of other people's luck and wonder why they don't have it. Capricorns often work very hard from a young age and wonder why the breaks don't go their way. They do—but later rather than sooner. Capricorn is the sign of the late bloomer, and life generally gets easier for them after forty. They are well advised to think about slowing down and enjoying life now rather than putting off being happy until they have earned the right.

In their quest for order, Capricorns can become iron-fisted dictators whose chief tactic is manipulation through guilt (a tactic learned from their parents). Richard Nixon, Stalin, Idi Amin and Mao Tse-tung were all Capricorns. They are not primarily remembered as great comedians.

Capricorns can also have a deadpan, matter-of-fact, take-it-or-leave-it way of expressing their opinions that can cause other people to see them as know-it-alls. This may be a mistake. They tend to regard it as your problem if you don't take their advice. Sir Isaac Newton, a Capricorn, was once involved in a discussion with Edmond Halley (of comet fame). Halley was pooh-poohing Newton's respect for astrology. Newton is reputed to have said, "Sir, I have studied the matter and you have not," promptly turning on his heel and leaving the room. This sums up the Capricorn attitude to argument. They will state their opinion and their reasons for it but have no interest in battering open closed minds. They do not tilt at intellectual windmills.

A final tip: Capricorns loathe inefficiency. You will never have a Capricorn's full respect unless you demonstrate competence and efficiency—especially in your work.

Capricorns need a partner who can help them learn how to live for today instead of tomorrow and how to have fun for fun's sake. If you can do this, if you have a strong sex drive, if you're honest and reliable, you're well on your way to having a great—perhaps lifelong—relationship with a Capricorn.

Must-Do's

Never fail to express appreciation of them.
Take responsibility for your own emotions and life.
Draw a clear line between your private and public lives.

No-No's

Don't add to their heavy load of responsibilities.

Never indulge in socially offensive behavior.

Never criticize them in public. Loyalty is highly prized among Capricorns. Save any criticism for a private moment.

How to End a Relationship with a Capricorn

■ ■ ■

The key to ending a relationship with a Capricorn is honesty and integrity. Capricorns can forgive a lot. When you break up with them, it may crack their stoic hearts for a while; their stiff upper lip will tremble. Even so, it generally won't alter their high opinion of you. But . . .

You can throw up on their brand-new carpet, you can even insult their taste in music and they won't blink. But . . .

Capricorn is actually one of the most tolerant signs. They have been known to put up with foibles that would make other signs murderous. But . . .

But . . . if you lie to a Capricorn, if you break promises to a Capricorn, if you repay loyalty with disloyalty, if you cheat them financially or, worst of the worst, if you go around gossiping behind a Capricorn's back, revealing embarrassing personal details or casting aspersions on their integrity . . . well, you deserve what you get.

Capricorns will not forgive betrayal and backstabbing. Like elephants, they never forget. As they value loyalty and consistency so highly, the betrayal of loyalty is felt in the deepest, darkest, saturnine realms of the Capricorn soul. They will brood on it; they will not forget. They may try to forgive but they won't be able to.

They may not admit it, but we assure you that a wronged or humiliated Capricorn subscribes to the eye-for-an-eye ethic. Worse still, they are shrewd enough to realize that a truly rewarding revenge may not be immediately possible. They have been known to wait thirty years.

So if you have committed one of the ultimate wrongs, be warned. First, instantly and irrevocably, Capricorn will freeze over like the South Pole.

Capricorn can refrigerate the exterior emotions like no other sign. There will be no communication, no postmortems, no recriminations, no let's-talk-it-through, no teary displays. *But* . . .

It may take twenty years, it may take thirty years, but paying you back will never be erased from their agenda. They don't believe life is fair and that you will get the comeuppance you so richly deserve. They believe the scales must be balanced. They're not prepared to leave it to karma.

Unlike Scorpios, Capricorns find it unnatural to go around plotting theatrical methods of revenge. It offends their sense of dignity. However, as Capricorns know, the world turns; and if an opportunity to exact revenge should present itself—months, years, or even decades later—then they will quietly do some small invisible thing that turns the life of the Judas from heaven to purgatory.

Remember the 1987 office Christmas party when you humiliated your Capricorn girlfriend by racing off with one of the very junior secretaries? Ms. Capricorn just turned to ice and never spoke one word of recrimination. Okay, maybe she's never given you the time of day since, but she's never attacked you either. This Capricorn woman somehow worked her way to a position above yours. The company is now restructuring—and you'll never know that it was Ms. Lucretia Capricorn Borgia who dropped a comment in the right ear at the wrong time and got you vocationally redirected to the unemployment lines.

So now you've been warned. Do not betray or humiliate a Capricorn's trust.

To break up with a Capricorn, be honest, be open, don't recriminate, keep your nose clean, and if you haven't done anything cruel or underhanded, they may well remain a reliable friend for the rest of your life.

Capricorns at Their Best

■ ■ ■

You have found a partner with emotional consistency, a sense of fair play, reliability, dry wit and sex drive above and beyond the call of duty. You will have a lover you can lean on in bad times and with whom you can enjoy increasingly good times as they mellow and improve with age. With encouragement, they will also display their loving, giving, romantic heart. You will be impressed at how they try to make their own life and your relationship better and better.

Capricorns at Their Worst

■ ■ ■

You will feel like a corporate widow or widower as your emotional and sexual life take a distant backseat to their endless march up the hill of achievement. You may feel you're in a relationship with a printed résumé rather than a human being. You will crave for them to open up their heart and trust you. The dour, cold, materialistic, frequently depressed and depressing Capricorn will weigh down your soul. You will despair that it would take a major archaeological dig to find their heart. You will hunger for more romance, more fun, more warmth, more trust, more spontaneity and more silliness in your life with someone who is not a sad sack and a party pooper.

Sexy Capricorns

■ ■ ■

Marlene Dietrich, Muhammad Ali, Elvis Presley, Howard Hughes, Anthony Hopkins, Isaac Newton, Joan of Arc, Martin Luther King, Jr., Gypsy Rose Lee, Cary Grant, Lord Byron, Ava Gardner, David Bowie, Humphrey Bogart, Kevin Costner, Mel Gibson, Dolly Parton, Ted Danson, Sissy Spacek, Donna Summer.

Unsexy Capricorns

■ ■ ■

Aristotle Onassis, Richard Nixon, Josef Stalin, Joe Frazier, Shari Lewis, Oliver Hardy, Mao Tse-tung, Janis Joplin, Ethel Merman, Mary Tyler Moore, George Burns, Idi Amin, J. Edgar Hoover, Hermann Goering, John Denver.

AQUARIUS

January 21st to February 19th

•••

Hang loose, hang free,

hang out, hangups.

The Lure of an Aquarius

■ ■ ■

Are you tired of partners who want to own you body and soul? Who want to monopolize all your free time? Are you weary of relationships in which you feel trapped? Wouldn't you just love a relationship with someone who wasn't trying to handcuff you to them? With someone who really, truly understands your need to be free and to be your own person?

Well, consider the attractions of breezy, independent, unpossessive Aquarius.

If you want a freewheeling relationship with someone who will give you space and won't talk about settling down and getting married on the third date, why not give friendly, open, zany Aquarius a try?

Indeed, their emotional aloofness and detachment can drive people positively wild with a desire to get them on their backs—or stomachs.

Moreover, here is a Sun sign you don't have to impress with a big-time front, someone from whom you won't have to hide your oddities and eccentricities. Indeed, that's what they'll like about you—that you are different. They won't mind that you're an unemployed actor with tattooed feet or a struggling musician with an earring in your nose—in fact, that makes you all the more *interesting*.

Indeed, you'll find yourself positively showered with interest and compliments. Mind you, they're also very interested in that person staring into space so intently, and see that girl expounding on the effect of Jupiter on the stock market or that man with the dreadlocks and John Lennon glasses. Must meet them—they would be fascinating.

Aquarians are interested in everyone—that is, everyone who does something interesting or has something interesting to say. They are particularly impressed by anyone who is brave enough to sweep away convention in search of the truth.

Aquarians are rarely snobs. Informal, inquisitive and humanitarian, they are as happy to share a bag of potato chips with the men working in the street as to dine on trout with diplomats.

Like the other two Air signs, Gemini and Libra, Aquarius feeds off ideas and generally has a plethora of views on how to fix up the world and how technology is creating the postindustrial society and whether society as we know it is of any use at all and perhaps we should restructure the whole thing or all drop out and become anarchists or revolutionaries—or just build mud-brick houses.

Aquarians like to think of themselves as futurologists and visionaries. If you want to discuss the fate of humanity, where it's all headed, whether the Aquarian Age has started—or whether it ever will—Aquarians are happy to talk about it before, after—and often instead of—sex.

But hold on to your amethyst crystals. If this doesn't sound like an Aquarian you know, there is a perfectly sound astrological reason. Aquarius is ruled by two very different planets:

Uranus, which is the planet of eccentricity, innovation, individuality, humanity, personal freedom, originality, the New Age and the loathing of mediocrity.

Saturn, which is the planet of practicality, structure, organization, restriction and tradition.

The Uranus-dominated Aquarian is the latter-day hippie whose T-shirt reads "Don't fence me in" and whose motto is "Let's play it by ear." These Aquarians don't want to be locked into responsibility. They find interpersonal devotion and closeness very claustrophobic and are mortally afraid of dependency.

By contrast, the Saturn-dominated Aquarian will be more like a Capricorn—more conservative, serious, materialistic, security-obsessed, eager to appear ordinary and respectable if not to be invisible. Unfortunately, they lack the famous Capricorn libido and tend to come across as uptight worriers. Frankly, if you're hormonal enough to be reading this book, you are unlikely to be in pursuit of an overly Saturn-dominated Aquarian.

The ideal Aquarian will have the forces of wild Uranus and practical Saturn in balance.

How to Interest an Aquarius

■ ■ ■

Key tactic: Come across as being independent, individualistic and ahead of your time.

Aquarians are looking for someone beyond the norm. You have to strike them as being a cut above the mundane. It could be that you have made a million from ethical investments—that would intrigue them. But it might fascinate them just as much if you were a dropout from the civil service eking out a living painting waterproof pictures on surfboards and planning how to turn this into an international business.

Artists, people on the fringe of mainstream society and those in the vanguard of new fields fascinate them: composers, poets, spokespersons for minority groups, refugees, drug counselors, research scientists.

They are interested in the bizarre and unusual. Quickly slip into the conversation some mention of one of your unique talents or interests that is well beyond steak-and-potatoes suburbia.

Even if they themselves don't have the guts or opportunity to drop out and say to hell with the establishment, they admire tremendously people who do. So make scathing remarks about yuppies and their trendoid habitats—boardrooms, BMWs, dance clubs and Club Med. Declare disdain for whatever is popular at the moment. Highlight the odd and eccentric in your nature. Lay bare your antiestablishment tendencies. Reveal your countercultural tastes. Drape yourself in Moroccan or Tibetan clothing or jewelry, wear Indian sandals, talk about the ashram you lived in for six months, your investment in a water-purifier factory, the book you're reading on how people who drop out of college are smarter and make more money, how you're writing a computer program on stock-market cycles.

Don't appear limited, predictable, average, boring or conformist.

Earning a big salary or being rich is desirable—after all, money buys the freedom Aquarians love so much—but make sure they know you've got a nonconformist streak. A combination dropout and financial genius. Great! A self-made software-wizard millionaire who wears frayed jeans and is into macrobiotics. Divine! A rich hippie. Perfect!

If you do happen to work for a multinational or you're (shudder!) a civil servant, make sure they realize you are a force for change within the bosom of the establishment. Admit you've got a reputation as a rebel. Aquarians love to send up the establishment, especially if they're part of it themselves. Your biting new joke about politicians or public figures could be very well received.

Aquarians have no time for social sham—your Giorgio Armani won't necessarily impress. They can be quite stingy—and tasteless—when it comes to their own clothing. This is why some middle-aged Aquarians look like remnants from the sixties; often they are still wearing the jeans, sandals and shoulder bag they wore to Woodstock or Ban-the-Bomb marches.

Key tip: The way to get an Aquarian interested in you is primarily through their passion for talking.

They like a good talker and a good listener. They are good listeners themselves because they are interested in everyone and everything—but they expect to be listened to as well.

Don't hesitate to plunge tongue-first into intense exchanges on politics, sex or religion. There are no inhibitions in Aquarian conversations. When you sense you've hit on a subject they are passionate about say, "I'm really into this, you know. I really want to know more about it. Why don't I come around to your place tomorrow with a bottle of wine and some take-out Chinese so we can talk some more?" Aquarians love a free meal and usually don't enjoy cooking, so the prospect of your bringing over the food and wine will be most appealing.

The next morning, quickly bone up on whatever the topic of conversation was. (Probably how to fix the world, how to get rich quick, how to drop out of society—or how to do all three simultaneously.)

Aquarians are very big on how to fix the world. Please note that this does not mean they are interested in getting involved in hands-on stuff. They have strong opinions on what should be done to help the Third World but don't feel compelled to go there personally and distribute food to the starving—and so risk coming face-to-face with malaria, tuberculosis and exotic microbes.

Another worthwhile ploy is to find out in advance that they are an Aquarian, then positively stun them by "guessing" their Sun sign. Tell them you are studying astrology and that you'd like to apply your burgeoning skills to their horoscope. You're certain their horoscope must contain unique, if not extraordinary, aspects. The average Aquarian will glow at the mention of their uniqueness. They'll also be tempted by the idea of a *free* reading.

Suggested opening line: "Hi. I'm . . . I had to come over and say hello because you have this aura of great energy. Can I get you a drink?"

What to talk about: The New World Order, the future of the United Nations, protest marches, the need for personal freedom, the social impact of computers and other new technology, social and power dynamics at your work or their work or anywhere else, ethically sound investments, conspiracy theories, whether Big Brother is watching us, how to make a lot of money easily and drop out and grow your own vegetables, the latest machinations in Washington, Marxism, the price of gold, the stock market.

Where to take them: Coffee shops for intense talks, restaurants (remember Aquarians only cook under duress), back to your place for a meal cooked by you, Greenpeace meetings, Amnesty International meetings, bookshops, weekend flea markets, most New Age venues. Aquarians can be more than a bit allergic to what they see as the close, suffocating aspects of personal relationships, so don't make the mistake of taking them to visit your mother with a view to sitting around making small talk over tea and scones.

What to give them: Ethnic jewelry and clothing, crystal pendants, a futon, unusual decorative items or curios either antique or futuristic, books on popular science, books on science fiction, books on where the world and humanity is heading, personal growth books, books on contemporary gurus, books on inventions, books on how to think and grow rich, books on avant-garde poets—in fact, books on just about anything.

How to Seduce an Aquarius

■ ■ ■

There is only one commandment for those who set out to seduce an Aquarian: "Verily thou shalt impress deeply upon them that thou art not out to entrap them nor doth thou intend to move in with them nor art thou out to change their lifestyle in even the smallest way."

Make sure they fully realize that you don't equate a naughty weekend with a prenuptial agreement. Aquarians have a cautious eye out for anyone trying to annex their freedom. This aversion to feeling fenced in often keeps Aquarians celibate for long periods. This is the sign most likely to pull back from togetherness and sentimentality. They like to have an escape hatch ready and waiting.

It's not that Aquarians have moral qualms about sex. Any pulling back from sex is generally connected with their fear of being owned and their fear of exposing themselves in any way—mentally or physically. It is not uncommon for Aquarians to be so "free-spirited" that they have two or three relationships going simultaneously. Mind you, they probably wouldn't call these "relationships"—too many connotations of closeness.

Doing it on the first date may not be seen as vulgar or loose by an Aquarian—just the way to go. If the chemistry is right, go with the flow and don't be worried about being seen as promiscuous.

Aquarians will try to protect their freedom above all else. They are quite likely to say, "I don't know where this is heading . . . I'm not ready for a permanent relationship . . . You realize I don't know how long this will last . . . I'm not at a point in my life where I feel I can make a long-term commitment."

You must *wholeheartedly* and *completely* agree with anything they say about the need for space and personal freedom. You must indicate that in this regard you are entirely of like mind. You might even preempt them by saying, "I don't want a 'relationship.' I just want to go with the moment." It might be salutary to avoid the word "relationship" altogether—especially if they do, which is likely.

But, if the "R" word should arise, reassure them that no matter how long the whatever-this-is lasts, you will always be their friend. Aquarians have been known to forgo having sex with people they are highly attracted to because they "liked" them. They may even say: "I'm attracted to you but I really like you and I don't want to risk ruining our friendship."

You might try pointing out to them that the corollary of this attitude is that they would end up only going to bed with people they didn't like! This appeal to logic in itself might be a leg-opener. Remember, Aquarians are turned on by intellect.

Be prepared to help talk them through all their emotional doubts about jumping into the sack with you. Some Aquarians, sensing their own need for freedom, will be worried that they only feel lust toward you and will worry about "using" you.

If they express this worry, say, "Use me."

Quickly add, "I can take care of myself. I want my freedom. Use me."

If this doesn't break their freedom obsession, give up.

Once you've finally convinced them that you're not going to propose marriage or move in, it should be pretty clear sailing after that. They will literally breathe a sigh of relief.

If the seduction is to take place at your place, put your most bizarre and unusual trinkets from around the world on display. More importantly, you must remove from display any absorbing reading matter that they could pick up and become fascinated by. They are quite capable of burying their nose in a book until three in the morning or, worse still, borrowing it and waltzing immediately out the door to go home and read it.

A final warning: be prepared to take full responsibility for contraception.

Seduction 1: The Reassurance of Freedom

As freedom at all costs is so important to Aquarians, it is wise to consider using a seduction technique that guarantees their freedom—or at least loosens them up so much that they temporarily let go of this obsession. Here are three suggestions:

Seduction 1(a): The Friendship-Deepening Ploy. The idea here is to convince the Aquarian that hopping into the sack with you will only deepen your friendship. Say something like "I feel our friendship is so deep and special that the only way we can deepen it any further is to take it to a physical level. I've always become better friends with every person I've been to bed with."

Seduction 1(b): The Preemptive Strike for Freedom.

Knowing that the object of your desires is an Aquarian and is almost certainly freedom-obsessed, one of the best tactics is to make a preemptive strike declaring your need for freedom. "I'm really attracted to you, but, you know, I just feel the need to be free. I want you badly but I don't want to be hemmed in. Do you think there is any way we could have sex without having a relationship? Because I'm just at this stage where I really need my freedom."

Seduction 1(c): The Moving Experience.

One way to convince the Aquarian that you won't impose on their freedom is to tell them that you're only going to be living in the area for a short time. Tell them that in a month you're going overseas indefinitely—or headed to Bali for three months to just "like, you know, work things out." The fact that you are moving on means you won't be around to trap them. "It means that if we start something that it can only last a month. But hey, all the sex manuals say length doesn't matter."

Seduction 1(d): The Prior Engagement.

This is an outrageous idea for a seduction, but it has been known to work. Aquarians often have multiple relationships—that way they feel less trapped than by the emotional hothouse of a one-on-one. They don't, in turn, demand sexual fidelity from their partners. The idea behind this seduction is to make use of this Aquarian tolerance for multiple partners.

It consists of presenting yourself as already in a relationship with somebody else (but note, most importantly, not a friend of theirs). An Aquarian may be persuaded to see this as an advantage. After all, if you're in a relationship with somebody else, you won't be pressuring them emotionally. "Look, I'm in a relationship with someone but sexually they're just not enough for me. You get me so hot . . . ."

Seduction 2: Seduction by Humor

Humor is a tried-and-true tool in Aquarian seductions. It can be used to relax the Aquarian's grip on their free-flight joystick. They love the over-the-top bizarre. If you can exploit this and get them laughing, then you've got them halfway to bed. Here are a few outrageous suggestions.

Seduction 2(a): The Transcendental Fuck. Turn up in religious robes carrying a shopping bag full of candles, incense and a picture of Krishna with the cowherd girls. Tell Aquarius that you have just received a transmission from your guru/spirit-guide/deceased-but-psychic Aunt Martha in which the Aquarian's name was mentioned. There is a unique astrological configuration that very night linking the Aquarian constellation with your own. The two of you must physically and spiritually conjoin that night to achieve samadhi in this lifetime.

Seduction 2(b): The We'll-Have-Nun-of-This. Come dressed as a nun or a monk. Tell them you are entering a convent/seminary the next day and you've come for a first and final fling before taking your vows. Say that you're a virgin and must experience sex so that you know what it is you're renouncing. Tell them you need something worth confessing for the next forty years.

Seduction 2(c): The Twilight Zone Naughty. Come dressed as a Martian. Talk in robotic tones. "I have been sent by the Intergalactic Council to commence sexual relations between our species, to investigate the possibility of intergalactic sexual compatibility. You have been selected to conjoin with me because you have been analyzed and found to be the best lay on the planet." Hopefully, they'll be so taken with your sense of daring that they'll play along and boink you just to join in on the outrageousness of it all.

Seduction 3: The Freebie

This is mainly a good one for women to try on Aquarian males. It appeals to Aquarians on many levels: it goes beyond bourgeois values, it guarantees their personal freedom and it offers them something for free.

Turn up dressed as a high-class call girl. Tell your Aquarian you are actually a hooker who works from home and generally solicits her clients by newspaper ads. Tell him you give free trials to potential regular clients. Say you are his for the night to use in any way he wants. Absolutely free and with no obligation.

At what stage you explode this myth is up to you. Maybe you can keep it going for a few nights. Hey, maybe it'll bring in some pocket money.

Even if he doesn't believe your story and laughs, he may still play along just for the outrageousness of it. Turn it into Seduction by Humor.

Seduction 4: The We-Shouldn't-Do-This-So-Let's

Key tactic: evoke the rebellious teenager inside every Aquarian.

Like Eve, Aquarians can be tempted to bite at the forbidden apple just because it is forbidden. Forbidden fruits taste sweeter!

The idea to implant in their heads (perhaps subtly, perhaps not) is that someone they regard as an authority figure would *hate* the idea of them boinking you.

It harks back to their childhood. They are probably carrying around the usual baggage of "Mommy and Daddy wouldn't approve"; opposed to this they have the legendary Aquarian desire for rebellion.

Accordingly, they tend to think: "If Mom/Dad/the school principal/Mother Superior/the Sunday School teacher would have been shocked by it, it must be worth trying."

It's ultimately up to you how you present yourself as irresistibly illicit.

It may not be you but the venue that is the forbidden fruit. Exploit a naughty scenario. A few suggestions: the back row of the synagogue, the crypt of a cathedral with High Mass being conducted upstairs, the parents' bed, outside the window of their old school principal. Consider organizing a dirty weekend in a hotel in their hometown where they are sure to be recognized.

Use your imagination.

Seduction 5: *Cogito Ergo Fornicatio* (I Think Therefore I Hump)

This seduction makes use of the Aquarian belief that the main organ of sex is the brain. If you can engage their mind, you're well on your way to engaging their body.

If you take them back to your place, your abode needs to look like a cross between an alchemist's laboratory and an artist's garret. Have something on display on which you are working—a book, an article, a musical score, a painting, a thesis, an invention—something that will provoke an earnestly in-depth discussion. You need to get them into an impassioned discussion of something about which *you* have new and exciting ideas—preferably something you have a hands-on interest in.

You must show how this work of yours opens up new frontiers in . . . well, in anything—art, philosophy, science, literature, music, political theory, whatever. Aquarians are in love with the future, so the trick is to convince them that you are already a part of the future and an important harbinger of it. They must see you as avant-garde, new-wave, New Age, futuristic, a prophet, a genius.

Once their mind is entranced, their body will follow.

If they think you are tantamount to the next Einstein, Picasso, Beethoven, Tolstoy, Jung, Madame Curie, they may want to drop their undies on the spot. They would hate to miss out on being part of the life experience of the next Einstein. They may hope to pop up in your memoirs.

Stop abruptly in the middle of your impassioned exposition of your earth-evolving vision for the future, kiss them wildly and go from there.

Aquarians are very likely to respond to the ad hoc seduction. In fact, many Aquarians prefer it this way—nearly unpremeditated. Don't worry about making it to the bed. Take them on the table.

Seduction 6: The Experimental Seduction

Aquarians are always on the lookout for new knowledge. They are often tempted to try out new things just to see what they can learn from the experience.

See if you can use this predilection to tempt one to try out you.

Aquarians are often science freaks. Challenge them with sex as a research project. Discuss how you have become most interested in the Chinese theory that certain sexual positions can be used to heal bodily ills, heighten awareness and increase creativity. Say that you want to try an experiment to see whether it is really true that screwing for fifteen minutes in the position of "goat butts a tree" will increase creativity during the following twenty-four hours. Even if they don't believe you, they will be so impressed by the level of your bullshit, they may laugh and comply anyway. Turn it into Seduction by Humor.

Seduction 7: Seduction by Reputation

Please note that Seduction by Reputation is not to be confused with the Egomaniacal Sales Pitch (see Sagittarius).

In Seduction by Reputation, you must in no way advertise your own proficiency. The world-shaking details of your erotic virtuosity must be transmitted by members of the other sex and be subtly conveyed in the long, friendly tête-à-têtes that Aquarians so love.

You may have to prime a few friends to have coffee with the Aquarian object of your desires, during which delicious details of your sensual skills will be conveyed *sotto voce*. "I never knew what sex was before. I'd never even heard of some of the things he/she did." They must also drive home to the Aquarian that attached to your great body is an equally impressive brain.

Even if it doesn't work, don't despair. The Aquarian is bound to spread the news. You never know what you might catch. Another Aquarian (or nearby Aries or Pisces) may overhear.

Seduction 8: The "Stranded!"

An Aquarian can be lured to bed on a trail of stimulating conversation. They *love* talking.

If you've come by public transportation, you could get them talking until two in the morning, no problem. And, "Heavens, is that the time, oh dear, I've got no way to get home . . . what, no spare bed? Oh well . . . if you don't mind sharing . . . nothing heavy, of course. Which side of the bed do you . . ."

Other good Aquarian seductions:

Unexpected Bedfellows (see Aries)

The Public Provocation Proposition (Gemini)

The Fax of Love (Gemini)

The Vamp—especially the Don't-Get-Excited-Please (Scorpio)

The Mutual Mental Masturbation Method (Scorpio)

The Passport to Unscheduled Delights (Sagittarius)

The I'm-Available (Sagittarius)

The Ideologically Sound Seduction (Sagittarius)

The Marcel Marceau (Capricorn)

Portents of Passion (Pisces)

Sex with an Aquarius

■ ■ ■

If Aquarians shy away from intimacy, it is not because they don't want sex.

They are the ones most likely to say, "I'm sleeping with So-and-so, but we're not really having a relationship . . . it's nothing serious . . . I'm not ready for anything too heavy."

Especially in public, Aquarians often resist physical touching—even hand-holding. This is symptomatic of their general resistance to true emotional intimacy. They hesitate to reveal their emotional depths. For this reason, they can lack sexual abandon, trying to keep a cork on the emotional and sexual volcano that lurks underneath.

Indeed, attempts to make them emotionally intimate and to get them to open up may turn them off sexually.

What they often want is wild experimental sex *so long as it doesn't involve any danger of their exposing themselves emotionally*.

Aquarians have a deep inner need to shock people. They see it as part of their purpose in life: to jolt middle-class values with off-the-wall jokes, off-color stories and off-the-planet theories. They may try to shock you with sexual stunts they claim to have performed or claim to want to. Be prepared.

But don't get too excited by these stories. Aquarians tend to talk big about wild, abandoned, off-the-Richter-scale polymorphously perverse sex. But they aren't necessarily prepared to follow through. Their minds are open to all manner of way-out things—including way-out sex. But their bodies can be a lot shyer than their minds. Like the guy who boasts about his huge equipment, be prepared to see them come up short.

On the other hand, knowing that they are so open-minded at least gives you the scope to share your wildest sexual fantasies with them. They won't be shocked and may volunteer to help make one or two of them come true.

They like to be surprised by the new and unexpected. Read through all the seductions in this book. Try out as many as possible on your Aquarian partner. The unpredictability will keep up their interest for a long time.

Many Aquarians are techno-freaks and computer buffs. This is one sign with whom you can try out high-tech sex gadgets.

You can also try out some piece of sexual arcana on them. The response you are after is "Where did you learn that!" Refer vaguely to ancient Tantric texts or previously untranslated parts of the Kama Sutra described to you by a French Oriental scholar the last time you were in India. Most likely they'll know you are pulling their leg and get a good laugh out of it.

Aquarians have erratic habits. There are many Aquarians whose bodies don't seem to have the regular daily needs of other human beings. They sleep and eat at odd hours. This can either frustrate the hell out of you, or you can make it work to your advantage. This is the sign you can arouse at 2 a.m. for an active sexual encounter.

You wouldn't want to be depending on this relationship for regular sex two or three times a week. You may get it seven times in one week and then nothing for a month. They tend to run hot and cold. Strike while the iron is hot—and keep striking as many times as possible while it is still glowing. Keep it free and easy, keep foreplay unpredictable and be ever ready with an innovative position.

Aquarians like a good laugh. See if you can bring laughter and genuine humor into the bedroom. Keep sex fun and free—nothing too heavy or serious. Your rewards—at least on the physical level—could be great indeed.

How to Handle a Relationship with an Aquarius

■ ■ ■

Aquarians are at their best sitting on a beanbag chair holding forth on what needs to be done to raise our consciousness and rectify Third World debt.

They want to be seen as standing in the vanguard of ideas. They have a fascination with all types of humanity on all levels—with what makes people tick. They're found in the front ranks at protest marches for dolphins and demonstrations for orphans in Africa. But many don't seem to realize that charity begins at home—with their personal relationships.

They're not good at sorting out relationships. They are frequently reluctant to accept the responsibilities that go with intimacy. They find interpersonal devotion and closeness very difficult. For many, commitment is a four-letter word.

Try to emphasize that first and foremost, you will always be their friend. They are good at friendships. Indeed, you must never set yourself up so as to appear opposed to their friendships. Many an Aquarian has been known to walk away from a relationship or a marriage when they felt their partner was interfering with their friendships.

Key tactic: Don't make too many demands on them.

The way to go is free and easy. Observe the great Aquarian maxim: Hang loose.

Never say, "I'm her boyfriend," or "I'm his girlfriend." Too possessive. It can make them feel trapped—as if you were staking a claim. Expect them to introduce you as "a friend"—and introduce yourself that way.

They are not big touchers and cuddlers. They find it cloying. At parties, don't stick to them like a Band-Aid, don't put your arm around them too often, don't stop them from mingling.

Even though they are the "freedom freaks" of the Zodiac, they are also a fixed Sun sign—one of the major areas of their fixity being freedom. They will doggedly cling to their right to be flexible and loose.

The worst type of Aquarian will always seem detached from the relationship—or always be attempting to detach from it. They will always be moving to somewhere further away from you—if not physically, then emotionally.

They can come to dominate you and the relationship via this emotional aloofness. In this way they protect themselves from hurt and subtly exercise power over you at the same time. You are the one always chasing them, trying to make the relationship work, trying to make the compromises, trying to fit in with them, trying not to "impose."

Be warned: they are notorious for turning up when you need them least and disappearing when you need them most. They may not phone you for weeks on end and then breeze in as if they saw you yesterday. (However, if they haven't phoned you for six months, you probably can deduce that the relationship is over.)

Aquarians are notorious for discussing all aspects of their intimate relationships at length with their friends—but won't talk about their feelings to the person they are in a relationship with.

You must expect your Aquarian to have some wacky habits. They are famous for frying bacon and eggs or ordering pizza at 3 a.m. Many of their meals can't easily be labeled breakfast, lunch or dinner. "Play it by ear" is their watchword. You should always call up before a prearranged date to confirm that it is still on and that they are still in the mood and still living in the same place.

Aquarians tend to equate housework with drudgery and see the kitchen as a small prison. Be wary if they invite you to dinner. Nine times out of ten, this will be a nominal gesture to repay your hospitality. They are rarely good cooks and tend to see cooking as a form of penal servitude. If they invite you over for a meal, don't arrive hungry. Snack beforehand. The meal is unlikely to hit the table on schedule. You may even end up cooking it yourself. And be prepared to eat whatever's going. Don't give prior warning of any dishes you hate or are allergic to. You will be perceived as fussy and demanding. Then again, you could volunteer to do the cooking—after all, that's what they were hoping to hear.

If you want someone who'll do their fair share of home cooking, you'll be severely disappointed. Unless you're an enthusiastic cook yourself, it's better to plan lots of meals out—Aquarians don't mind slumming and they are confirmed patrons of take-out food.

Inside revelation: Aquarians are actually a good deal more interested in money than they will ever let you know.

They can be singularly tight. Usually nobody knows how much money an Aquarian has. Fancy clothes are a low priority. Many dress poorly—often foraging in secondhand shops. Lots of Aquarians look unintentionally retro. Many Aquarians talk about how poor they are and refuse to eat anywhere that's more than ten dollars a person while secretly building up a nest egg with which they hope to retire early or achieve the Aquarian nirvana of independence from job, family, partner—independence from anyone or anything.

Don't anticipate lavish presents for your birthday. They may even pretend they don't remember, or say, "I'm not into birthdays." You might try testing out this theory when their birthday comes around.

This is a symptom of one of their most common tactics: construction of a persona that provides them with an excuse for not holding up their end of a relationship.

Aquarians can chafe under responsibilities. Either mentally—or, worse, out loud—they can keep harking back to "the good ol' days" when they had no responsibilities or ties. At least that's how they remember it. They idealize this as the most blissful time of their life.

If you really want to interest an Aquarian in moving in with you, you might try emphasizing the adage: "Two can live as cheaply as one."

The highest manifestation of the Aquarian freedom ethic is: *freedom within structure*. Freedom without structure is chaos by another name. Proper organization creates more freedom, not less. You will be much valued by your Aquarian if you find ways to help them create a structure within which they can feel free. Establish your relationship as a structure that they perceive as providing them with more space and free time, not less.

Must-Do's

Expect that they will exhibit as much interest in a stranger as in you.
Be self-sufficient; they hate having demands made on them.
Respect their need for space and free time.
Learn to cook for yourself and them.
Learn where all the good take-out restaurants are.

No-No's

Never expect to be the only interest in their lives.
Never refer to yourself as their boyfriend/girlfriend/partner/lover. You are simply "a friend."

Never make demands on them that take them away from their established circle of friends. They are great believers in the saying that lovers come and go but friends are forever.

Never expect to be included in family gatherings.

Never expect a home-cooked meal.

Never expect TLC when you are sick.

Avoid talking commitment.

How to End a Relationship with an Aquarius

■ ■ ■

You don't usually have to worry on this score—most likely, they'll break up with you.

Aquarians are notorious for having difficulties with long-term, committed relationships. They have been known to disappear overnight (even after years of marriage) or simply stop calling. When you eventually phone them, you may find yourself in a superficial conversation that makes you feel like a casual acquaintance calling for the first time in months. "Oh, hello—how are you?"

You might have to go from being a lover to being a friend overnight—even in the course of one party.

One way for you to break up with them is to simply absent yourself. They will assume it's off after about six weeks without anybody's ever having to broach the awkward topic of relationships.

Perhaps you might have to "go off" somewhere to "you know, get in touch with myself" and "like, just work things out." Aquarians understand the idea of having to "go off" somewhere. They are very, very unlikely to pursue you to another state—or even to the next street.

They are generally quite intuitive and will often just sense that the affair has come to the end of its natural life span.

If they actually try to pin you down about why you're ending the relationship, a good idea is to say something like "I felt trapped, you know. I just felt the need to be free."

Aquarians at Their Best

■ ■ ■

Unpossessive Aquarius will let you have the space and time you need. You can relax in comfort, not having to cover up your messes, quirks, eccentricities and undone laundry. You will have someone with whom you can share your wildest dreams, thoughts, theories, passions. They will bring with them not only their own individualistic and unconventional ideas but also a wide variety of unusual and stimulating friends. You will also have someone who appreciates your cooking.

Aquarians at Their Worst

■ ■ ■

Your relationship with an Aquarian won't feel like a relationship at all. You'll find yourself exasperated with trying to break down their emotional and physical barriers. You'll get only brief glimpses of emotional intimacy and only the most perfunctory of commitments. You'll be frustrated by the incompetent persona they assume as an excuse to escape housework and the practical nitty-gritty of sharing life with another person. Their opinionated nature and sporadic sex drive won't lend a warm glow to the relationship either.

Sexy Aquarians

■ ■ ■

Tom Selleck, Nastassja Kinski, Mozart, Humphrey Bogart, Eartha Kitt, Paul Newman, Clark Gable, Ida Lupino, Robert Wagner, Kim Novak, Burt Reynolds, Princess Caroline of Monaco, Germaine Greer, Natalie Cole, Geena Davis, James Dean, Neil Diamond, Jane Seymour, Mikhail Baryshnikov.

Unsexy Aquarians

■ ■ ■

Ernest Borgnine, W. C. Fields, Gertrude Stein, Ronald Reagan, Zsa Zsa Gabor, Jack Benny, Sonny Bono, Oprah Winfrey, Phil Collins, Dan Quayle, Carmen Miranda, John McEnroe, Yasir Arafat.

PISCES

February 20th to March 20th

...

Life's too hard. Couldn't I try

something easier—like astrophysics?

The Lure of a Pisces

■ ■ ■

If you've been spiritually, emotionally or even physically mangled by an aggressive Aries, a critical Virgo or a manipulative Scorpio, you might like to try a gentle, sympathetic Pisces.

Pisceans are normally shy, diffident, compassionate, caring people who like to give out sympathy and support nearly as much as they like to receive them.

They are prepared to listen to all the dreadful things other people have done to you and will dish out enormous amounts of genuine empathy. (However, they will be very turned off if they get wind of any dreadful things you've done to other people.)

If you've been struck down by the flu or other illness, Pisceans will turn into your instant home nursing service. In turn, they expect you to be there with aspirin and chicken soup when they are laid low.

Pisceans are not usually too critical about the bodily shortcomings of their partner. So if you're wondering if you're a candidate for a tummy tuck or a bottom lift, Pisceans are likely to pretend they don't notice or say it doesn't matter. Pisces is the least judgmental sign. They are the sign most likely to tolerate your peculiarities and accommodate your minor peccadilloes.

The Piscean personality can be hard to pin down. They adapt to the moods and characters of others. Some are veritable Zeligs, able to undergo complete character transformations depending on the company they are in. It's not that they are having a spontaneous identity crisis. They are pulling out of their personality file the card that they need to relate to you.

Pisceans are rather otherworldly, and often their soulful puppy-dog eyes are focused on the spiritual side of life. If you want someone who will give you a physically warm and affectionate love life and with whom you can share postcoital discussions on the importance of your spiritual life and the origin of the universe (first the Big Bang and then discussions thereof), you would do well to consider Mr. or Ms. Pisces.

The Piscean is a vulnerable and sensitive soul, notoriously poor in the selection of sexual partners. Suggestible, even gullible, they can easily be taken for a ride by less scrupulous signs—don't you be one of them.

To Catch a Fish, First Know Your Variety

■ ■ ■

The symbol of Pisces is two fish moving in opposite directions: one swimming up to spiritual heights, one swimming down into decadence and physical indulgence.

Two planets rule Pisces: Neptune and Jupiter.

Neptune is the planet of compassion and self-denial. Kindness is the greatest Piscean virtue. Neptune draws the Pisces up into the highest reaches of the mystical and imaginative. The downside of Neptune can draw them into fantasy, escapism, living in their heads, living with their heads in books; it can even lead them into alcohol and drug dependency—in fact, it can lead them into anything but dealing with the practicalities of everyday life.

Pisceans share their other ruling planet, Jupiter, with Sagittarians. Like Sagittarians, Pisceans have a philosophic streak and believe in the value of a good time. But Jupiter can draw the aimless, negative sort of Piscean into overindulgence in worldly pleasures and fatuous socializing. Instead of escaping into the spiritual realms, they escape into the material world. Pisceans are well represented in the ranks of shopaholics, gamblers and soap-opera addicts. Anything to filter out harsh reality.

As the last sign of the Zodiac, Pisces incorporates elements of all the previous eleven signs. One astrologer has called it "the garbage can of the Zodiac." More kindly, we may think of Pisces as the melting pot of the Zodiac. This can make Pisces the hardest sign to pick—it also makes it the hardest sign to give specific advice about.

That's why the first step in handling a Piscean is: know your variety of fish.

Pisces dropoutus—This fish will not be found in the fast-running streams of worldly interests; it needs to be searched for in the deep backwaters of esoteric bookshops, weekend flea markets, beaches at sunset, double-feature movies, church choirs and ashrams.

Pisces misteriozus—Rarely found in schools, this variety is a slow-moving, solitary fish that can be found in deep pools, exploring the profound spiritual undercurrents of life.

Pisces spongeoffus—This is a blood-sucking fish that tries to latch on to a larger, more stable fish and draw off its food, its energies, its dwelling place, its finances and its practical abilities.

Pisces superficialis—A lively fish found exclusively in shallow waters, this one is easily lured by baubles, beads, bright lights and noisy parties.

How to Interest a Pisces

■ ■ ■

To get a Piscean interested, you need to tread a fine line between the ethereal and the sensual.

You need to come across as caring and good but still sexy and wicked.

They must suspect that you are erotic Hot Property, but they also want to be reassured that the spiritual side of your nature is strong.

A male Piscean is looking for a cross between Florence Nightingale and Greta Garbo. A female Piscean is looking for a cross between Phil Donahue and Tarzan. So present yourself as a sexual beast with a heart of gold: the heart of Mother Teresa inside the bodice of Madonna; the soul of St. Francis inside the body of Jean Claude Van Damme.

Key tip: Above all else, you must persuade them that you have a good heart. If you can convince them of this, they will forgive you for a lot of physical and even social flaws.

Impress them with your kindness and sensitivity. Be genuinely interested in how they are. "Do you want a drink? Are you comfortable, can I get you a cushion? Do you like the atmosphere here? It might be quieter outside— wouldn't you like to go outside to look at the moon?"

Pisceans love animals, so show them photos of your dog and talk adoringly and sentimentally about your pets. Indeed, believe it or not, a good line might be: "I really want you to meet my dog. I want my dog to meet you." When you are around your pets or their pets, you must spoil the little beasts silly. If you go to visit them, take something for their cat or dog as well as for them. Be unconcerned as the animal sheds all over your best suit or shreds your favorite socks.

Or invite them to spend the night so that they can see the possum you can't bear to kick out of your garage. (Pisceans have even been known to resist killing their resident cockroaches—good grief, some even name them, like pets.) Tell them about any person or animal you sponsor—a child in Africa, a dolphin at the zoo.

Another good way to interest a Piscean is to talk a lot about *the atmosphere, the vibrations.* "What do you think of the atmosphere at this party? The vibes are a bit funny. Doesn't it seem a bit strained and artificial to you?" This will help them see you as intuitive, as someone who shares their sensitivity—as a soul-mate who understands the importance of vibes. Talk about any psychic or occult experiences you've had or any mystical or spiritual books you've read recently.

Above all, never, never display a lack of interest in them and what they are talking about. They have the most fragile egos in the Zodiac, so they need to be reassured that they are attractive and interesting.

Suggested opening line: "I find the mood here a bit strained, don't you? Would you like to go somewhere quieter?"

What to talk about: Your dog, your cat, the vibes, astrology, the origins of the universe, how to meditate, how to read tarot cards, alternative healing, the meaning of dreams, whether there is an afterlife, who's sleeping with who in the TV soaps and the state of royal marriages.

Where to take them: Secondhand and mystical bookshops, ballet, theater, galleries, museums, historical churches, comedies, to the water: lakes, rivers, boat trips, walks along the beach in the early morning and evening, walks in the country, a trip to a country inn to have a nice hot lunch on a cold winter's day. Pisceans often dislike crowds, so you can invite them home right away— to eat dinner with you. Be wary of taking your Piscean to noisy crowded places like bars or to see bands.

What to give them: Pisceans like things they can enjoy at home alone: CDs, occult books, a VCR, videos of old 1930s films, silk cushion covers, candles, oil lamps, incense, flowers, houseplants, a kitten, bird feeders, cashmere sweaters, antique knickknacks, an aromatherapy massage, things to do with water: seashells, bath oils, an aquarium, a water purifier, a fountain. Pisces rules the feet, so slippers or beautiful socks often go over well.

How to Seduce a Pisces

■ ■ ■

A warning here is that many Pisceans are very intuitive—so they may know about your intentions almost before you do.

Pisceans like to be reassured that they are sexually attractive—whether they feel attracted to you or not. Quite early on, tell them you find some aspect of their anatomy very arousing. "You've got beautiful eyes. You've got fabulous lips. What great hair." They can be a bit shy and coy about receiving such compliments, but they will hear and remember.

Pisceans—especially the women—want a mixture of the gentle and the strong in their partners. They are attracted to strength because they so often lack energy. But they are revolted by anyone with an uncaring attitude. They want a controlled, caring brute. A gentle monster. A macho pussycat. An Arnold Schwarzenegger exterior with a Tom Hanks heart.

You must skillfully cater to both these needs. Be their knight or Amazon in shining armor. Help them with their shopping, fix their dripping faucet, chauffeur them, assist them with their tax return. Then suddenly expose your vulnerable heart. Sob during a sentimental movie. Break down and confess how vulnerable you feel inside; people see you as tough but all you really want is someone who understands you. Best of all, arrive at their place with a puppy or a kitten inside your jacket. Tell them it's a stray you found that you simply couldn't abandon—perhaps they could look after it for a few days while you find a home for it? Not only will you make an impression with your caring nature—you will never get that animal back.

Pisceans are notorious ditherers. You may have to help them make key decisions. They are not likely to drag you off to bed at the first encounter. You may have to be the one who suggests coffee back at their place.

Pisceans love to feel comfortable all over. There is an easy progression from the comfortable to the sensual and from there to the sexual and passionate. Make them comfortable and they may well let you lead them all the way down the primrose path. Accordingly, the first key tactic in seducing a Piscean is: provide warmth and comfort.

Pisceans hate the cold. (You've heard the expression "a cold fish." A cold Pisces will act just that way.) Any seduction scenario must occur somewhere warmed to subtropical temperatures.

Pisceans are not much interested in luxury per se; a five-star hotel may be fine but it won't appeal on the grounds of opulence and glamour alone. They are very attached to their personal creature comforts, so they may prefer the seduction to occur in their own home.

Pisces may get very excited by the ripping off of clothes at the first passionate encounter—but make sure you do this with an artistic touch. You can be animalistic but not barbaric.

Seduction 1: The Cuddle Litmus Test

Pisceans are devotees—even connoisseurs—of the cuddle. They are after a quality cuddler. They also believe that cuddling is an underestimated indication of your technical skills in other intimate areas. Fail the cuddle test and you are likely to be labeled not worth the effort. Practice cuddling.

One well-executed, well-timed cuddle may be all it takes. Conversely, you can also use cuddling to gauge your prospects. Here is some body language to be aware of:

The A-frame cuddle. Here the Pisces hugs you with the top half of the body but keeps the pelvis well away from yours. Sexual prospects: zero.

The shoulder-tapping hug. Another distancing hug. The Pisces hugs you but taps or slaps you on the shoulder rather than continuing contact. This shows they are not comfortable with intimate contact with you. Sexual prospects: very poor.

The dead-zone hug. The hugging equivalent of a dead-fish handshake. The Pisces hugs you but just freezes in position, zombie-like. Sexual prospects: poor.

The warm hug. The Pisces hugs you affectionately but their body doesn't mold to yours. Sexual prospects: maybe.

The sensual hug. The Pisces hugs you and their hands don't stay still but move around your back. This shows a desire to caress your skin and feel you. Sexual prospects: a definite possibility.

The reverse hug. The Pisces comes up and hugs you from behind. Your bottom is pressed against something interesting. Sexual prospects: excellent.

The body-molding hug. The Pisces molds their body against yours, warmly snuggling in, crevice to crevice. Sexual prospects: what are you waiting for, you idiot?

The octopus hug. Body molding plus wandering hands. Speaks for itself. Sexual prospects: you may have to fight them off.

The Cuddle Litmus Test Stage Two: The Erotic Move. If the hug is

going well, why not try a segue into the Erotic Move?

Pisceans are sensitive by nature, so they're after a lover with a deft and artful erotic touch. The idea here is to do something tactile calculated to get the right nerves firing. It must be something that proves that you have The Touch. It should leave them in no doubt as to what is going on in your devious little mind and so give them an opportunity to call a halt if they don't want you to proceed. Some artful strokes to consider:

1. Unbutton a cuff of their shirt or blouse and stroke the soft flesh on the inside of their arm.

2. Take their hand, turn it over, kiss the palm.

3. Caress an earlobe—or the back of the neck—or everything.

Ideally you will cause a *frisson*—an involuntary shudder caused by an electric charge rushing from tip to toe.

If so . . . repeat on some other part of their anatomy.

The Cuddle Litmus Test Stage Three: The Artful Octopus. If the

Erotic Move goes well, why not become the Artful Octopus? Timing is everything. The well-timed Octopus ends up in bed; the poorly timed Octopus ends up on the doorstep; the completely mistimed Octopus ends up in the hospital wondering why the Pisces never mentioned their black belt in jujitsu.

Seduction 2: Whispers in the Dark

One useful supplement to the cuddle is darkness. Darkness can be used to overcome Piscean shyness. It also encourages the Piscean proclivity to mental fantasy.

Get your Piscean in the dark—inside or outside, so long as it's warm. Here the cuddle—or the arm around the shoulder—may go on for a long time. There could be an extended exchange of intimacies and confidences. Make sure they are comfortable, relaxed and that you have convinced them what a caring, sharing person you really are.

This then leads to the next obvious step: The Erotic Move (see previous page). (For a variation on this approach, see Seduction by the Stars! under Sagittarius.)

Seduction 3: Seduction by Lethargy

Pisceans are not usually the athletes of the sexual Zodiac. They are more the sensual indulgers. The key principle to keep in mind is the natural Piscean progression from relaxation to sensuality to sex. All you have to do is get them in that liquid relaxed state and merge.

Seduction by Lethargy (i): The Xanadu Pleasure Palace. The idea behind this seduction is to take advantage of the notorious Piscean love of physical indulgence. Ensconce them in a warm room, on a palatial soft couch or on a mountain of cushions. Wait on them hand and foot with wine, warm drinks, comfort foods: soup, chocolates, etc. The idea is to get them so deliciously, lethargically blissed out that they simply cannot get up to go home. Nor will they have the energy to resist you. Get them replete, content and purring. Proceed to the Cuddle Litmus Test Stage Two or to Whispers in the Dark.

Seduction by Lethargy (ii): The Wet Sunday Afternoon Indulgence. A good way to reinforce Seduction by Lethargy is to have the scenario take place when there are not only serious reasons to stay inside (all this comfort and indulgence) but also serious reasons not to go outside (cold, rain, snow, tempest). A wet Sunday afternoon is the perfect time. Wet and cold outside, warm and comfortable inside. Internal heat turned up to Central Africa at noon. Again, get them on the couch and cushions. Indulge them to the hilt and beyond. Piscean heaven. How could they say no?

Seduction by Lethargy (iii): The Massage. Possibly apres bath, offer your skills as a masseur/masseuse. Bliss them out. Roll them over.

Seduction by Lethargy (iv): Unexpected Bedfellows—Piscean Style. The basic idea here is to sneak into their bed early in the morning or late at night. Pisceans hate to leave a warm bed. "Just lie back and enjoy it."

Seduction 4: The Bath

Pisceans have an incurable weakness for water. As we said before, it is a small Piscean step from the sensuous to the sexual, and nothing is more sensual for a Piscean than the Bath. The Bath is a bona fide Piscean sex aid. It is a Piscean institution, a religious ritual.

Here are some ways to use this to your advantage:

Find out their bath time. It will usually be on a regular schedule. Pisceans hate having their daily timetable of eating, sleeping and bathing disturbed.

Contrive to arrive when they have just had a bath—when they are warm, glowing and freshly dusted with talcum powder. Move to Seduction 1, 2 or 6. Or try something bolder. Knock on their door when they have just climbed into the tub. Assuming they don't leave you standing there (a genuine possibility, by the way), they will come to the door wrapped only in a towel or robe and primarily interested in getting right back into their precious bath. Now say, "Good evening," remove your clothes and attempt to join them in the bath. Or ask politely, "Can I be of any assistance?" then remove your clothes and climb in.

If you have a luxurious bath of your own, you could invite them to make use of it. If you need a reason, first get them to help you do something messy or smelly like spreading manure on your garden or bathing your Irish wolfhound. Then you'll both need a bath.

All sorts of things are possible in a bathtub and almost every home has one. Pisceans understand the artistic potential of a bar of soap.

Seduction 5: The Sexual Sorcerer/Sorceress

The idea of this is to take advantage of the wicked element lurking inside many a mild-mannered Piscean.

Pisceans at their best/worst can be devils for the erotic. They can be *very* self-indulgent all around—food, drink and sex. The most unlikely-looking Piscean may well shock you with the contortions of their sexual fantasies (and experience). Most of them are only waiting for the right partner to come along to do it all with them (or so they fantasize!).

Your job is to convince them that you are the one.

How you do this will be ultimately up to you. You could try a variation on the Egomaniacal Sales Pitch (see Sagittarius). You could try a variation on the Seduction by Reputation (see Aquarius). Best of all you could just give them the Jack Nicholson evil eye.

But you have to serve up the aperitifs first: you need to display proof of your potent potential: the raised eyebrow, the subtle touch, the wicked innuendo.

This seduction is not to be undertaken by the untalented, the inexperienced or the unimaginative. You must convey that you know exactly what to do. An effective appetizer for the Erotic Move.

Seduction 6: The Tides of Passion

This is mainly one for men to try on Piscean women. Never forget that Pisceans are fantasy freaks. For many a Piscean woman, the chief sexual fantasy of the twentieth century remains *The Sheik*, starring Rudolph Valentino. Fantasy, true romance and unbridled lust all in one package.

The idea is to sweep her off her feet. Flowers, smoldering looks, the promise of eternal passion. Take her in your arms and carry her to the boudoir.

Either you can pull this off or you can't.

It could work.

Go for it.

If spurned at the critical moment, disappear for a week. Proceed to Portents of Passion. "I didn't tell you this before but . . ."

Seduction 7: Portents of Passion

Pisceans have a decidedly mystical bent. It could be useful to take advantage of this and Pisces' susceptibility to suggestion: "Fate has drawn us together. This was foreseen in the stars. It's karma. It's meant to be. It's beyond our control. Who are we to resist the forces of destiny?"

The idea is to suddenly latch on to some apparently inconsequential fact that they reveal about themselves. For instance, that they come from Walla

Walla, that they have a twin brother, that they have a birthmark in the shape of a swordfish on their left forearm.

Leap upon this revelation with astonishment, amazement and wonder. Explain that it was foretold years ago that you would meet someone who came from a town that was twice-named, had a twin and carried the sign of the Fish. "You are the One! You are the subject of the portents of passion!" (Gasp.) If asked to elaborate on the further predictions of this soothsayer, proceed to demonstrate the unbridled passion she foresaw.

If you fail to carry this off convincingly, you have the option of turning it into Seduction by Humor (see Aquarius).

Seduction 8: The Erotic Movie Move

Another way to influence the malleable Piscean psyche is via your VCR. Pisceans often like sensually erotic movies (we don't mean smutty). Rent an appropriate video, install your Piscean on your couch and ensure that the pause button, your hands and everything else are at the ready. Some suggested videos: *Women in Love, Henry and June, The Unbearable Lightness of Being,* possibly the early Emmanuelle films.

Other good Piscean seductions:

Seduction by Curiosity (see Gemini)

The Stray Dog (Cancer)

The Bacchanalia (Leo)

The Five-Star Seduction (Leo)

The I-Need-You (Virgo)

The Gold-Plated Seduction (Libra)

The Gothic Thriller (Scorpio)

The Striptease (Scorpio)

Seduction by the Stars! (Sagittarius)

The Marcel Marceau (Capricorn)

Sex with a Pisces

■ ■ ■

Sensuality rather than raw manic passion is the primary desire of your typical Piscean. They need lots of nurturing, yet they want a strong, technically excellent lover too.

Aim to get a Piscean into a position in which all they have to do is lie back, indulge and succumb. They favor the soft rather than the athletic side of sex. They want to languidly enjoy it rather than feel that they've just done the equivalent of a four-minute mile.

They have a very sensitive relationship with their bodies. They are not much interested in sexual activities that would leave them with cuts and abrasions. Muscle-straining positions, clawing fingernails, contortionistic venues—forget it. Even sex in the great outdoors might be too much—too many pebbles, twigs and ants, ouch.

However, Pisces is a mutable sign. Pisceans are very suggestible. Once they are in a relaxed, languid state, you may be able to initiate all manner of activity that they might turn their nose up at when less liquid.

They can be ditherers, so you might have to take a gentle, leading hand in sex. They like to be seduced rather than to seduce. However, once in that sensual state, they respond well.

They need to feel needed and are sensitive to the moods of others. If you can sweep them up in the tide of your passion, they may well respond likewise.

In fact, many Pisceans have a sort of "concubine" mentality—they want to learn their lover's fantasies and bring them to life with intuitive flair. Share your fantasies with your Piscean and see if they don't gently try to bring this dream into orgasmic life. They love to please and try to make sex a work of art.

They often have an intuitive touch. You might find that certain parts of your anatomy receive loving attention they haven't enjoyed for a long time. You'll love the times they roll you over and say, "Just lie back and enjoy it."

Like Virgos, Pisceans want you clean—but they also like moisture, including sweat. The thought of two sweaty bodies meeting can be quite a turn-on. You might even try two oiled-up bodies.

One thing to watch out for is the legendary Piscean apathy. Pisces can become apathetic about any aspect of their lives—as if it's too hard, too much trouble, and easier to just give up and have a cup of coffee instead. This attitude can at times include sex: too much trouble and mess. Better to lie around and just daydream about it. Beware these periods of sexual apathy.

Pisces can be very hot for sex for a while but then go on a sexual vacation and withdraw totally for recovery. Do not fear, the tide is likely to turn. Meanwhile, perhaps you could catch up on your reading.

And never forget that they are highly suggestible.

Pisces needs a lover free of inhibitions—this will help them get over their shyness. With the right lover, they are prepared for any possibility their sexual partner can imagine.

A final warning: Piscean women are rarely robust but are notoriously fertile, so take care.

How to Handle a Relationship with a Pisces

■ ■ ■

The three key things to remember with typical Pisceans are:

1. their heads tend to be in the clouds;

2. they often lack energy;

3. they need regular time alone to emotionally and psychically regenerate.

You will make yourself very welcome and valued if you provide them with help in the day-to-day practicalities of life, which they often find very difficult. Many have trouble coping with the real world. Pisceans are the great drifters and dreamers of the Zodiac. They tend to have one foot in another world. If you want to really impress them, do some practical and organizational things for them: paint their cupboards, help move their furniture. Your rewards in terms of returned affection could be great indeed.

Beware though of *Pisceus spongeoffus*, who wants you to provide *all* the comfort, food, goods and security in their life.

You need to provide them with a combination of kindness and organizational efficiency. You need to tread the fine line between being a kind, sensitive New Age kind of person and a wimp.

They tend to convert the lover of the moment into the idealized princess or knight in shining armor. No one can live up to these sorts of images. Because of this, Pisceans tend to get engaged more than they get married.

You may have to have long discussions with them to convince them to enter into a relationship with *you* rather than the soul projection they have placed on you.

Because they are nonjudgmental and tend to drift through life, they can end up spending years with a partner who is not really suitable.

Pisces are the least naturally energetic Sun sign. You may be surprised at just how often your Piscean partner can complain about lack of energy. This has to be respected and is all part of their soul's unwillingness to live in a body at all.

As such, it is important never to interfere with their good night's sleep. They are not usually bright and cheery early-morning risers. You may have to creep around quietly in the morning until they are ready to face the world. Also you need to respect their ritualistic approach to going to bed and rising. Their routines are one of the most important ways they cope with the horror of everyday life.

Pisceans can find other human beings very draining emotionally and psychically. They need periods of reclusion. Give them time to themselves, but still be there for them. Many Pisceans are more comfortable living separately and keeping assignations with their lover. But between these meetings, you need to contact them frequently and ask how they are.

If you do cohabit with a Piscean, you'll have to allow them to set up a little "temple" just for themselves—a room of their own into which they can retreat.

Pisceans are devoted to creature comforts rather than luxury. They can spend a lot of time and money on music, incense, perfumes, pretty pictures, quilts, cushions. They love comfortable, soft furnishings.

They are usually loyal to their current lover. Indeed, they often mistake commitment for dependency. They quickly come to feel dependent on their current lover, so great is their need to feel loved and protected.

Frustratingly, they often have difficulty asking for what they want and difficulty receiving. They spend their lives adapting to the other person's wants and never honoring their own needs. In consequence, they can feel drained and secretly resent their partner, who is supposed to read the Piscean's mind. They usually have a lot of trouble expressing anger for fear of disturbing the psychic vibrations. They need to be encouraged to tell you when they're upset and not bottle it up for years.

Many a Piscean has a martyr complex. The female Piscean, for instance, may see herself as the tragic princess abandoned and betrayed by black knights whose armor she thought shone purest white.

Pisceans change.

They are a mutable, spiritual sign apt to completely overhaul where they live, how they look, what they do. They need a partner who will not only adapt to such changes but also gently push them from lethargy and day-dreaming into action. They need someone who can help them from self-absorbed fantasizing into planning and execution. Many Pisceans become New Age self-help workshop junkies. They need a partner who will not only allow such growth but help them to focus and commit and not be drowned in a spiritual stew of bits and pieces from everywhere.

Pisceans need a gentle but strong, caring yet prodding partner. When they find one, they give back loyalty, tenderness, compassion, tolerance and sensuality.

Must-Do's

Be kind, sensitive and attentive.

No-No's

Don't be vulgar.

Don't be a wimp.

Never criticize them. They don't criticize others, so extend the same courtesy to them. They tend to accept people "warts and all."

How to End a Relationship with a Pisces

■ ■ ■

The simplest way to end a relationship with a typical Piscean is by being honest—while buttering up their usually fragile egos. Reassure them that you still think they're wonderful, that you still want to keep them as a friend; tell them you deeply respect them but, deep down, both of you know the energy has gone out of the relationship. If you are both to keep spiritually progressing in this life, you must follow the energy that is calling you elsewhere; you have to be by yourself to honor that energy . . .

If, for some strange reason, you want the Piscean to go off and leave you, the best tactic is to convince them that you are a low, unevolved, cold-hearted bastard. If you can convince a Pisces that you are not a nice person, you are likely to be dropped quite smartly.

You might try to have crude sex with them when you are covered in dirt from gardening. Yuk. They'll be very offended. If this doesn't work, try whipping yourself into a violent fury about something and smash a glass. You'll never see them again.

The qualification to this is that Pisceans will stay in a relationship with a person who is quite horrible to them if they are convinced that in some way that person *needs* them or that there is some way the Piscean can change them. So if you want the Piscean to lose interest in you, you have to show that you are beyond redemption. One way to do this is to speak uncaringly of animals—Pisceans may put up with being mistreated them-selves but would never put up with having their pets mistreated. Confess that you dislike animals. Say something like "Actually, I've always hated cats. If I see a cat in an alley and no one's looking, I see how far I can drop-kick him."

Your relationship with the Piscean is now terminated.

Tell them that you don't like dolphins and are just as happy to eat them as eat tuna. What's the difference anyway?

They'll never call you again.

Which is a shame, really, because they are usually nice, sensitive people. Why not try the honest but noncritical approach first?

Pisceans at Their Best

■ ■ ■

You will feel you are in a relationship with the most caring, sympathetic, accommodating person on the planet. They'll tolerate your foibles, forgive your lapses, intuit your needs, sympathize with your difficulties and adapt to your sexual desires. You'll find yourself enchanted when they share their love of music, poetry and fantasy with you. You'll feel you have found a soul-mate for your own spiritual quest into realities beyond the grossly material.

Pisceans at Their Worst

■ ■ ■

You'll believe you are in a relationship with a marshmallow man or woman. You'll be exhausted by their inability to cope with everyday life and feel that they are relying on your organizational abilities, practicality, energies and finances. You'll lose all respect for this weak, directionless creature who drifts through life in a daydream and poses as a victim of the world. At their very worst, you'll find you have a total emotional and financial sponge on your hands.

Sexy Pisceans

■ ■ ■

Sidney Poitier, Elizabeth Taylor, David Niven, Rex Harrison, Jean Harlow, Albert Einstein, Chopin, Harry Belafonte, Cyd Charisse, Vaslav Nijinsky, Rudolf Nureyev, Jon Bon Jovi, Enrico Caruso, Bruce Willis, Nat King Cole, Kurt Russell, Drew Barrymore.

Unsexy Pisceans

■ ■ ■

Ted Kennedy, Jim Backus (the voice of Mr. Magoo), Jackie Gleason, Fats Domino, Zero Mostel, Jerry Lewis, Glenn Close, Billy Crystal, George Harrison, Patty Hearst, Ron Howard, Liza Minnelli, Tony Randall.

FURTHER READING

Judith Bennett, *Sex Signs: Every Woman's Astrological and Psychological Guide to Love, Men, Sex, Anger, and Personal Power* (New York: St. Martin's Press, 1980). A brilliant look at astrological archetypes and their sexual and relationship proclivities. Though the book was specifically written about women, almost everything is also applicable to the male of the sign.

ABOUT THE AUTHORS

Ren Lexander. Being a sensitive New Age type of guy, with Moon conjunct Venus in Aquarius, Ren was moved to consult an astrologer to find out whether there was any arcane explanation for what seemed like an overendowment of basic animalistic urges. "It's perfectly clear," he was told. "You were born under the sign of the Goat. And Mars—the planet of lust and passion—falls exactly on the cusp of your house of sex. To sum up: you are a sexual predator." These are his astrological qualifications for writing a book he wishes he'd had when he was eighteen.

Ren is the author of *Three Nights on Nowhere Street,* about the time he spent living with the homeless; *The Complete Guide to Translating Bullsh*t,* a humorous look at the fact that we are seldom brave enough to say what we mean; and *Eye of the Shadow,* a thriller about murder, sex and rebirth. He has a Ph.D. in philosophy.

Geraldine Rose. Geraldine is a Pisces and therefore enjoys a rich fantasy life, especially since Venus, the planet of love, occupies her house of sex. Twelve years of working as a professional astrological counselor have revealed how, when and where the passions of each sign of the Zodiac are most likely to be ignited. She decided it would be safest to express the upcoming conjunction of her Mars and Ren's Venus by conjoining with him in print only. Like Ren, she has her Sun in the ninth house of writing and publishing. She writes an astrological advice column for a national magazine.